Imperial Encounters

Imperial Encounters

RELIGION AND MODERNITY IN INDIA
AND BRITAIN

Peter van der Veer

PRINCETON UNIVERSITY PRESS

PRINCETON AND OXFORD

ISBN 0-691-07477-1 (cloth)
ISBN 0-691-07478-X (alk. paper)

This book has been composed in Sabon

The paper used in this publication meets the minimum
requirements of ANSI/NISO Z39.48-1992 (R1997)
(*Permanence of Paper*)

www.pup.princeton.edu

Printed in the United States of America

10   9   8   7   6   5   4   3   2   1

FOR JACOBIEN, JAN ANNE, AND SJOERD

Contents

CONTENTS

Acknowledgments

ONE OFTEN ENCOUNTERS the idea that India is a deeply religious, traditional society, whereas Britain is a deeply secular, modern society. My motivation in writing this book is to counter such stereotypes that are based on Orientalist assumptions about East and West. By writing a comparative study of the simultaneous development of nation and religion in India and Britain I offer a critique of secularization theories as well as theories of nationalism, and clear the ground for a better understanding of modernity.

This book works on a large canvas, in time (a century), in place (India and Britain), and in subjects (gender, race, sacred scripture, secularism, and spiritualism). Thus the challenge has been to write a coherent narrative. To go into a detailed interpretation of primary sources would simply have been impossible. My book is not an exercise in archival research or literary criticism in which the close reading of a primary text against a historical context provides new insights, but an exercise in historical sociology in which larger historical developments are sociologically interpreted and illustrated with examples of major issues, such as the sati debate, the age of consent controversy, the Mutiny, and so on. Historical protagonists, like Annie Besant, Vivekananda, or Gladstone play an important role in the story as exemplars of the broader trends that I want to lay bare. For any of these figures there is a huge body of scholarship available, based on their writings and other sources, but it frames them in the narrow context of national history and thus neglects exactly what I want to bring out. Writing thus would have been impossible without the support of the extraordinary group of scholars gathered in the Research Center on Religion and Society at the University of Amsterdam: Gerd Baumann, Birgit Meyer, Patricia Spyer, Peter van Rooden, and Peter Pels. I am especially indebted to the latter two for their criticism and advice. A conference on "The Morality of the Nation-State," held at the Center in 1996 and published in 1999 under the title *Nation and Religion: Perspectives on Europe and Asia*, provided a strong intellectual impetus for this book. The process of my research began in 1995–96 in the rarefied environment of the School of Social Sciences at the Institute for Advanced Studies in Princeton, New Jersey. I am grateful to Clifford Geertz for his invitation and to the Institute and the Mellon Foundation for its support.

I am also grateful to Nicholas Dirks for inviting me to the University of Michigan's International Institute which provided me with a series of fascinating discussions about my work and with a Sawyer Fellowship to enable my stay. I have been extraordinarily lucky in having good friends and colleagues who have stimulated my work through the years. Arjun Appadurai, first in Philadelphia and later in Chicago, has, through his own early work on religion and power in India and later his pathbreaking work on the cultural dimensions of globalization, given me lots to think about regarding my own project. Nick Dirks, first in Ann Arbor and later in New York, has always inspired me by the subtlety of his conceptualization of history and power. Small wonder that both were students of the pioneer in this field, Bernard Cohn. Gauri Viswanathan has over the last couple of years been my most demanding critic and a great support through her own example and the seriousness of her work. Tom and Barbara Metcalf, Gyan Prakash, Chris Fuller, Daud Ali, Webb Keane, Arjun Appadurai, and Jackie Assayag invited me, respectively, to Berkeley, Davis, Princeton, London, Ann Arbor, Chicago, and Pondicherry to discuss my work. All these occasions have been very helpful. My greatest intellectual debt is to Talal Asad and Edward Said for reasons that will be clear to any reader of this book. Finally, I am grateful to Mary Murrell at Princeton University Press for supporting this project and to Rita Bernhard for her copyediting.

Imperial Encounters

Introduction

THE NINETEENTH CENTURY witnessed both the expansion of British power over the world and the creation of a national culture in Britain. These two processes are commonly understood to be either unconnected or only connected in insignificant ways. The nineteenth century is also the period in which a gradual colonization of India took place and an anticolonial nationalism emerged. While these two processes were obviously related, their interaction is often perceived as having left British culture untouched. The present book challenges these views. It examines issues of religion, race, gender, and language, all of which are foci of national identity, in the historical interaction of Britain and India. It is inspired by Edward Said's claim, in *Culture and Imperialism*, that the historical experience of empire is a common one among both the colonizers and the colonized.[1]

This book argues that (1) national culture in both India and Britain is developed in relation to a shared colonial experience; (2) notions of religion and secularity are crucial in imagining the modern nation both in India and Britain; and (3) these notions are developed in relation to gender, race, language, and science. I thus reject the common assumption—sometimes hidden, sometimes explicit—that the metropole is the center of cultural production, while the periphery only develops derivative, imitative culture. The book aims at problematizing oppositions between modern and traditional, secular and religious, progressive and reactionary, on which nationalist discourse depends and which the historiography of Britain and India adopts. It can only do so in an essayistic fashion by attempting to show that what is often assumed to be opposite is in fact deeply entangled, and that what is seen as unconnected is in fact the product of close encounters. The issues chosen for analysis are strategic ones, but they are by no means thought to be exhaustive. The approach combines historical anthropology and comparative religion. The book offers a reflection on the history of Britain and India informed by anthropological theories of the nation-state and religion. What it tries to show is that religion has been crucial in the formation of national identity not only in India but also in supposedly secular and modern Britain. It argues that the interpretive framework that is commonly used to approach modernity, religion, secularity, and nation has to be problematized by looking at colonial interactions.

India is often imagined to be the land of eternal religion, and Britain the land of modern secularity. In such an imagination India appears to exist outside history, whereas Britain is understood as the agent of history. Another and more subtle way of presenting the opposition between India and Britain can be found in Louis Dumont's work on Indian sociology. Dumont argues that India's history cannot be grasped with the historiographical concepts developed in the West, because secular history (as significant development) is religiously devalued in India.[2] India is different and needs a historical approach that appreciates a cultural difference which, in Dumont's view, is primarily located in the religiously sanctioned caste system. Dumont's major work on the Hindu caste system, *Homo Hierarchicus*, argues that traditional India had a holistic system of group religion (*dharma*) that regulated all spheres of life according to the hierarchical interdependence of castes (*jati*). The modern nation, according to Dumont, is based not on group religion but on separate values for separate spheres of life as well as on the ideology of the individual.[3] If one looks for historical development in Hindu cultural terms one can find it, according to Dumont. But if one looks at India with Western concepts, as both Hegel and Marx did, the conclusion is, inevitably, that India's development stagnated long before the nineteenth century. For Hegel, Hindu religion denied the possibility of individual rationality and freedom and thus the unfolding of Rationality in the State.[4] For Marx, India's economy was still in the phase of primitive communism in the village, since the caste system prevented the development of individuality, private property, and the state.[5]

Britain, on the contrary, is clearly the land of history. The Industrial Revolution, individual property, individual freedom, class conflict, the rise of the nation-state, the victory of science, the decline of religion are all clear markers of history. Indeed, history is the sign of the nation-state, of modernity, as much as the denial of history is the sign of the colony, of tradition.[6] This is exemplified by the extraordinary interest taken in historical arguments by British politicians and philosophers alike during the transition to the modern nation-state between 1750 and 1850.[7] Modernity is at issue here and it can only be defined in relation to antimodernity, and, historically, to an antecedent state of affairs. John Pocock has asserted that British arguments about modernity in this period identified three antecedents: ancient, medieval, and preindustrial.[8]

However, not only antecedents in Britain's history, narrowly conceived, but also comparisons with societies that were colonized by Britain were crucial elements in identifying one's modernity. In eighteenth-century Britain there is, in fact, a rapidly growing readership for books about exotic people. A particularly interesting example is George Psalmanazar's *A Historical and Geographical Description of Formosa, an Island Subject to the Emperor of Japan,* published in 1704.[9] This book was highly successful till it was discovered that Psalmanazar was a forger and impostor who had never been to Formosa. Forgeries, however, sometimes lay bare what are the tropes of writing in a given period. The main trope in Psalmanazar's forgery is his conceptualization of the difference between Formosa and Britain in terms of "false" religion—that is, priestly superstition—against "true" religion—that is, Anglican Protestantism. This trope connects anti-Catholicism with aversion to religions encountered in the period of British expansion. It is also found in perhaps the most influential history of a non-European society, James Mill's *History of British India,* written a century later by a writer who was not a forger or impostor like Psalmanazar but who, like Psalmanazar, had never been to the place he wrote about. The difference between the two is that Mill (1773–1836) argued that his authenticity derived precisely from his lack of direct acquaintance with India. Mill claimed to possess a judgment that was untainted by unmediated contact with India and its civilization, unlike his opponents, the Orientalists, who had "gone native."

James Mill finished the three-volume *History of British India* at the end of 1817, and the book brought him employment by the East India Company a few months later. Mill, one of the great products of the Scottish Enlightenment and a close associate and follower of Jeremy Bentham, wrote his *History* as a frontal attack on both Indian traditional institutions and the British Orientalists whom he accused of defending a degraded and degrading society. Like Psalmanazar, Mill was against the rule of priests who, in his view, had greater authority in India than in any other part of the world (except Rome, perhaps). Mill's description of the authoritarian irrationality of India's religion closely resembles Psalmanazar's Formosan fantasy:

Everything in Hindustan was transacted by the Deity. The laws were promulgated, the people were classified, the government established, by the Divine Being. The astonishing exploits of the Divinity were endless in that sacred land. For every stage of life from the cradle to the grave; for every hour of the day; for every function of nature; for every social transaction, God prescribed a number of religious observances.[10]

Besides having a backward religion, India was, in Mill's eyes, an example of immoral feudalism that had to be destroyed both there and in Britain. There was no doubt that India occupied a much lower stage in the evolution of "utility" than Britain, but, still, in Britain a battle also had to be waged against antimodern political forces. It is worth noting that Mill was simultaneously criticizing Indian society and British society, and connected the Orientalists, who wanted to maintain the ancien régime in India, with "the establishment" that had the same desire for Britain. *A History of British India* is definitely not Montesquieu's *Lettres Persanes* (1721), in which oriental despotism is depicted to criticize absolutism in France, but its mode of comparison is perhaps even more interesting. It connects India and Britain in a general treatise of utility, morality, and progress. Mill is the first major thinker who identifies the need to push India into modernity as one of the main objectives of the East India Company (which was gradually transforming from a trading company to a branch of the British state during the first half of the nineteenth century). This thought, much later in the century and in a very different political context, was endorsed by no other than Karl Marx himself.

Mill's view that the Company had the task to civilize the Indians, "push them into history," was most eloquently put into practice in Thomas Babington Macaulay's *Minute on Indian Education* (1835), which argued not only that "a single shelf of a good European library is worth the whole native literature of India and Arabia" but also claimed that the proposed educational system would produce "a class of persons, Indian in blood and colour, but English in taste, in opinion, in morals, and in intellect."[11] The belief of Utilitarians like Mill and Macaulay was that the English educational system would annihilate Hinduism and wake the Hindus from their oriental slumber. In this belief they were supported by their contemporaries, the evangelicals. Zachary Macaulay, Thomas B. Macaulay's father, was one of the Clapham evangelicals who had successfully lobbied for the opening up of India as a mission field, which happened in 1813. Education had become religion's primary instrument for conversion and expansion, and its growing importance in the nineteenth century only enhanced its status. While the evangelicals reached out to the lower classes in Sunday Schools, missionary schools targeted the Indian elites. The great challenge for the Company, however, was to promote education while at the same time establishing its policy of religious neutrality which was deemed necessary to prevent unrest among the natives. Colonial policy made the teaching of the Bible impossible in secular education in India but was then faced with the difficulty of how to impart British civilizational values. According to Gauri Viswanathan, the solution was found in the teaching of English literature as a way to impart Christian morality. She shows brilliantly how English literary study was introduced in British India at a time when the classical curriculum was still well established for the higher classes in Britain.[12] The study of English literature, in the Arnoldian sense, taught the way to moral improvement, and was in that sense similar to religion. As such, not only literary study but also secular literature as a means to moral improvement was first tried out not in Britain but in India.

In the early decades of the nineteenth century Utilitarians were trying to define modernity in terms of utility and rationality, while evangelicals were trying to define it in terms of Christian morality. Both groups developed their concepts in constant reference to India and communicated them not only to audiences in Britain but also to Indian audiences. Indians were not passive recipients of these concepts but were actively involved in shaping them. For instance, in Bengal, Rammohan Roy (1772–1833) studied Christianity and felt great affinity with the rational critique of religious orthodoxy, launched in Britain by Unitarians like Channing. He wrote two major works on the ethical teachings of Jesus and became a Unitarian leader.[13] In 1827 he founded the British Indian Unitarian Association.[14] At the same time, however, Rammohan also studied the Vedas and Upanishads. This led him to explore the limits of Unitarian universalism, which continued to be based on Christianity. In 1828 he decided that a universal, rational religion had to be based on the Vedas and Upanishads, and he created the Brahmo Samaj. What Indian intellectuals like Rammohan did was to explore the universality of modernity and point out its limits and contradictions.

In this way, Indians and British develop in the nineteenth century a shared imaginary of modernity. This puts Dumont's problematic, with which we began this introduction, into another perspective. The conceptual difficulties of defining modernity in relation to the "ancient" or "feudal" antecedents of modernity in Europe also apply to defining modernity in relation to "coeval" India. Such a definition cannot be based on an irreducible cultural difference between India and Europe. A comparative approach of "civilizations," like that of Louis Dumont, makes India into a holistic universe, signifying antimodernity, and Britain into another, signifying modernity. However, modern India and modern Britain are products of a shared colonial experience. Key concepts of modernity, like secularity, liberty, and equality are created and re-created in the interaction between colony and metropole. No doubt, this is a history of power and knowledge, but not simply one of the impositions of British knowledge on Indian barbarism, as Macaulay liked to think. Both colonizer and colonized were intimately connected and transformed through a shared process of colonization.

The challenge this book has taken up, therefore, is to write from an interactional perspective about the location of religion and secularity in nineteenth-century India and Britain. This entails an engagement with notions of science, language, gender, and race. Before proceeding, let me first elaborate what I mean by *interactional perspective*. When reading the historiography of nineteenth-century English history, it is striking how "little Englandish" it is. The relation with the colonies is left to imperial/colonial historians who specialize in such things, while mainstream history is not affected by these histories from the margins. Inversely, in Indian nineteenth-century history one reads much about the role of the British in India, but it is often cast in a nationalist theater of "foreign power" against "native" resistance. The parallel to "little Englandism" is "big Indianism," namely, the idea that India simply absorbs all foreign influences without changing fundamentally. Moreover, Indian historiography is too fascinated by India to be interested in the impact of the colony on the metropole. The difficulties in challenging this situation are obvious. Besides problems of a conceptual nature, there are problems of scale, focus, and methods of inquiry. If one engages in a form of interactional history, how can one contain the narrative and how can one avoid a further simplification of what are already simplified summaries of immensely complex local, regional, and national histories? Nevertheless, an escape from the essentialisms of British modernity versus Indian antimodernity is perhaps possible by attempting to lay out fields of historical interaction and encounter, however fragmentary. In fact, the fragmentary nature of the enterprise is a blessing in disguise, because it works against the grain of national history, which is written to put fragments into a whole, signifying the nation, or else put them to oblivion. Interactional history is precisely an attempt to go beyond the national story and get at some of the fragments without losing coherence in the telling of the tale.

Interactional history is different from global history. Attempts to use comparative frameworks that go beyond the nation-state and amount to global history generally stand in the tradition of two nineteenth-century classics of the social sciences, Marx and Weber. Sociology only becomes the science of the new industrial society as an isolated entity between 1920 and 1950 in the new metropole: the United States.[15] Before the Great War "it was the structure of empire as a *whole* that provided the basis of sociological knowledge. Sociology's comparative method embodied the imperial gaze on the world."[16] It is certainly true that evolutionism, race science, and the notion of progress dominated these comparisons. They showed a common understanding of the modernity of the nation-state in terms of a theory of global difference. What they ignored is the extent to which these differences were not cultural essences but rather were produced by the power relations of empire.

Marx obviously wanted to write a global history of the evolution of labor and value, and his example has been followed by materialist historians of the world system, including Braudel, Wallerstein, and Frank. According to these authors, peripheral societies are subjugated by the core societies of capitalist development, and they either suffer this development or become, in turn, agents of it. They are part of history only when they have agency in the unfolding of this global history, as the anthropologist Eric Wolf implicitly argues.[17] Since European societies are the core societies it is hardly feasible to write a history of peoples without Europe. Neo-Marxist historians have made two major modifications to this general perspective: first, that significant developments in the direction of capitalism have come about in these peripheral societies without European intervention; and, second, that the development of capitalism in the core societies depended more on imperialism than was previously assumed. So capitalism in India, for example, developed without Britain, but capitalism in Britain could not develop without India. An extreme example of the shifts that have taken place in economic history is the turn from replacing Europe by Asia as the center of world history in the latest writings of Andre Gunder Frank.[18]

According to Frank, China and India, till 1800, were much more central to the world economy than Europe was, because of their productivity in manufacturing by which they created an export surplus. The history of European dominance is therefore very short and explainable in terms of Kondratieff cycles and the availability of cheap energy (coal). In Frank's view, European dominance is again being replaced today by that of Asia. Frank severely criticizes the work of Braudel and Wallerstein and his own earlier work for its Eurocentrism and argues for a complete "re-orientation" of historiography. The centering of Asia and the de-centering of Europe is occurring entirely in terms of the global economic system. The telos of history remains world capitalism, whether capitalism comes from outside or inside.

The problem with the global history of imperialism from the Marxist perspective, both in its past and current incarnations, the latter being less dogmatic about modes of production, is that it primarily remains a material and economic history, and, as such, engages in a particular homogenizing style of writing history as if the economy is the determining principle "in the last instance." The colony in the end creates the wealth of the metropole and is shaped in accordance with metropolitan interests. Whatever the subtleties in the analysis of economic and material interaction, the model remains that of a system of economic determination that has a center and a periphery and, crucially, is the cause of the center's development and of the periphery's stagnation. The colony is shaped by the metropole in this process, while the metropole profits and makes progress thanks to its peculiar relation with the colony. However, cultural imperialism as an evolving political practice that simultaneously shapes both metropole and colony cannot be accounted for in this materialist view. A history of power that extends beyond economic relations seems to escape materialist historians despite the fact that it is not economical power but political power (including military force) that, even in Frank's view, ultimately explains Britain's ascendancy and India's decline. As Gauri Viswanathan has convincingly shown, it is even true for a Marxist student of politics and culture, such as Raymond Williams, that his work curiously fails to apply its own theory of culture to British imperialism and its effects on English culture. For Williams, imperialism is only understable in terms of a system of economic determination that escapes cultural analysis; therefore he chooses to ignore it for his analysis of English society and culture.[19]

Marxism, however, is only one example of nineteenth-century attempts to understand the modern world as a stage in global development, although it is still one of the most influential explanations today. The modernization theories of the twentieth century have inherited this nineteenth-century tradition. When they depend more on Weber than on Marx, as they often do for political reasons, they place higher value on a scale of civilization than on the evolution of material conditions, yet they remain teleological and evolutionist. Unlike Marx, Weber did not assume that there was an ultimately determining element in history, but, in his analysis of Protestantism's unique contribution to the development of capitalism, he saw rationalization as an evolutionary process. Weber was a comparativist, but he compared civilizational essences and not networks of historical interaction. He wanted to explore the reasons why modern capitalism emerged in the West and nowhere else. He argued that disenchantment, as brought about by Protestantism, was of singular importance in the emergence of capitalism and that this dominant feature of modernity was lacking in other world religions he examined, such as Hinduism, Buddhism, and Islam. It escaped him that nineteenth-century Protestantism, which had shaped his understanding of sixteenth- and seventeenth-century Protestantism, had been formed precisely during that transformation of the modern world in which colonial interactions had been crucial. The location of religion shifts dramatically in nineteenth-century Europe and India, and this affects Weber's understanding of religion and rationality in ways that are impossible for him to historicize.[20]

My critique of both the Weberian culturalist approach and the Marxist materialist approach makes it clear that in order to describe the history of global modernity from 1800 one must focus not only on historical interactions and the field of power in which they play themselves out but also on the categories with which one studies them. Also apparent is that there is not a world-systemic teleology that connects imperialism of the past with globalization in the postcolonial world today. Indeed, the story of increasing integration and unification obscures the coexisting tale of increasing disintegration and disunity along ethnic and religious lines that we find everywhere. If imperialism is not only an economic practice but also a political and cultural one—and one requiring a holistic approach in the anthropological sense—historical interactions must be studied across the globe, with special attention paid to the conceptual frameworks that develop in these interactions and become the unquestioned categories of historiography.

The aim of this book is to disturb both the complacency of national histories and that of an imperial history centered on the primacy and priority of Western history. It seeks to problematize our understanding of modernity but does not claim to provide a totalizing, global theory. The objective is not to show, in a kind of quid pro quo evenhandedness, that everything in Britain was preceded in the colony or that everything is connected; rather, the more modest intention is to discern significant connections while avoiding the pitfalls of both nationalism and evolutionism more than a century after their early conceptualizations. Such an exercise is a necessary condition for a critical understanding of modernity.

This book, then, is about national religion and empire. The first chapter examines the ways secularity and religion presuppose each other in nineteenth-century India and Britain. It argues that the rise of voluntary, religious movements which come to dominate the emergent public sphere in India and Britain shapes the understanding of the secularity of the state and the nature of religious belief. These movements are part of the imperial landscape and interact with each other in a number of ways. Both

11

British Christianity, signifying the British nation and the imperial state, and Indian Hinduism, signifying the beliefs and practices of "the majority" of the Indian nation, are products of this interactional history.

The second chapter goes on to explore the moral nature of the nation-state. It argues that modern notions of religion, language, race, and gender are constructed in the process of forming a nation-state. This is true both for the metropole and the colony. Religion becomes a defining feature of the nation and for that purpose is nationalized. It becomes one of the fields of disciplinary practice in which the modern civil subject is formed. The moral mission of the nation-state is to organize the education, health, and social welfare of its subjects; to do so, it must acquire knowledge about the targeted populations. Such projects of documentation in themselves have the effect, at least partly, of producing the realities they purport to describe. This spirit of scientific exploration, so often seen as the hallmark of modern secularity, produces modern ideas of body and mind, of spirituality and materiality, of language and culture, of race, and of gender and character. In all these ideas, religion as the site of the nation is crucial.

Chapter 3 explores the relationship between spiritualism and anti-imperialist radicalism. However irrational spiritualism may seem, scientific empiricism and rational explanation are crucial to it. It is a site from which the superiority of elite Christianity could be contested and the spirituality of the East (especially India) could be claimed. The Spirit of the Age was nationalism, and the battle fought by the spiritualists concerned who was allowed to participate in the public sphere.

Chapter 4 explores the role of Christianity in constructing the masculine Englishman and the role of Hinduism in constructing the masculine Hindu. A connection between physicality and morality, between effeminacy and sexuality, is made in response to anxieties about national degeneration in the context of empire. Sports in public schools, Boy Scouts, religious martiality are all developed in the service of a moral nation felt to be under threat.

Chapter 5 looks at Scripture as the basis of civilization and at the practice of comparative philology in order to discover civilization. While in Britain philology became marginalized when it was replaced by race science as an instrument of colonial rule, in India it became an authoritative science for the transformation and translation of Hindu traditions. This chapter also examines the career of the leading Orientalist of the second half of the nineteenth century, (Friedrich) Max Müller, the founder of comparative religion and, in India, the recognized authority on Hinduism.

Chapter 6 deals with the rise of race science in Victorian Britain in the context of empire and its appropriation and use by Hindu nationalists in India. Race comes to replace religion as the defining characteristic of the British nation and its right to imperial rule. The Mutiny of 1857 creates an anxiety about the immutable barbaric nature of the Indian race and a pessimism about "real" conversion. Religion, however, continues to address the problem of the criminalized poor, both in Britain and India, and thus becomes a field of social practice in which populations are targeted for "moral uplift."

The book makes no pretension to be an alternative history; instead, it offers alternative ways to look at familiar problems and material. It is not a full account but a collection of essays that lays out a problematic. Its goal is to challenge social scientists—anthropologists, sociologists, historians, political scientists, and students of comparative religion—to explore beyond the received narratives of colonialism, nationalism, and secularism.

Secularity and Religion

SECULARITY AND RELIGION, more than anything else, is the site of difference in Britain's and India's close encounters. As this chapter attempts to show, notions of progress, liberty, tolerance, democracy, civil society, and public sphere converge in the all-embracing notion of secularity. In secularity one finds the essential and irreducible difference between modernity and tradition. The usual way to approach the cipher of secularity is by means of the secularization thesis.[1] Till recently, this was the most successful element of any sociological theory of modernization; however, it has come under increasing criticism over the past two decades, especially in response to the growing significance of political Islam after the Iranian Revolution of 1979.[2] On the one hand, the secularization thesis offers a master narrative that attempts to explain everything concerning religion in the modern world; on the other hand, it leaves major historical developments, such as the emergence of the national form of societies, outside the picture. Jose Casanova's recent summary of the thesis describes its three essential features: (1) the separation of religion from politics, economy, and science; (2) the privatization of religion within its own sphere; and (3) the declining social significance of religious belief.[3] Casanova rejects the second feature but maintains that the first and third are still viable. I suggest that all three features be thoroughly historicized, that they not be understood as a unilinear teleology but as a number of diverse developments related to the rise of nation-states. One pitfall of the secularization thesis is that it subsumes divergent genealogies of secular modernity in one narrative of secularization.

In the European discussion of secularization, decline in church attendance and in the number of churches are good indicators of change. Starting with the last decades of the nineteenth century, such a decline seems evident in England, although there is considerable debate about the periodization and interpretation of that decline. Catholicism, for instance, continues to grow substantially till the Second World War. In the Netherlands—to take another European example—decline begins only in the 1960s. Again, in the United States there is a somewhat different picture. American churches have always been very creative in recruiting church members, as evidenced over the last decades by "televangelism." For Christianity, church membership and church attendance are good indicators of change, and these factors indicate that the historical picture differs among Western societies. Thus a generalized secularization story will not do. This is true not only for the facts and figures of church attendance and membership but also for the causal explanations of industrialization and rationalization, offered by secularization theory. For example, there is more evidence during the Industrial Revolution in England for religious expansion than for secularization.[4] Similarly, a consensus now exists among historians that the impact of scientific discoveries, such as those of Darwin, on the decline of religion has previously been much exaggerated.

If the secularization thesis does not account for the history of Western Christianity, it is even less applicable to the history of Islam, Hinduism, Buddhism, and most other religions. In the latter cases, the question about church attendance and membership cannot even be raised since there are no churches, and congregational worship in temples or mosques either does not exist or differs significantly from that in Christianity. The organization of religion, the place of religion in society, and the patterns of recruitment are so different that not only does secularization theory itself become meaningless but so, too, do the empirical and theoretical problems derived from it in the context of Western Christianity. This has not prevented social scientists from universalizing this ill-founded story about the West to include the rest. The rhetoric, dressed up as argument, goes as follows: Since all societies modernize and secularization is an intrinsic part of modernization, than all societies secularize.[5]

In recent years, much doubt has been thrown on the secularization of India and the ultimate triumph of secularism. The anthropologist T. N. Madan has, for instance, argued that "secularism as a widely shared worldview has failed to make headway in India."[6] Since Indians are Hindus, Muslims, Buddhists, or Sikhs, the majority are not Protestant Christians (although some are). They cannot and will not privatize their religion.[7] Madan points out that in sociological theory, especially that of Max Weber, there is an essential linkage between Protestantism, individualism, and secularization. He argues, accordingly, that secularism is a "gift of Christianity to mankind" and that it is part of the unique history of Europe.[8] Madan expresses what appears to be a general consensus among both social scientists and the general public that the modern West is uniquely secular and the East uniquely religious. The problem with this consensus is that it reduces complex and diverse histories to the binary opposition of secularity and religiosity. We have already seen that the history of secularity in Western societies is varied and complex; the same can be said about the development of religious institutions in India. Nevertheless, the appeal of these essentializations cannot be dismissed by providing ever more complicated narratives of social change. It is, in fact, hard to go beyond theories of modernization and secularization, however much one tries to get away from them. One is compelled to address the conceptual complexities and contradictions contained in them.

Historically, it is important to understand the secular and the religious as mutually interdependent. Their definition cannot be separately reached but depends on this structural relationship. This interdependence is crucial in the formation of the nation-state, but that formation follows different historical trajectories in different societies. In the next chapter I look more closely at Indian and British processes of state formation, but here I limit the discussion to what I see as the central feature of the idea of secular modernity, the separation of church and state.

The Separation of Church and State

According to the historian Owen Chadwick, Britain developed a "secular" atmosphere of public life between 1860 and 1890.[9] The question is not whether in this period we find the three elements of the secularization thesis, as outlined by Casanova, because we do not. The question is rather what a "secular" atmosphere entails in this period of high nationalism and high imperialism. Perhaps the most significant historical development in this regard is the building of a "wall of separation" between church and state, to use Thomas Jefferson's language.[10] The European wars of religion of the sixteenth and seventeenth centuries were concerned precisely with the question of the relation between political and ecclesiastical authority. They were fought around the central issue of political loyalty: Can one be loyal to the state when one is not following the religion of the state?[11] As Hobbes and other political thinkers realized, it was the nature of the state that was at issue here. The outcome of the political revolutions of the late eighteenth century was that political loyalty could rest on citizenship instead of membership in the state church. The relationship between these two, however, was decided differently in different societies depending on their historical trajectories. Both the American and the French Revolutions put an end to the association between royal absolutism and the established church. The French Revolution developed into something decidedly anticlerical in its secularism (*laicité*) and carried a direct attack on religious institutions. The American Revolution carried the spirit of religious dissent from Britain to the American shores and was aimed at gaining religious freedom from oppressive state interference. In Britain itself, disestablishment has not even been carried out fully today, although the early nineteenth century saw the gradual enfranchisement of Catholics and Dissenters. The location of religion is therefore different in these societies, and the expression "secular society" does not do justice to these differences.

Secularism, as a set of arguments in favor of separation of church and state, has a genealogy in the Enlightenment, but these arguments work out quite differently in a variety of historical formations. If it does so already in the interconnected spheres of philosophical and political radicalism of France, Britain, and America, one should not be at all surprised that it also does so in the interconnected spheres of Britain and India. The separation of church and state is often conceptualized in relation to liberty, and a way to approach the secular is thus through the question of freedom as posed in the liberal tradition by John Stuart Mill (1806–1873).

In his celebrated essay *On Liberty* (1859), Mill argues for complete liberty of opinion and the expression thereof and thus advocates a free exchange of ideas, close to what Jürgen Habermas has called "*bürgerliche Öffentlichkeit*" or "bourgeois public sphere." Critics of this view have generally objected that the liberal public sphere excludes certain groups of people. In that connection it is interesting to read the motto of Mill's famous essay, taken from Wilhelm von Humboldt's *Sphere and Duties of Government* (1792): "The grand, leading principle, towards which every argument unfolded in these pages directly converges, is the absolute and essential importance of human development in its richest diversity."[12] This in fact contains the principle of exclusion in Mill's views on liberty:

It is, perhaps, hardly necessary to say that this doctrine is meant to apply only to human beings in the maturity of their faculties. We are not speaking of children, or of young persons below that age which the law may fix as that of manhood or womanhood. Those who are still in a state to require being taken care of by others must be protected against their own actions as well as against external injury. For the same reason, we may leave out of consideration those backward states of society in which the race itself may be considered in its nonage. The early difficulties in the way of spontaneous progress are so great, that there is seldom any choice of means for overcoming them; and a ruler full of spirit of improvement is warranted in the use of any expedients that will attain an end, perhaps otherwise

17

unattainable. Despotism is a legitimate mode of government in dealing with barbarians, provided the end be their improvement, and the means justified by actually effecting that end. Liberty, as a principle, has no application to any state of things anterior to the time when mankind have become capable of being improved by free and equal discussion. Until then, there is nothing for them but implicit obedience to an Akbar or Charlemagne, if they are so fortunate as to find one. But as soon as mankind have attained the capacity of being guided to their own improvement by conviction or persuasion (a period long reached in all nations with whom we need here concern ourselves), compulsion, either in the direct form or in that of pains of penalties for noncompliance, is no longer admissible as a means to their own good, and justifiable only for the security of others. (78–79)

I have reproduced this long quotation from Mill's essay because it lays out so clearly that his concern is with liberty in the service of progress. It depends on the notion that some societies are at a lower stage of evolution. Such a notion of evolutionary stages had already been developed in the Scottish Enlightenment and is the basis of all historical thought in the nineteenth century. Societies at lower stages of evolution have to be educated like children to make them capable of enjoying freedom. Mill is not in any simple way prejudiced in racial or religious terms, as evidenced in his position in the controversy over the behavior of Governor Eyre in Jamaica and in his response to the Indian Mutiny shows. For instance, in a long footnote on the British response to the Mutiny later in the essay he accuses both evangelicals and the state of persecuting Muslims and Hindus. His position allows for the toleration of diverse religious opinions, but only if they already belong to modern civilization and thus contribute to the moral principle of progress. One has to be free to be able to express oneself freely; that is the idea. Mill's view allows him to be, at the same time, a radical advocate of freedom and a supporter of enlightened (progressive) imperialism. It is not insignificant to remember here that it is not only evolutionary theory that leads him to claim freedom at home and support despotism in the colony but also his lifelong employment in the service of the East India Company where, at the end of his career, he held the highest administrative position, a post previously held by his father, James Mill. Evolutionary theory is therefore not just a grand narrative of progress and modernity but belongs to the joint predicament of nationalism and imperialism.

The evolutionary difference between metropole and colony is simply asserted by Mill, not argued. His argument is about progress and liberty, and it uses religion as its foil. Both the Roman Catholic Church ("the most intolerant of churches") and Calvinist churches are depicted by Mill as intolerant institutions which only when they cannot convert others to their opinion by force or persuasion reluctantly accept a difference of opinion (76). It is of great concern to Mill to defend the right of atheists and blasphemers to express their opinion, and he defends that right by arguing that Christ was put to death as a blasphemer (93). The persecution of Christians as heretics is his main historical example in his argument for liberty. He firmly rejects the idea that Christian doctrine provides a complete morality, while at the same time arguing that the recorded teachings of Christ contain nothing that contradicts what a comprehensive morality requires (118).

As remarkable as his defense of unbelief and blasphemy and his attacks on Calvinism are Mill's examples from comparative religion. He cites the Muslim prohibition of the eating of pork and the tendency to prohibit the eating of pork in a society in which the majority is Muslim. He compares that to the Puritanical prohibition of dancing and music in regions where Puritans are in the majority and to Sabbatarian regulations. Mill's conclusion is unequivocal. Individuals and minorities have to be protected against the religious sentiments of the majority. Again, this line of argument has a history in the persecution of dissenters by the state and the established church in the seventeenth and eighteenth centuries and the response to that in America by Jefferson (as well as Madison and other "founding fathers") with the separation of church and state.

The idea that religion especially is a threat to freedom of thought and expression and therefore to an open public sphere as the basis of a democratic nation-state thus has a history in the Enlightenment and is firmly established in the liberal tradition, and indeed is expressed till the present day. An example is a recent argument by the philosopher Charles Taylor. According to Taylor, "Secularism in some form is a necessity for the democratic life of religiously diverse societies."[13] In his view, democracy needs "what used to be called patriotism, a strong identification with the polity, and a willingness to give of oneself for its sake."[14] The legitimacy of modern nation-states depends on participation and a relatively strong commitment on the part of citizens. When groups are systematically excluded from the process of decision making, the legitimacy of rule is challenged. That is why the nation, according to Taylor, should not be defined in religious terms, since that definition would exclude groups with religious allegiances that differ from those of the population's majority. He suggests

19

that exclusion by religious majorities often goes from barely tolerating the presence of a minority to its expulsion.

The "secular atmosphere" in the second half of the nineteenth century, to which Owen Chadwick refers, may indicate that the question of political loyalty does not immediately emerge when citizens follow different religions in the modern nation-state. The loyalty to one's king and state does not follow from one's religious affiliation but from one's national identity, of which religion may be one ingredient among others. It is nationalism that replaces religion in this regard, and one can come to nationalism via a variety of religious affiliations. Another way of expressing this is that in the modern era religions are nationalized. Regarding the treatment of minorities in a modern, democratic polity, there is not much reason to fear a religious majority more than a secular majority, but an understanding of European history based on a particular Enlightenment tradition, as highlighted, for instance, in Peter Gay's work, leads Eurocentric thinkers to assume a connection between secularity, tolerance, and freedom.[15] The assumption that religious views are absolute and allow no tolerance for difference may be true in theory, but the historical record shows that people with different religious opinions have lived in a variety of polities without immediately coming to violent conflict with one another. The historical record also shows that, in Britain, the nineteenth century is one of considerable religious expansion in a number of spheres of life without open, violent conflict. Although anti-Catholicism continues to be a strong element in forging a Protestant national identity during the nineteenth century, the Gordon Riots of 1780 are the last seriously violent outburst of that antagonism. The kind of violent religious conflict in which Britain is involved in the nineteenth century is increasingly directed outward and, of course, related to the colonial project. Separation of church and state does not lead to the decline of the social and political importance of religion. With the rise of the nation-state comes an enormous shift in what religion means. Religion produces the secular as much as the reverse, but this interaction can only be understood in the context of the emergence of nationalism in the nineteenth century. And, in the case of Britain, dealing with the national means dealing simultaneously with the imperial.

The question of political loyalty in the colony is different from that in the metropole. The culturally diverse plural states that preceded British imperial control over India depended on the collaboration of Muslim and Hindu elites of a variety of sectarian affiliations. That the people would have religions different from that of the rulers and that these rulers would extend royal patronage to these other religions had long been a historical fact in most of these states. The British East India Company initially just conformed to this established pattern of rule. From 1817 on, the government of Madras took over direct responsibility for the administration and upkeep of Hindu temples and rituals. This looks like the establishment of a direct relation between British rule and Hindu religion, which makes Robert Frykenberg speak of a de facto "Hindu Raj."[16] In Britain this led to strong protests from evangelicals who formed an Anti-Idolatry Connexion League. These Christian protesters demanded of the government that the British would be at least "neutral" toward native (Hindu or Muslim) institutions and at best would support Christian missionization in India.

The anti-Hindu rhetoric of the opponents of the government's policy aroused public consciousness among Hindus that their religion was under attack.[17] This consciousness was further strengthened by the fact of missionization and conversion. A great number of organizations emerged in South India in the 1820s and 1830s to resist the missionary onslaught. We thus find an extraordinary situation in which the colonial officials desire to infiltrate the native, religious institutions and to rule by patronage in the Indian tradition but also one in which movements outside the state challenge these policies, demand a secular state, and significantly transform the nature of religion. According to Frykenberg, this dialectic of aggressive missionization and Hindu resistance created a public sphere in South India in the nineteenth century that does not at all evoke the image of a "secular atmosphere." Secularity and religion receive particular historical meanings in this atmosphere of debate, however. The government of Madras was forced by the anti-idolatry activists to retreat from their policies and accept a new policy of "noninterference," made into law in 1863. This left the administration and upkeep of Hindu temples and rituals to new, emergent elites which used the British legal apparatus to create a new, "corporate Hinduism" that was fully modern.[18] These elites were not only interested in controlling Hindu institutions, which especially in South India were quite powerful and immediately connected to political control, but they also had a reformist agenda concerning religious education, ritual action, and customs that is crucial even today.[19]

The question of political loyalty in India led the British first to follow the established pattern of religious patronage, but religious activism in Britain made them change this policy into "noninterference," that is, secularity. The shift of their policy toward religious institutions is similar to the shift from Orientalism to Anglicism in the educational policy of colonial India. It is remarkable to see that in both the American colony and the Indian colony it is the Christian dissenters who try to erect a "wall of separation" between church and state. The hostility of religious people toward liberty, which Mill assumes, is belied by dissenters' great push toward freedom of religious opinion. Obviously their aim is not to create a "secular atmosphere" or a secularization of society; on the contrary, their minimal goal is not to be hindered by the state in their efforts to convert people in a free market of opinion and, at most, to have that aim supported by the state. Certainly white settler society in America had a very different relation with the British state than with the Indian colony, and therefore the reasons for a secularized state were quite different. The effects in both cases, however, were not that dissimilar in allowing an expansion of religious activity in civil society.

The separation of church and state in Britain took place gradually and partially in the nineteenth century. A major step was the enfranchisement of religious minorities, such as the Catholics and Dissenters, which resulted in a shift of political loyalty from religious identity to national identity. Religious institutions and practices were crucial in the formation of national identities, but gradually, in the second half of the nineteenth century, the opposition between Britain as a Protestant nation and France as a Catholic nation became less relevant than the opposition between a Christian, civilized nation and colonized peoples without civilized religions. Race replaced religion as the most important marker of difference, although religion and race were often combined. Enlightened Christianity belonged to a stage in the process of civilization that the British had already achieved. The conclusion is that, *pace* Taylor, it is not so much that religion cannot be allowed to enter the public sphere in order to let the modern nation-state exist but that religion creates the public sphere and, in so doing, is transformed and molded in a national form.

In India, obviously, political loyalty could not be transferred from the religious to the national. When the period of religious patronage of native institutions had come to a close under evangelical pressure, the British not only attempted not to interfere with native religions but also did much to disavow any connection to the missionary project and to Christianity as such. One can indeed speak of a definite secularity of the British state in India that was much stronger than in Britain itself. The British considered a sharp separation of church and state essential to their ability to govern India. Their attempts to develop a neutral religious policy in a society in which religious institutions played an important political role could not be anything but ambivalent. In the management of both South Indian Hindu temples and North Indian Sikh and Muslim shrines the colonial government remained involved, despite all efforts to the contrary.[20] Nevertheless, externality and neutrality became the tropes of a state that tried to project itself as playing the role of a transcendent arbiter in a country divided along religious lines. Again, however, this did not contribute to a secular atmosphere in society. Indian religions were transformed in opposition to the state, and religion became more important in the emergent public sphere. As in Britain, religion was transformed and molded in a national form, but that form defined itself in opposition to the colonizing state. The denial of participation in the political institutions of the colony led Indians to develop an alternative set of institutions of a jointly political and religious nature. Indians did not conceive the colonial state as neutral and secular but rather as fundamentally Christian. As Nita Kumar puts it, "the Sanskritists of Banaras today have a collective memory of a threat in mid-nineteenth century when government wanted to Anglicize and Christianize them."[21] Similarly, popular conceptions of British rule, as evident in the Cow Protection Movement of the 1880s, portrayed it as having an alien, Christian nature. When, in 1888, the North-Western Provincial High Court decreed that the cow was not a sacred object and thus did not have to be protected by the state, the decision galvanized a movement not only against Muslims but also against the Christian rule of "cow-eaters."[22] When the state started to use religion among its census categories, it itself came to be understood in religious categories. A distinct feeling that the modernizing project of the colonial state was based on Western values and thus Christian in nature remained important. This feeling was further enhanced by the fact that many high-ranking officials were self-conscious Christians who felt it their duty to support the missionizing effort. Perhaps one of the best examples of this kind of official was John Muir (1810–1888) who served in the northwestern provinces as an administrator and was a qualified Sanskritist who reorganized the Sanskrit College at Benares in the mid-1840s. Muir wrote a critical examination of Hinduism in Sanskrit, the *Matapariksha* (1839), to which three Hindu pandits responded.[23] While these were intellectual challenges and responses, one must remember that John Muir was not simply a philosopher posing intellectual questions but was a high-ranking colonial official whose views greatly impacted educational issues. At the same time it is important to see how Muir's theological position,

23

vis-à-vis Christianity, develops in the course of his dialogue with Hindus from a more negative evangelical stance to a more conciliatory and intellectual one.

Although the legitimizing rituals and discourses of the colonial state were those of development, progress, and evolution and were meant to be secular, they could easily be understood as essentially Christian. The response both the state and the missionary societies provoked was also decidedly religious. Hindu and Islamic forms of modernism led to the establishment of modern Hindu and Muslim schools, universities, and hospitals, superseding or marginalizing precolonial forms of education in Muslim *madrasas* and Hindu *pathshalas*. Far from having a secularizing influence on Indian society, the modernizing project of the secular, colonial state in fact gave religion a strong new impulse.

The separation of church and state as the sign of secularity did not result in a secular society in Britain or India; rather, it indicated a shift in the location of religion in society from being part of the state to being part of a newly emerging public sphere. This historical development takes place between 1750 and 1850 and is perhaps best exemplified by the emergence of voluntary, missionary societies in the 1790s and the emergence of Hindu voluntary, revivalist societies in the 1820s. The crucial term here is *voluntary*, that is, fully independent of the state, responsible for financing its own activities. It is also important to observe here that while there is an element of "response" to missionary activities in Hindu revivalism, it is also true that the missionary societies themselves respond to the imperial project and receive their significance within that project. This is a shared, historical space of interaction.

RELIGION

Defining "religion" is at least as difficult as defining "secularity." Talal Asad recently pointed out that the universalization of the concept of religion is closely related to the coming of modernity in Europe and to the European expansion over the world.[24] The modern understanding of religion, which is exemplified in Clifford Geertz's influential article "Religion as a Cultural System," is very different from what medieval Christians would have regarded as religion, and this is, a fortiori, the case with Muslims, Hindus, and other non-Christians.[25] This raises the broad historical question of how a modern Western understanding of religion has become

24

dominant and applied as a universal concept. The project of modernization, which is crucial to the spread of colonial power over the world, has provided new conceptual frameworks in which both colonizing and colonized subjects understand themselves and their actions.

Talal Asad has summarized some of the crucial shifts in the understanding of religion in modernity. He points out, following Reinhard Koselleck, that "older, Christian attitudes towards historical time (salvational expectation) were combined with newer, secular practices (rational prediction) to give us our modern idea of progress."[26] This is a shift that Benedict Anderson has identified as a crucial element in the formation of a national imagination. Following Erich Auerbach and Walter Benjamin, Anderson argues that the medieval Christian conception of the simultaneity of past and future in an instantaneous present, marked by prefiguring and fulfillment, is replaced by an idea of homogeneous, empty time, marked by temporal coincidence, measured by clock and calendar.[27] What I would stress, however, is that the new conception of progress and simultaneity did not replace the older conceptions but were transformations of them. It is fascinating to see how, in the nineteenth century, Protestant conceptions of guilt and atonement, of "the few elect," of God's grace were transformed in conceptions of progress, of grace extended to all inhabitants of the world, of the "white man's burden."

As mentioned above, an important development is the universalization of religion as a category. Where the Christian churches had always been involved in distinguishing superstition and false belief from true religion, in the seventeenth century attempts are made to define *natural religion*, that is, beliefs, practices, and ethics said to exist in all societies, in all religions. This development is related both to the need to pacify religious conflict in Europe and to the intensified contact with other societies and religions in the emergent world system.[28] As Talal Asad argues, "the emphasis on belief meant that henceforth religion could be conceived as a set of propositions to which believers gave assent, and which therefore could be judged and compared between different religions and as against natural science."[29] This makes the theoretical exercises of comparative religion and anthropology possible in the nineteenth century, but also a modern Christianity that is located firmly in activities in the world (secular, so to say) and affirms the laws of nature that can be "read' as God's creation. The recognition of a multiplicity of religions, however, in no way prevents the identification of the essence of religion with Christianity. Modern Christian theology is full of attempts to identify Christianity as the highest form or the essence of religion and to replace outright attacks on other religions, targeted as forms of devilish paganism, with more subtle attempts at conversion by recognizing elements in them that lead to Christianity. It also enables attempts at conversion through education that affirms a higher morality and a stronger conformity with natural science than the practices and beliefs of the unconverted. Attempts to convert Christians to another form of Christianity, say Catholics to Protestantism, become marginal. Indeed, they are all seen as forms of Christianity within the emerging nation-states. Central in the nineteenth century is conversion to modernity, that is, a transformation of the lives and practices of both the lower classes in the metropolitan societies and the entire populations of the non-Christian colonies. It is this new field of moral uplift and conversion that Christians are exploring in the nineteenth century.[30]

These considerations are crucial when we try to analyze the modern religions of India. This book focuses on India's dominant religious tradition, but it has often been noted how difficult it is to speak of a religion called "Hinduism." The term *Hindu* is derived from Sanskrit *sindhu* and refers to the people who live near the great river Indus. *Al-Hind* is an early Arabic term used by Muslims who settled in this region. *Hindu* is thus a term used by outsiders to speak about this region and its population. Later the term *Hindustan*, again a geographical designation, came into vogue. The term used in the early period of European expansion into India is *gentoo* (Latin: gentiles) or *heathen*. It is European Orientalism of the eighteenth century that gradually systematizes knowledge about the people of India and their various beliefs and practices into an integrated, coherent religion called Hinduism. This is part of a larger, empirical enterprise to "map" India and its inhabitants, an enterprise framed in metropolitan theoretical concerns. It is often asserted that no such thing as Hinduism exists but rather a great variety of heterogeneous practices of a devotional and ritual nature as well as metaphysical schools that are only lumped together by the foreign term *Hinduism* in the early nineteenth century. Such an assertion contains a lot of truth, but less true is that Hinduism is an exceptional case in this regard, as a number of authors argue.[31] The same can be said about Islam or Buddhism or, in comparable ways, about that strange category, "tribal religions." It is important to realize that religion itself is a modern category that is applied to Christianity as much as to Hinduism. The difference, however—and this remains crucial—is that Christianity, at least from Kant on, is portrayed as the rational religion of Western modernity, whereas Hinduism is mystified as Oriental wisdom or irrationality. It is in the field of historical interaction, established by imperial expansion, that the category of religion becomes significant.

In an influential contribution to the study of Hinduism, the historian Romila Thapar has argued that in India of the 1980s there is a political attempt to restructure the indigenous Hindu religions (in the plural) to a "syndicated Hinduism" that is a monolithic, uniform religion, paralleling some of the features of Semitic religions like Christianity and Islam. She rightly connects the current Hindutva movement in India to the nine-teenth-century Hindu response to "missionary activity and Christian co-lonial power."[32] Revivalist movements, like the Arya Samaj, discovered in Hinduism a monotheistic God, a Book, and congregational worship. This is a substantial transformation of a set of polytheistic traditions with a great variety of scriptures, none of which is really dominant, and domes-tic and temple worship that is only seldom congregational. What these movements wanted to create is a modern Hinduism that is respectable in the eyes of the world (monotheistic and text-based) and that can be the basis for a morality of acting in the world (secular) as in Mohandas Gan-dhi's use of the Bhagavadgita as the foundational text for social work (*karma-yoga* and *seva*). The creation of Hinduism as a religion in the modern period entails a profound transformation of ideas, practices, and institutions and cannot be simplified by pointing at premodern tolerance of diversity or by rejecting it as a political ploy of right-wing Hindus. The political struggle against the anti-Muslim Hindutva movement in India today would gain from a better understanding of the transformation of Hinduism in the modern period.

A development that Hinduism and Christianity as modern religions share is the formation of an informed, religious public. Religion is crucial for the creation of the public sphere. This may come as a surprise to those who accept Jürgen Habermas's understanding of the rise of "the public sphere." In his *Strukturwandlung der Öffentlichkeit*, Habermas argued that private individuals assembled into a public body began, in the eigh-teenth century, to discuss openly and critically the exercise of political power by the state.[33] These citizens had free access to information and expressed their opinion in a rational and domination-free (*herrschafts-freie*) manner. Crucial to this development was the emergence and expan-sion of a market for newspapers and other printed materials. Another critical element was the rise of the bourgeoisie, the reason why Habermas speaks of the bourgeois public sphere. These bourgeois turn out to be secular liberals rather than religious radicals. In my view, Habermas's analysis of the Enlightenment tradition belongs, at the theoretical level,

27

very much to a discourse of modern, European self-representation. A striking element in this self-representation is the neglect of religious, public opinion since it cannot be regarded as rational and critical.

In Habermas's model we have a picture of European development in which secularity is one of the distinguishing features of modernity. This picture is simply false. Enlightenment did not do away with religion in Europe. On the contrary, in the eighteenth century there continued to be a direct connection between natural science and natural religion, as well as between political debate and religion. As Margaret Jacobs has argued: "Habermas's individuals are far too secularized."[34] Jacobs focuses on the new religiosity of the enlightened few, such as the Deists in England.[35] The productive side of Habermas's argument, however, is his focus on the sociology of the public sphere: both the discursive possibilities of critical debate and the tendency of the public sphere to expand and allow a growing number of participants. In that connection I would like to draw attention to the organizational activities that developed out of eighteenth-century evangelism. While early evangelism—for example, Methodism—was already developing new communication networks, this development received a very strong impetus at the turn of the century. I am thinking here of antislavery societies, Bible societies, and missionary societies around 1800 that—at least in Britain (the prime subject of Habermas's analysis)—were instrumental in creating a modern public sphere on which the nation-state could be built. I would therefore suggest that the notions of "publicity," "the public," and "public opinion," captured by Habermas's concept of "the public sphere," are important and can be used for comparative purposes if we are not constrained by Habermas's secularist perspective.

CONCLUDING REMARKS

Let me briefly summarize what I have tried to express in this chapter. First, I have argued that the location of religion and secularity has to be related to the emergence of a public sphere that is relatively independent of the state. In the creation of the public sphere in Britain the role of evangelical movements is crucial. In India these missionary movements are mirrored by a whole range of religious movements that are instrumental in creating a public sphere in India. In Britain a modern sense of the Christian self is created that connects theological notions with progress and a sense of a "mission in the world." The Christian self in nineteenth-century Britain is formed in connection to the "white man's burden" in India, missionary and colonial. In India the Christian missionary activities demand a secularity of the state, and this leads to a public sphere in which religious movements produce an anticolonial Hinduism that is fully modern.

Second, I have argued that the opposition between religious intolerance and secular liberty is mistaken. The rise of the nation-state and the related emergence of a public sphere makes new, modern forms of freedom and unfreedom, tolerance and intolerance, possible. Nonconformist Christians demand freedom of religious opinion, and evangelical movements are crucial in the formation of the public sphere at the beginning of the century but embrace notions of evolutionary progress that underpin the colonial project. Hindu movements resist the colonial project while adopting some of its most important features, but they create a Hinduism that is becoming more and more anti-Muslim.

The Moral State: Religion, Nation, and Empire

IN 1988, when British Muslims petitioned their government to ban Salman Rushdie's *Satanic Verses*, they discovered that the existing blasphemy law did not prohibit insults to the Prophet Muhammad. It only applied to Christianity, and, accordingly, the government rejected the petition. The home minister for race relations, John Patten, subsequently wrote a document lecturing the Muslims and the general public "on being British." Talal Asad has brilliantly analyzed the political implications of the liberal views expressed in this text. A crucial aim of Patten's text was to delineate "a common national culture." According to Patten, this commonality was to be found in "our democracy and our laws, the English language, and the history that has shaped modern Britain."[1] In this chapter I address two issues that are omitted in Patten's discussion of "being British": Christianity and empire. It is, of course, quite understandable that a politician would not mention Christianity as a major component of British culture at the height of the "Rushdie affair." Nevertheless, the laws to which Patten referred included a blasphemy law that only protected Christian sentiments. Moreover, no one will doubt that Christianity is a crucial element in the history that shaped Britain.[2]

Similarly, there is a silent assumption in Patten's document that "being British" has nothing to do with empire. In other words that the problem of conflicting values, as it emerged in the Rushdie case, was a new problem, brought to Britain by immigration; that it only had to do with empire in so far as the immigrants came from the former empire, another instance of "the empire strikes back." Nevertheless, one might contend that Patten's arguments, calling for acceptance of a common, national culture, as well as those of Muslim leaders, calling for the religious neutrality of the state, as shown by the political protection of the beliefs of all religious communities, are rooted in the same history of empire but experienced on opposite sides of the colonizing process. It is sometimes said that the British are unaware of their history because it took place elsewhere. My own reading in British history suggests that the imperial connection is indeed too seldom consciously reflected upon by historians of Britain, let alone British politicians. In this chapter I attempt to show structural similarities and differences between the development of religion and nationalism in Britain and India.

That Patten could get away with not mentioning Christianity as a component of Britain's national culture is because organized Christianity has been gradually marginalized in British society over the course of the twentieth century. Britain is now a so-called secular society, in which Christianity, assumedly, has become a private matter for individuals with no political relevance in the public sphere. Without denying significant changes in the location of religion in British society in this century I am wary of that assumption. Even in 1980 a leading article in *The Times* argued that it would be undesirable for the Prince of Wales to marry a Roman Catholic.[3] In the meantime a number of undesirable events appear to have happened in the British royal house, and one wonders whether this particular opinion would be expressed today. Nevertheless, this quite recent opinion from a leading newspaper in a so-called secular society is quite remarkable in its insistence on the Protestant nature of the nation. The opposition between Protestants and Catholics is obviously much less important in the twentieth century than in previous centuries, but it is exactly in oppositions of this kind that the religious nature of the nation-state is expressed. Despite Patten's omission of Christianity in his definition of "being British," there is sufficient evidence that the arrival of Muslim immigrants in Britain has made Christianity again an important element in the defense of national identity.[4]

In my view, the crucial relationship that needs to be analyzed is that between state, nation, and religion. The modern state is a nation-state, and the hyphen indicates that the modern state requires a nation and vice versa. In the colonial period only Britain was a nation-state, while in the twentieth century India was a colony struggling against Britain to gain its independent status as a nation-state. This, at least, seems to indicate a time lag in which colonizing Britain was an established nation-state and colonized India became one. However, one must remember that the nation is a nineteenth-century historical formation, so that the time lag is a relatively minor one. In other words, in the same period that Britain was colonizing India, England was colonizing Great Britain, trying to unify what was not yet (and will only partially be) the united kingdom.[5] We can see the historical outcome of the latter process even today in Northern Ireland and Scotland.[6] I mention this simply to point out that Benedict Anderson's notion of a time lag, in which blueprints of a finished nation-state are exported to less-evolved societies via colonialism, may lead us to miss the processual and differential nature of nation-state formation.[7]

It may also cause us to overlook the fact that this process involved Britain and India simultaneously, within the same historical period.

Often raised is the question, What comes first in this hyphenated phenomenon, nation or state? Does the state produce the people, or the people the state? On this I am in agreement with Marcel Mauss who, in his unfinished work on "the nation," argues that the idea of "nation" combines in the collective spirit the ideas of "fatherland" (patrie) and citizen:

> These two notions of fatherland and citizen are ultimately nothing but a single institution, one and the same rule of practical and ideal morals and, in reality, one and the same central fact which gives the modern republic all its originality, all its novelty and its incomparable moral dignity. . . . The individual—every individual—is born in political life. . . . A society in its entirety has to some extent become the State, the sovereign political body; it is the totality of citizens.[8]

In his provocative and profound way Mauss does away with any sharp distinction between state and society. Where Renan suggested that the nation is a daily plebiscite, a deliberate choice, Mauss argues that it is a collective belief in homogeneity, as if the nation were a primitive clan, supposedly composed of equal citizens, symbolized by its flag (its totem), having a cult of the fatherland, just as the primitive clan has its ancestor cults. In Mauss's view, the modern nation believes in its race ("It is because the nation creates race that one believes that the race creates the nation"),[9] its language, its civilization, its national character. This collective belief is recent, modern, and to a very considerable extent the result of public, obligatory education. The idea of national character is intimately tied to the idea of progress.[10]

What we find in Mauss is a rejection of the common distinction between civil ties and primordial bonds, between citizenship and ideas of ethnicity, race, language, and religion.[11] In his view, they all go together in a complex transformation of society into the nation-state. For Mauss, one of the most interesting aspects of this process is that it produces simultaneously the individual and the nation. In Foucault's terms, the state is totalizing and individualizing at the same time.[12] The boundaries of the state are notoriously difficult to define. The state appears to be a sovereign authority above and outside society, but Foucault has pointed out that the modern state works internally through disciplinary power not by constraining individuals and their actions but by producing them. The individual, civil political subject is produced in churches, schools, and factories. Timothy Mitchell has argued that it is the peculiarity of the modern state phenomenon that "at the same time as power relations become internal in this way, and by the same methods, they now appear to take the novel form of external structures."[13] The state is thus to be analyzed as a structural effect.

Where does this leave religion? In Mauss (as in Durkheim) there are constant references to the idea that nationalism is the religion of modern society, just as clan totemism is the religion of primitive society. If that is the case, could one then say that Christianity (or Hinduism or Islam or Buddhism) is the religion of the ancien régime and nationalism the secular religion of modern society? Our previous argument about the secularization thesis has already shown that the idea of one thing replacing another is much too simple. An implication of Mauss's argument appears to be that what happened to race and language in the age of nationalism also happened to religion. It becomes a defining feature of the nation, and for that purpose it is transformed in a certain direction, that is, it is nationalized. Thus religion becomes one of the fields of disciplinary practice in which the modern civil subject is produced—not the only one, obviously, since language, literature, race, civilization are other fields producing what Mauss called "the national character."

That religion is important in producing the modern subject should not seem strange to those familiar with Weber's discussion of the Protestant Ethic. That it also is important in producing the modern public is perhaps more startling, especially if one stresses that in the nineteenth century not only is Protestantism nationalized but so, too, is Catholicism and many other religions, such as Islam and Hinduism in India. One may immediately object that Protestantism became the national religion of England and the Low Countries already in the sixteenth century. I would suggest, however, that although Protestant state churches existed in these countries in the early-modern period , they were not yet nation-states and thus there was no national religion. In other words, in the eighteenth and nineteenth centuries many major changes in religion were under way that affected its organization, its impact, its reach. These changes had to do with the rise of that hyphenated phenomenon, the nation-state.[14]

Implicit in my argument thus far is that the "modern subject" is produced together with the "modern public." Consequently, religion is not only important in the shaping of "individual conscience" and "civilized conduct," but also in the creation of the public sphere. In the remainder of this chapter I explore the nationalization of religion in Britain and India. I hope to show that the developments in the metropole and in the colony have important features in common, but that there are also substantial differences having to do with the way state, nation, and religion are related in these two sites of the empire.

The Moral State in Britain

In nineteenth-century Britain two major religious developments connect religion to nationalism. The first is the enormous growth and impact of evangelicalism on the entire religious culture of Britain. The second is the inclusion and enfranchisement of Catholics in the nation. Let me start with evangelicalism. Evangelical revival starts conventionally with John Wesley in the first half of the eighteenth century, but there was an important second wave in the 1790s that lasted into the nineteenth century.[15] The growth of evangelical movements in the first half of the nineteenth century is spectacular, but more significant than these numbers is the considerable impact evangelicalism had on religious groups and individuals of every kind. The evangelical expansion coincided largely with that of the Industrial Revolution, which has led to all kinds of more or less economistic causal explanations, ranging from those given by Elie Halevy to those offered by Edward Thompson. All these explanations have subsequently been subjected to substantial criticisms, which I will not discuss here. Whatever the causalities involved, it is important for my purpose to point out that evangelicalism aimed at inward conversion but also had an outward goal of converting others. Itinerant preachers and later Bible societies and missionary societies ranged far and wide. Indeed, evangelicalism exerted a strong civilizing and educational effort aimed at transforming people's personal lives. There can be little doubt about the importance of the evangelical movement in producing modern, civil, and hard-working individuals.

At the same time, evangelicalism had a significant political impact. The term *evangelicalism* obviously covers a broad range of ideas and attitudes, but its campaign for the abolition of slavery in the first decades of the nineteenth century shows how evangelicalism, despite its diversity, could have a strong political message. Here we see also how evangelicalism at home was connected to the empire, as exemplified in the words of William Wilberforce, one of the leaders of the evangelical Clapham sect:

> I consider it my duty to endeavour to deliver these poor creatures from their present darkness and degradation, not merely out of a direct regard for their well being . . . but also from a direct persuasion that both the

colonists and we ourselves shall be otherwise the sufferers. The judicial and penal visitations of Providence occur commonly in the way of natural consequence and it is in that way I should expect the evils to occur.[16]

David Brion Davis suggests that the abolition of the slave trade in 1807 and of slavery in 1833 were "genuine rituals," evoking fantasies of death and rebirth, and were "designed to revitalize Christianity and atone for national guilt."[17]

These attitudes toward the rest of the world were new and thoroughly modern. Until the 1790s there was hardly any interest in missionization abroad. Missions such as the Society for the Propagation of the Gospel, founded in 1701, employed chaplains, but their task was mainly to minister the trading company's men.[18] The 1790s proved a turning point, however, perhaps best captured in the title of William Carey's book *An Enquiry into the Obligation of Christians, to Use Means for the Conversion of the Heathens*.[19] A great number of missionary societies were founded, including the well-known London Missionary Society (LMS) and the Church Missionary Society (CMS). All these societies saw themselves engaged in a battle against idolatry and an endeavor to save heathen souls. Not only were these souls thought to go to hell if not saved, but saving them came to be seen as a Christian duty. One can only wonder about the extent to which Christian imagination in Britain was fueled by the imagery of the poor Hindus, Muslims, and others being lost for eternity. What we do know is that one out of two missionary speakers at provincial anniversary meetings of missionary societies between 1838 and 1873 came from India.[20] There can be little doubt that the simultaneous evangelical activities of Bible societies, missionary societies, and Sunday Schools created a public awareness of a particular kind of world and of an imperial duty of British Christians in the empire.

I see evangelicalism as a very broad, religious force, active both within and outside the established church.[21] By 1850, about one-third of Anglican clergymen, including many of the brightest and the best, could be designated "evangelical" and so could the vast majority of Nonconformists.[22] I take this to imply that the earlier strong divide between the established church and Nonconformism was, to some extent, bridged by evangelicalism. This divide obviously continued to exist in political debates about church-state relations, but dissent appears to have lost its radical antiestablishment politics within evangelicalism, which basically promoted a middle-class piety with strong elements of civil and frugal behavior and national honor. Certainly, one can point at the extremist elements

35

within the movement with their millenarian, Adventist antinomianism that seem to perpetuate the earlier characteristics of eighteenth-century dissent. These elements remained significant throughout the nineteenth century and into the twentieth. In a number of cases their outbursts of religious fervor pushed influential men, like Gladstone (1809–1898), from evangelicalism toward High Church. Nevertheless, one continues to see in the Liberal leader Gladstone a strong evangelical streak that informed his political views and actions.[23] Similarly, several generations later, C. F. Andrews (1871–1940), missionary and later friend of Tagore and Gandhi, left the Irvingite congregation in which his father was a minister, for High Church only to become a missionary and later a moralist supporter of Indian nationalism. Andrews did not feel close to the religious atmosphere in which his father, who had the powers of prophesy and healing, conducted his services. Nevertheless, he became a missionary who soon felt the constraints of High Church Anglicanism as too limiting. One can easily see the influence of evangelical moralism in C. F. Andrews's positions.[24]

In mainstream evangelicalism, religious enthusiasm was channeled into public activity, spreading middle-class values over the larger population. By and large, it does not seem correct to see the evangelical movement as an antirational movement. Rather, it was a movement that tried to combine rational thought and religious "feeling," sense and sensibility. In that and other respects I interpret it as a typical nationalist movement that tries to combine enlightenment with romanticism. Although there is constant debate between utilitarian liberals and evangelicals, evidence of their common ground is considerable. This common ground is exemplified in the way John Stuart Mill tried to distance himself from the hyper-rationalism of his father.[25] The evangelical project was to convert people to a morally inspired existence in which individual conscience of sins and atonement are catchwords, within a nation with a colonizing mission that is interpreted as liberating.

Gladstone is an interesting example of the combination of liberalism and evangelical moralism. Brought up in a devoutly evangelical family, he began his career under the influence of the poet-philosopher Coleridge's book, *On the Constitution of Church and State*.[26] To defend the established church in the aftermath of Catholic emancipation, he wrote a book entitled *The State in Its Relations with the Church*, in which he endows the state with a conscience that transcends that of individuals.[27] In this treatise he argued not only for a strong tie between church and state, but he endowed the state with high moral qualities:

The State is properly and according to its nature, moral . . . It means that the general action of the State is under a moral law . . . In the government and laws of a country we find not a mere aggregation of individual acts but a composite agency . . . This composite agency represents the personality of the nation; and, as a great distinct moral reality, demands a worship of its own, namely, the worship of the State, represented in its living and governing members, and therefore a public and joint worship. To sum up then in a few words the result of these considerations, religion is applicable to the State, because it is the office of the State in its personality to evolve the social life of man, which social life is essentially moral in the ends it contemplates, in the subject-matter on which it feeds, and in the restraints and motives it requires; and which can only be effectually moral when it is religious. Or, religion is directly necessary to the right employment of the energies of the State.[28]

Since Gladstone, later in his career, became a defender of the rights of dissenters and Catholics, it has been argued that he completely repudiated his earlier views.[29] I would suggest, however, that we see in Gladstone a shift from the early-modern view of the public church to the moral nation-state in which not the state bureaucracy but individual and national conscience were paramount. What remains constant is the moral/religious nature of political activity. Instead of excluding others from this moral life of the nation he now wanted to include them all. This meant a repudiation of a strictly Calvinist notion of the "few elect" to be replaced by a moral universalism that extended grace to all the inhabitants of the world. There is a vision here of a national church or the nation as a church that goes beyond the visible, institutional Church of England.

Such a fusion of church and nation-state was also crucial to the civilizing mission, as envisioned by Thomas Arnold in his *Principles of Church Reform*.[30] Although Arnold was still doubtful of the desirability of including Roman Catholics (Irish barbarians) and concerned that dissenting groups would join this Christianizing and civilizing mission, his doubts were soon overtaken by new realities—the liberal doctrine to improve society, which fits extraordinarily well with Christian moralism. In this regard, it is interesting to note that Coleridge not only influenced Gladstone and Arnold but also that principal spokesman of liberal ideas in the nineteenth century, John Stuart Mill.[31] Instead of the usual evangelical views of damnation and the end of times, there is in Gladstone a liberal view of progress, but added to this is the notion that progress is the Christian improvement of society and that in such progress we see the hand of

God. This mixture of liberal and evangelical ideas leads to a quite general emphasis on the moral character of the English people and their duty to lead the world.[32] These views of progress and grace for all were not confined to the British isles but included the "white man's burden" to bring the gospel to the colonies.

The shift from an Anglican exclusivist vision of the nation to an inclusivist nationalism is reflected in the other major religious development of the period, the emancipation of the Catholics. Eighteenth-century England had been very much a Protestant state, but the creation of the British nation-state required the inclusion of the Catholic minority. There was a considerable history of anti-Catholic hostility in England, which resulted in the exclusion of Catholics from most areas of public life. From 1800, Roman Catholicism, like evangelicalism, experienced a tremendous growth. In England this was the result of both an increase in English Catholics and a great influx of Irish immigrants. In Ireland there was an expansion of Roman Catholic activity, marked by the foundation of an Irish priest-training college at Maynooth in 1795. Roman Catholicism, like evangelicalism, also had an influence outside its fold. This is most evident in the Oxford movement (also called the Tractarians), a movement from 1833 on toward emphasizing the Catholicity of the Church of England, called Anglo-Catholicism. John Henry Newman (1801–1890), one of the movement's luminaries, replaced "Anglo" with "Roman" in 1845 and rose to become a Roman Catholic cardinal in 1879.

Evangelicals viewed the growth in the numbers of Roman Catholics as a threat, which was compounded by their understandable fear of "the enemy within," namely, the Oxford movement. In the 1820s the political struggle concerned the right of Roman Catholics to sit in the united Parliament of Great Britain and Ireland, which was decided in 1829 by the Catholic emancipation. Not only were Roman Catholics now allowed to become part of the nation but also dissenters whose civil disabilities were revoked by the Test and Corporation Acts in 1828. One has to interpret the books of Coleridge, Arnold, and Gladstone in the light of these events, which definitely served to transform significantly the religious and political character of British society.

The enfranchisement of the Catholic minority in the British isles did little, however, to prevent the strong connection that grew between Roman Catholicism and Irish nationalism.[33] This connection emerged very clearly in the Repeal agitation of 1843, in which the Roman Catholic clergy and Irish nationalists worked hand in hand to attack the legislative union between Britain and Ireland. This movement, supported by Roman

Catholic organizational structures, drew huge popular support. It is no exaggeration to see Irish nationalism as the strongest example of religious nationalism in "Greater Britain." Thus the emancipation of Catholics had not succeeded in drawing the Irish Catholics into the British nation, which continued to be strongly English in character. Likewise, the Scottish Presbyterians were not immediately inclined to be part of an English/British nation that was marked by the Disruption in 1843, in which half the Established Church's clergy left to form the Free Church of Scotland. As in England, evangelicalism worked here to promote the cause of nationalism, but this time it was Scottish nationalism. The main inspiration to form the Free Church was an evangelical urge to be close to "the people," but, as a corollary, the Disruption was marked by anti-English sentiments (which still remain strong today) as expressed in opposition to Westminster as well as to Anglicized landlords. Not nearly as strong as in Ireland, nationalism in Scotland was nevertheless also marked by religious overtones. The same may be true for the connection between Welsh linguistic nationalism and Nonconformist religion.

Catholic emancipation undid any illusion people like Thomas Arnold may have had about Britain as a Protestant nation. Anti-Catholic feelings among the Protestant majority did not prevent Roman Catholics from growing into the largest single church in England in the twentieth century.[34] At the same time, building "Greater Britain," including Ireland, into a nation proved impossible in the face of the successful combination of Roman Catholicism and Irish nationalism. Anti-Catholicism was very strong in the evangelical movement, but it should be emphasized that both Catholicism and evangelicalism—in a dynamic fed by mutual rivalry—expanded substantially in the first half of the nineteenth century. Both movements were simultaneously expanding and trying to dominate an emerging public sphere that made nationalism possible. Evangelical Awakening and Roman Catholic Revival are most profitably seen as two connected movements that derived much of their expansionist energy from their mutual rivalry.[35] In this connection it is interesting to note that evangelicalism, despite its anti-Catholicism, even influenced the nineteenth century's most famous convert to Catholicism, John Henry Newman, as he candidly admitted in his *Apologia Pro Vita Sua*.[36]

From the 1830s till the 1860s anti-Catholicism and anti-ritualism within the Anglican Church were major themes of what John Wolffe has called "the Protestant Crusade."[37] This implied widespread agitation and popular mobilization of both Protestants and Catholics. Again, I would suggest that we see them in their interaction. Both evangelicals and Catholics were eager to underline their nationalism. Protestants in particular liked to emphasize their link to that paramount symbol of imperial nationalism, Queen Victoria.[38] While Irish Catholics obviously emphasized their Irishness, English Catholics were trying even harder to distance themselves from allegations of antinational allegiance to the Pope. My contention is that both movements helped significantly in creating an imperial and missionary nationalism, characterized by superior national qualities of a ruling race: a nation with a mission. As Mandell Creighton, Anglican Bishop of London, asserted at the turn of the century, "the question of the future of the world is the existence of Anglo-Saxon civilisation on a religious basis."[39] Creighton explicitly had the Church of England in mind when speaking about "the conquest of the world," but I would propose that religious diversity was encompassed by a notion of the duties of a superior race.

The notion of racial superiority in the second half of the nineteenth century depended to an important extent on comparison. Civilization was defined by its antithesis: barbarism or savagery. The internal rivalries, animosities, and political conflicts within British Christianity faded into the background of what came to be seen as the difference between British Christian civilization and the barbarity of the colonized peoples. The biblical affirmation that humankind was one, derived from one single pair in the Garden of Eden, as well as the Enlightenment notion of universal sameness and equality were rapidly giving way to ideas of radical racial difference in the second half of the nineteenth century.[40] Philologists like Renan and the early Max Müller equated race and language, and Renan asserted the right of superior races to colonize inferior ones. Where Thomas Arnold had been concerned about the relation between religion and nation, his son, Matthew Arnold, the author of *Culture and Anarchy*, relocated that concern by emphasizing a racialized view of culture. That the Arnoldian view of culture continued to be religiously inspired should be clear from the following quotation from *Culture and Anarchy*:

> The aim of culture [is to set] ourselves to ascertain what perfection is and to make it prevail; but also, in determining generally, in what perfection consists, religion comes to a conclusion identical with that which culture . . . likewise reaches. Religion says: The Kingdom of God is within you; and culture, in like manner, places human perfection in an internal condition, in the growth and predominance of our humanity proper, as distinguished from our animality. . . . Not a having and a resting, but a growing and a becoming, is the character of perfection as culture conceives it; and here, too, it coincides with religion.[41]

It is important to note that Arnold was Inspector of Schools and in that capacity responsible for the education of the British in the new racialized mission of the nation. Modern science supported this ideological formation of national culture in which language and race took central stage, and the culture of the colonized was turned into an object of academic study, with its own university chair.[42] Gradually race comes to take precedence over religion as the dominant element in British nationalism in the second half of the nineteenth century.[43]

THE COLONIAL MISSION IN INDIA

One of the great policy debates in the East India Company in the early nineteenth century was between Orientalists, who argued that the Company should continue its policy of supporting native religious and educational institutions, and Anglicists, who argued that there was little of value in these native institutions which should be replaced by the more civilized and advanced institutions of England. This was clearly a complex debate that was, more or less decisively, won by the Anglicists when Thomas Babington Macaulay's *Minute on Indian Education* of 1835 was accepted as the basis of official policy. In this battle, evangelicals sided with Anglicists. Evangelicals, such as those of the Clapham sect (William Wilberforce, Zachary Macaulay, John Venn, Samuel Thornton, and Charles Grant) who were prominent in the antislavery campaign, were indignant at the support the Company had given to Hinduism and Islam in India. They concurred with the Utilitarian Anglicists in their disdain for the native institutions and literatures of India. William Wilberforce told the English Parliament that the Orientalists were as skeptical about Christianity as the French revolutionaries whose actions it regarded with horror.[44] Not only should the Company allow missionaries to work in India (which it did after 1813), but it should stop the support of native institutions.

As we have seen in the previous chapter, in the early decades of the nineteenth century the Company was still giving patronage to Hindu temples and festivals, especially in the South. Under strong pressure from the evangelicals, the Company had to withdraw from that policy. It did so hesitantly. Even as late as 1838 a committee had to be formed in England for the purpose of "diffusing information relative to the connection of the East India Company's Government with the superstitious idolatrous systems of the natives, and for promoting the dissolution of that connection."[45] We have to see this as a withdrawal of sorts, however, since the British became active in setting up systems and committees to manage religious endowments. These committees became important arenas for organizing the public sphere, for Hindus and Muslims alike. As such, it was another instance of a new colonial politics of representation that replaced the older patronage networks in which the Company had participated to further its prime purpose, trade.

Utilitarians and evangelicals agreed that the religious institutions of India needed to be dismantled and replaced by Christian civilization. They disagreed, however, on how to bring civilization to the natives. Religious neutrality was seen as essential first for trading purposes and later for British rule in India. The Company continued to resist direct support for missionary projects. The Anglican Society for the Propagation of the Gospel in Foreign Parts (est., 1701) had always been a colonial church providing clergy for the British in the colonies until it was transformed in the 1830s under evangelical influence.[46] Serious missionary activity among the natives originated only in the nineteenth century outside the Company in evangelical circles that raised money from the British public. The Company's neutrality, however, did nothing to prevent attempts to reform Indian society through education, an endeavor fully supported by the Utilitarian Anglicists. This, however, turned out to be a field in which missionaries were extremely active.

Whatever the debates between evangelicals and Utilitarians—and they were considerable—none of them would have denied that civil society and the forms of knowledge on which it was based were ultimately part and parcel of Christian civilization. Gauri Viswanathan has argued forcefully that the teaching of "secular" English literature, as recommended in Macaulay's *Minute*, amounts to a relocation of cultural value from belief and dogma to language, experience, and history.[47] This relocation can be detected in the intellectual differences that simultaneously divide and connect Matthew Arnold with his father, Thomas, as well as Thomas Babington Macaulay with his father, Zachary. Despite their differences, these people are in the same moral universe. Their differences are not about the moral mission of the state but about matters of policy. The developments in that universe are similar in Britain and among the British in India. For evangelicals and Utilitarians, the world was no longer limited to England or Greater Britain. The antislavery campaigns had made the British public aware of Britain's role in a larger world. That that role had to be one of reform and uplift friend and foe could agree on.

However much the British tried to hide the Christian roots of their colonial policies behind the mask of religious neutrality, the colonized "natives" were not to be fooled. It is often rightly observed that there were great differences between the operations of the missionary societies in India and those of the state, but these were differences within a shared colonizing project. It is certainly true that the officers of the company and later those of the colonial state looked down on the missionaries and that, in general, there was a substantial social gap between them. Nevertheless, their concerns colluded in the crucial fields of education and reform, as they did back home in Britain. The real difference was obviously not between the colonial state and the missionaries but between the colonizing British and the colonized Indians. Whereas in Britain the state would gradually occupy the social spaces opened up by the religious organizations, in India these spaces were occupied by rival religious organizations of native "subjects." Their ideas and actions could not be incorporated in a British nation characterized by its Christian civilization. In due course they became oppositional toward the colonial state and, by the same token, toward bearers of Indian nationalism.

Despite the official policy of religious neutrality, the British interfered with every aspect of Indian religion and society. Considering the nature of the colonial project there was actually no choice, and the tropes of "withdrawal," "secularity," and "neutrality" only tried to hide that discursively. Although I limit myself here to a discussion of the British involvement with Hinduism and its consequences, I would suggest that the developments that took place in Indian Islam and Sikhism were not altogether different. The policies of the British set off a whole chain of reformist reaction in Hinduism. As in the case of the evangelical "awakening" in Britain, the causalities involved are extremely complex, and I do not see reform merely as a reaction to the colonial project. As I have argued elsewhere, reform is certainly, to a considerable extent, an "invented tradition" in response to colonial modernity, but it is as much a product of religious discursive traditions of longue duree. Debates about the worship of saints and images had been going on long before colonization.[48] What I wish to highlight here, however, is the creation of a public sphere by reformist organizations in a way that reminds one of the evangelical activities in Britain. Let us look briefly at the construction of "Hindu spirituality" in the Brahmo Samaj and the Ramakrishna mission, as well as at the construction of the "Aryan race" in the Arya Samaj.

An early instance of a "Hindu public" responding to colonial rule was the abolition of sati (widow immolation) by the British in 1829. Sati was perhaps the most definite sign of Hindu depravity and Christian moral superiority evangelicals could get. Consequently, they focused their campaign against native institutions on the abolition of this particular practice. They succeeded in convincing Governor-General William Bentinck, who later also enacted Macaulay's Anglicist proposals for Indian education. A statue for Bentinck, erected soon after his departure from India in 1835, showed a sati scene under Bentinck's stern figure; an inscription on the rear of its base recorded that Britain was now committed to "elevate the moral and intellectual character" of its Indian subjects.[49] Beneath the evangelical moralism, however, one may well detect a sexual fantasy of "white men saving brown women from brown men."[50]

More important than the evangelical actions and the government's responses was the position taken by "enlightened" citizens of Calcutta. Rammohan Roy (1772–1833), sometimes called "the father of the Bengal Renaissance," wrote, between 1818 and 1832, a great deal on the subject. In January 1830 Rammohan, together with three hundred residents of Calcutta, presented a petition to Bentinck in support of the regulation prohibiting sati. Rammohan rejected the practice on the basis of his reading of Hindu scripture. He distinguished authoritative sources (such as the Vedas) from other sources. It is interesting to note that he did not refer to any authoritative interpretation of these sources by learned gurus but relied entirely on his private, rational judgment. This is certainly an important step in the laicization of Hinduism. What we also see here is the importance of scriptural authority to which a lay person may refer without mediation of a sacred interpreter. One of Rammohan's most important objectives was to abolish the rules of the caste-based, hereditary qualification to study the Veda.[51] Following Lata Mani, I would suggest that the colonialist insistence on the unmediated authority of written evidence for Indian traditions, enabled by the Orientalist study of these texts, made possible a gradual shift in emphasis from the spoken to the written in Hinduism.[52] I would add, however, that the evangelicals, who railed against the sati practice, also insisted on the centrality of the text. Rammohan's position participated in both the Orientalist and the Protestant ways of thinking. His privileging of his own rational judgment, based on reading and discussion, enabled the rise of a certain kind of public debate in Habermas's sense.

Rammohan was strongly influenced by English and American Unitarianism, a Christian creed characterized by a rational and universalist theology as well as a social reformist conscience. He contributed an interesting tract to its theology, namely, *The Precepts of Jesus*, published in 1820. He was very interested in Christian theology and became a Unitarian, but, as his involvement in the sati-debate shows, he also remained a Hindu. In 1828 Rammohan founded the Brahmo Samaj. This was a small movement propagating a deist and universalist kind of religion, based, however, on Hindu sources and especially the Upanishads and the philosophical commentaries on the Upanishads (together known as the Vedanta). It was particularly opposed to "superstitious customs" of "ignorant people," deceived by their Brahman leaders. The deception by Brahmans is a crucial point. It is, of course, tempting to see it as a straightforward adoption of British attacks on Brahmans, as, for example in James Mill's *History of India*, but it is certainly a bit more complex than that. Roy himself came from a Brahman family, and his attack is based on his reading of Brahmanical sources. The British attack on Brahman priests lent support to a particular argument against priesthood in a Brahmanical debate about religious authority. Christian rational religion and certain Brahmanical arguments of long standing fit together quite well as the basis of a Hindu rational religion. Reason and "the dignity of human beings" became as important for it as for its Christian counterparts in Europe. Also interesting was its attempt to come to a universal religion, reminiscent of the Deist view that the great truths of religion were all universal and that true religion was ultimately natural religion, not bound to particular historical events of revelation that divided one religious community from another.[53]

What I would emphasize here is the strong parallel between the development of Indian and European "rational religion." There is, however, a crucial difference: Whereas the European Christians tried to universalize their Christian tradition, Indian Hindus did the same with their Hindu tradition. This reproduced the Hindu-Christian opposition that was also the opposition of colonized-colonizer. Colonialism provides the discursive frame in which Hindu rational religion emerges. As Ranajit Guha demonstrates, this is also evident in the work of someone outside the circle of the Brahmo Samaj, the humanist thinker Bankimchandra Chattopadhyay (1838–1894), who was very much influenced by August Comte.[54] Bankimchandra (again a Brahman), like many European thinkers, centers his view of "humanness" (*manusyatva*) on the notion of the perfectibility of man. In contrast to European thinkers, however, he thought it possible to give examples of *Adarsa Purush*, "ideal man," whose perfection had to be emulated. These examples were taken from Hindu religious history, with the god Krishna at the highest rank. The most perfect man was thus a Hindu god. The Enlightenment question about the nature of man had thus found, in the colonial setting, a particular answer in terms of religious nationalism.[55]

The intellectual Vedantic and Unitarian views of the Brahmos left them, to an important extent, isolated from the larger Bengali Hindu society. In this larger environment a particular Bengali brand of Vaishnavite devotionalism had become important since the sixteenth century. This devotionalism focused on the God Krishna and on gurus who descended from the disciples of the great sixteenth-century guru Chaitanya. It is interesting that in the second half of the nineteenth century this devotional tradition had begun to exercise considerable influence on the rational religion of the Brahmos. In the 1860s Keshabchandra Sen (1838—1884), one of the most influential Brahmo leaders, introduced devotional singing in the Brahmo congregational meetings.[56] He also no longer spoke English, but Bengali. He moved to the rural outskirts of Calcutta and introduced an ascetic lifestyle among his followers. The next step seems to have been his encounter with the contemporary guru Ramakrishna (1836—1886), a priest in a temple for the Mother Goddess Kali in Calcutta. In his two newspapers (one in English, the other in Bengali) he introduced Ramakrishna to the wider, reading public as a true saint in the authentic Hindu tradition. In that way he authorized this illiterate Hindu ascetic as an acceptable guru for the Hindu middle classes. Partha Chatterjee portrays the meeting of these two personalities as constituting the "middle ground" occupied by the emergent middle classes, between European rational philosophy and Hindu religious discourse.[57] In his view this "middle ground" enables the anticolonial nationalists to divide the world into two domains —the material, outer world dominated by Western science and the spiritual, inner world of the home dominated by Hindu values. It is crucial to realize, however, that Keshabchandra was also a universalist who wanted to bring all religions together and that Ramakrishna was an unorthodox ascetic with a desire to transcend and transgress narrow boundaries of Hinduism. What we also have in this meeting, then, is the creation of a Hindu universalism.[58]

The spirituality of Hindu civilization, however, is not only signified by "the home" but also by reformist and political action, such as that seen much later in Gandhi's nonviolent activities (satyagraha). The theme of Hindu spirituality being in opposition to Western materialism definitely becomes the principal theme in Hindu nationalist discourse from this period on. A major step in the popularization of Hindu reformist ideas was made by linking it to emergent nationalism. "Hindu spirituality" had to be defended against the onslaught of colonial modernity. Perhaps the most important expounder of the doctrine of "Hindu spirituality" has been the founder of the Ramakrishna Mission, Vivekananda (1863—

1902). Vivekananda was an extremely talented student who had been thoroughly educated in contemporary Western thought. He joined the Brahmo Samaj briefly before he met Ramakrishna.

The encounter with Ramakrishna had a transformative impact on the young Narendranath Datta who adopted the name Vivekananda when he took his ascetic vows. As Tapan Raychaudhuri emphasizes, Vivekananda was "more than anything else a mystic in quest of the Ultimate Reality within a specific Indian tradition."[59] It is this tradition that was vividly presented to Vivekananda not by learned discourse in which he himself was a master but by the charismatic presence of a guru, Ramakrishna, whose trances had first been treated as "insanity," but later became regarded as possession by the Goddess. What I suggest is that the articulation of Brahmo "rational religion" with the religious discourse of Ramakrishna produced the specific brand of "Hindu spirituality" that Vivekananda came to propagate.

The typical strategy of Vivekananda was to systematize a disparate set of traditions, make it intellectually available for a Westernized audience and defensible against Western critique, and incorporate it in the notion of "Hindu spirituality," carried by the Hindu nation that was superior to "Western materialism" and brought to India by an aggressive and arrogant "British nation." His major achievement was to transform the project to ground "Hindu spirituality" in a systematic interpretation of the Vedanta (the Upanishads and the tradition of their interpretation). This project, which started with Rammohan Roy and had produced rational Hinduism, was now combined with disciplines to attain perfection from the ascetic traditions in what Vivekananda called "practical Vedanta." The practical side also included participation in social reform. This kind of "Hindu spirituality" was later carried forward by Mahatma Gandhi and Sarvepalli Radhakrishnan, but it has also become a main inspiration for the current brand of Hindu nationalism today.[60]

A major element of Vivekananda's message was nationalist. He saw his project in terms of a revitalization of the Hindu nation. In 1897 he founded an ascetic order, the Ramakrishna Mission, to make ascetics available for the nationalist task. National self-determination, social reform, and spiritual awakening were all linked in his perception. The Ramakrishna Mission established itself throughout India and also outside India. It did not become a mass movement, but Vivekananda's rhetoric of spiritualism exerted an immense influence on the way Hindu gurus in the twentieth century came to communicate their message. Vivekananda transformed Hindu discourse on asceticism, devotion, and worship into the nationalist idiom of "service to the nation" for both men and women.

Vivekananda's construction of "Hindu spirituality' gave the sacrificial notion of "self-sacrifice" a new meaning that drew simultaneously from Hindu traditions of devotion (*bhakti*) and evangelical notions of female morality. We have here a complex mixture, in which "femininity" is the signifier of "Hindu spirituality," while women themselves should be self-sacrificing in accordance with both Victorian notions of "domesticity" and Hindu notions of total devotion to their husbands. The debate about sati signifies a moment in a series of interactions through which both the Indian and British nations became defined.

While gender was the dominant issue in the prohibition of sati and crucial to the definition of "Hindu spirituality" with its emphasis on "feminine devotion and self-sacrifice,"[61] race and caste were the paramount issues in the formation of "Hindu Aryanism." The mutiny of sepoys of the Bengal army and the ensuing revolt in northern India in 1857, as well as its suppression in 1858, contributed immensely to the notion of racial and religious differences between the colonizers and the colonized. In this period of great anxiety about the loss of control over India, stories about inhuman atrocities inflicted on British women and children were rapidly circulated throughout Britain and confirmed the general view of the Indians' barbarity that had already been established in the depiction of sati. The suppression of the revolt demonstrated to the British once and for all that they were a superior race. This feeling was most clearly (and outrageously) expressed by Charles Dickens:

> I wish I were Commander in Chief in India. The first thing I would do to strike that Oriental race with amazement (not in the least regarding them as if they lived in the Strand, London, or at Camden Town) should be to proclaim to them in their language, that I considered my holding that appointment by the leave of God, to mean that I should do my utmost to exterminate the Race upon whom the stain of the late cruelties rested; and that I was . . . now proceeding, with all convenient dispatch and merciful swiftness of execution, to blot it out of humankind and raze it off the face of the earth.[62]

In the long run the revolt convinced most colonial officers that conversion to Christianity was an uphill struggle and reinforced the idea that religious neutrality was essential to colonial rule. For these officers it became difficult to see how the Indian barbarians would ever become equal to

British Christians. Lord Canning dismissed the evangelical Herbert Edwardes, Commissioner of Peshawar, as "exactly what Mahomet would have been if born at Clapham instead of Mecca."[63] Racial difference between the British and the colonized and among the colonized themselves became the explanation and legitimation of colonial rule.

While this reinvigorated racism in India colluded with the rise of racial nationalism in the metropole, at the level of scientific thought the notion that the higher castes of India belonged to the same Aryan race as the British was widely accepted. In India the idea of race had to be combined with that of culture or civilization to explain why the British as "younger brothers" of the Aryan family had to guide the "older brothers" to civilization. This intervening cultural element continued to be religious difference. The story of the Aryan race in India was a story of decline, caused by a variety of factors such as racial mixing or climate but especially by the inherent barbarity of Hindu polytheism.

Ideas of race were not exclusively theoretical but also informed recruiting patterns for the army that included "martial" races, such as the Punjabi Sikhs, and excluded "effeminate" races, such as the Bengalis. Another important distinction was between "the Aryans" and the "Dravidians" in South India. The missionary Robert Caldwell based his linguistic and ethnological theories about Dravidian languages and peoples on that distinction. In the second half of the nineteenth century he developed a myth of the Aryan (Brahmanical) invasion of South India and the subsequent subjection of the Dravidian people to a Hindu caste system in which the invaders were on top. His argument was meant to support his own missionary work among the "original" Dravidian population by delegitimizing Brahman priests, but ultimately his theory of a Dravidian race was used in the South for political purposes that had nothing to do with Christian conversion.[64]

The Aryan race theory was taken up in northern India by Hinduism's most important reformist movement, the Arya Samaj. Its founder, Swami Dayananda Sarasvati (1824–1883) was one of India's many gurus in the nineteenth century. He was initiated in the order of the Shivaite Dashanamis, a prestigious Hindu ascetic order that only allowed Brahmans to take the ascetic vows. Just like other ascetics of his order, Dayananda traveled through India, visiting sacred places. He became rather successful and seemed on his way to form his own, limited community of ascetic and lay followers. In 1872 Dayananda visited the Brahmo leader Debendranath Tagore in Calcutta for four months. This visit seems to have transformed his style. He abandoned his ascetic robe and exchanged his use of Sanskrit oratory for Hindi.[65]

Dayananda already had a strong reformist sense that the Hindu religion had degenerated and needed to be revitalized. In his own representation, he had been summoned by his own, blind guru of the Dashanami order to campaign for a return to a pristine Hinduism based on the Vedas. This was a command entirely within the Hindu discursive tradition in which the Vedas are seen as the ultimate, authoritative source of knowledge. Until Dayananda appeared on the stage, however, it was more or less an imaginary source. Knowledge of the Vedas was transmitted in Brahman families, largely orally with some help from manuscripts. Moreover, the Vedas are lengthy, obscure texts, riddled with internal contradictions, by no means a straightforward source for authorization of human practice. In this period, however, Max Müller, the towering figure of Orientalist scholarship in Britain, had provided a definitive edition and translation of the Rig-Veda, financially underwritten by the East India Company. This was one of the major gifts brought to India by the Prince of Wales on his tour in 1875–76. Dayananda thus accepted the degeneration doctrine, implicit in the Aryan theory. Hinduism, as it actually existed, was a degeneration of a pristine Aryan religion, as laid down in the Vedas.

It is not possible to follow here in any detail the development of Dayananda's thinking or of the movement, called Arya Samaj (the Society of Aryans), that he founded in Bombay in 1875. I will simply summarize the points that made Dayananda's Aryan religion (Arya Dharm) a radically new religious program. First, he proposed to get back to the basic Vedic mentators of these texts. He provided his own Sanskrit commentaries to these texts, in which he sought to show that all the scientific knowledge of the West was, in fact, already present in the Vedic revelation. He spoke of the Vedic teachings of telecommunications, about the construction of ships and aircraft, and about gravity and gravitational attraction. The importance given to science and its appropriation is, of course, extremely significant. Vedic religion was a universal, rational religion of an Aryan people. It was the cradle of all human civilization. In this we can see the influence of the "rational religion" arguments in Calcutta.

Like the Brahmos Dayananda argued that the Vedic revelation was monotheistic. A monistic argument could very well be developed from an early medieval interpretation of the Upanishads by Shankara, the founder of the Dashanamis, the order to which Dayananda belonged. Moreover, there is also a monotheistic tendency in the ascetic orders that focuses their meditation on one god. Dayananda, however, wanted to obscure the reference to many gods in the Vedic hymns. He did not use the traditional Hindu argument that one particular god is higher than all the other gods (or that he encompasses all the others). He wanted to get rid of the Hindu pantheon and the practice of image worship.

In the nineteenth-century European evolutionary worldview, monotheism was seen as the highest form of religion. A religion had to be monotheistic to be rational and to allow a scientific understanding of the world. In that sense, Dayananda's discourse on Hindu monotheism looks derivative, but I would like to draw attention to its very specific Hindu, discursive underpinnings. The reference to the Vedas, the monism of the Vedanta, and the monotheism of the Shaivites and their depreciation of image worship are all present in Dayananda's thinking. The lay response to Dayananda's message was also very much predetermined by existing Hindu discursive frames. Dayananda's rejection of image worship limited the appeal of his message considerably. Image worship is the dominant form of worship in popular Hinduism, and it is inconceivable that a radical iconoclastic movement would succeed in India. The Arya Samaj did, however, have a considerable following in the Punjab, where one finds a long history of imageless worship.

Second, an important point in Dayananda's program was an attack on the caste system which he saw as a degeneration of the original, natural ordering of Vedic society in four functional groups: priests, warriors, traders, and servants. This natural order was entirely rational and functional, if only it was based on achievement rather than ascription. Dayananda's privileging of this ancient social hierarchy may have been related to the fact that the census operations, starting in the 1870s, tried to use it to rank actual castes (whose social relations were only salient on a regional basis) hierarchically on an All-India basis. As Bernard Cohn has powerfully argued, the census operations enhanced the importance of caste distinctions in the new arenas for competition created by the British.[66] Dayananda's solution to take over the All-India grid of the census, explain it in functional terms, and do away with actual hereditary caste relations was original and radical. It was used much later in Gandhi's social philosophy to include the untouchables in the Hindu nation.

More than anything else this meant in the Arya Samaj that everyone—of whatever caste—could become a priest and officiate in the principal rite of the Arya Samaj, the Vedic sacrifice, which is commonly the strict prerogative of Brahmans. Despite his emphasis on Brahmanical scripture and Brahmanical ritual, here Dayananda launches a direct attack on the ritual hegemony of Brahman priests. In so doing, he continues a discourse on priesthood which, as we have seen with Rammohan Roy, has its roots both in Brahmanical debates and in colonial attacks on Brahmans. Dayananda takes his attack a crucial step further by allowing non-Brahmans to perform the Vedic sacrifice. Although this had an affinity (in the Weberian sense) with the aspirations of a new class of English-educated Indian officials, Dayananda's program was too radical for many. Again, it had most of its appeal in the Punjab, where religions like Sikhism had not only done away with the worship of images but also with Brahman priesthood. The radical novelty of Dayananda's program is clear: the Arya Samaj became a religious community in which all religious power gravitated toward the laity. Dayananda, after his death, was not succeeded by another guru but by a committee of lay members.

A third important innovation was the great emphasis the Arya Samaj placed on education. A large number of schools were founded in the Punjab and elsewhere that still today also attract many non-Arya Hindu students. This kind of social activity made the Arya Samaj a strong competitor of the Christian missions. Following the Arya Samaj, a great number of religious movements, with or without a core of ascetic gurus, entered the quickly expanding fields of education, social welfare, and medical care. The Arya Samaj had discovered the larger Indian public as the target of internal missionization. Special rituals were devised to purify those who had been converted to other religions and bring them back to the Hindu fold. The larger Indian public also came to include those who had left India as indentured laborers to work in British plantations overseas. Arya Samaji missionaries were sent to these areas and enjoyed considerable success.

What we see here is that the Arya Samaj became an important factor in the creation of a Hindu public. It brought the debate about the nature of Hinduism to the popular masses in a far more direct manner than Rammohan or Bankim had been able to do. Dayananda's message developed, in the colonial context, from important Hindu discursive traditions and remained close to them. Dayananda was a prolific writer and talker who was constantly in debate with other Hindu leaders, again following a long-standing tradition of the public contestation of religious opinion (*shastrartha*). At the end of his life he found the revolutionary issue, the Protection of Mother Cow against British and Muslim butchers, that would lead to mass participation in the public sphere.

Concluding Remarks

I hope to have conveyed that (1) religion has been crucial in the emergence of nationalism in both Britain and India; that (2) the processes of nation building in these two countries have been connected through empire; and that (3) the imperial relation has affected the location of religion in Britain and India. The modern state depends, in liberal theory, on the formation of a civil society consisting of free but civilized subjects, as well as on the formation of a public sphere for the conduct of rational debate. In that theory the notions of "freedom" and "rationality" are defined in terms of "secularity". I have tried to show that, contrary to that theory, religion is a major source of rational, moral subjects and a central organizational aspect of the public spheres they create. Antislavery societies, Bible societies, anti-Catholic agitation, anti-Sati petitions, Ramakrishna missions, Cow protection movements—all these have in common the creation of public spheres of political interaction that are crucial to the formation of national identities. The moral tenor of these movements is essential to the understanding of the mission of empire as well as the mission of anticolonial nationalism.

I also hope to have demonstrated the fallacy in the supposition that the British polity is secular and the Indian polity religious. I have suggested that one cannot make a sharp, structural distinction between nation and state. In the modern period the nation-state is produced as a hyphenated entity, that is, the two go together. There is, of course, a liberal notion that the state is outside civil society and can be criticized by that society, which limits state power. I contend, however, that the modern state is not an entity but a nexus of projects and arrangements through which society is organized. The externality of the state is an effect of these projects. It is especially through the project of education and legal arrangements that the modern subject is formed. As Mauss has suggested, language, race, and religion are also constructed in the process of nation-state formation. This is true for both the metropole and the colony. The moral mission of the modern state is to organize the health, wealth, and welfare of its citizens, and, to achieve that, it has to get to know them through various projects of documentation, such as the census.[67] The extent to which this knowledge is gathered through religious categories and the extent to which distribution of power and services is carried out through religious organizations are perhaps indexes of the "religiosity" or "secularity" of a particular society.

Though I have not dealt with this here, it might be that from the 1870s churches and other religious organizations gradually lost their previous importance in the organization of the nation-state in Britain as compared to labor organizations and political parties. Such a shift may have been enabled by the growing centrality of scientific race theories in the definition of the British nation as compared to Christianity. It was certainly also Britain's growing imperial power in the second half of the nineteenth century that allowed for racial fantasies of superiority. Moreover, the conceit of religious neutrality which was thought essential to imperial rule (perhaps even more after the revolt of 1857), made race a better marker of difference than religion. At least it allowed some government officials to steer away from the constant evangelical pressure to promote Christianity in India. These imperial designs of religious neutrality (a neutrality absent in the metropole), however, did not prevent Indians from seeing it as a moral state with a definite Christian morality.

Obviously, the crucial difference between the modern state in the metropole and in the colony is that in the former its project of political legitimacy is in terms of "the nation," citizenship, and national identity, whereas in the latter "the subjects" are excluded from citizenship and their national identity is either denied or denigrated. Both religious and racial difference are legitimations of differences of power. That is why anticolonial nationalisms are not only struggles for power in the political arena but also attempt to counter the cultural hegemony of the colonial theory of difference. They often do so, as in the cases discussed here, by posing an alternative interpretation of the grounds of hegemony, be it religion or race. Vivekananda posed the superiority of Hinduism's spirituality over Western materialism. In doing so, he denied that Britain's Christianity was morally superior, which allowed the British to rule India. Britain's ascendancy was, in his view, only a material one that in fact had jeopardized any spiritual value British Christianity might have had. Dayananda adopted the Aryan race theory from Orientalism; but instead of accepting the theory that Christianity was to redeem the "fallen state" of Hindu civilization, he proposed a return to Vedic religion, which had preceded Christianity and was the very origin of all morality.

The Spirits of the Age: Spiritualism and Political Radicalism

IN FEBRUARY 1879 an American man and a Russian woman arrived in Bombay. Col. Henry Steel Olcott and Mme. Helena Blavatsky had sold everything they owned and had come to India to stay. Their host in Bombay was Harishchandra Chintamani, president of the Bombay Arya Samaj. He was not the best of hosts, however, since he sent the newly arrived guests the bill for the lavish party he had arranged to welcome them, including the cost of his welcoming telegram. He may not have realized that these foreigners' assets were mainly cultural, or, more to the point, spiritual. Indeed, this was not a very auspicious start in the collaboration between the Theosophists and the Arya Samaj, a partnership that had seemed so promising on May 22, 1878. On that day Olcott and Blavatsky had changed the name of their small New York coterie to the "Theosophical Society of the Arya Samaj of India," with Swami Dayananda Saraswati as its head. Nevertheless, soon after their arrival in Bombay, Olcott and Blavatsky left the city to meet Dayananda in Saharanpur, traveled with him to Meerut, and eventually returned to Bombay. In December they again visited Dayananda, this time in Benares. Blavatsky arrived there in the company of Alfred P. Sinnett, editor of the *Allahabad Pioneer*, a man she had met in Simla. This made it clear that the two Theosophists no longer depended entirely on the Arya Samaj for their survival in India, for they had made valuable contacts in India's British society. That the Theosophical Society in India had influential contacts among both the Indian and the so-called Anglo-Indian (British colonial) elites remained one of its significant features.

Doctrinal differences between the Theosophists and Dayananda emerged soon after this meeting, and, on a visit to Bombay in 1881, Dayananda broke with them. In the typical polemical fashion of the time, Dayananda published a flyer entitled *Humbuggery of the Theosophists*.[1] The Swami denounced the trickery and irrationality of Olcott and Blavatsky as a show, a *tamasha*. He thought they were bogus people with very little understanding of the scientific nature of Hinduism. He particularly objected to the occult experiments of Madame Blavatsky which he thought were distracting from the spiritual truths of the Aryan religion.

Clearly the perspectives of the two parties in the debate on the true nature of Hindu spirituality differed considerably. It is obviously tempting to argue that Dayananda's perspective was the more "authentic" one. After all, he was a Brahman and a Dashanami ascetic whose guru, Virajanand Saraswati, had instructed him to reform Hinduism. He could read, write, and speak Sanskrit, although he had chosen to use Hindi in order to reach a larger audience. Certainly he knew more about Hindu discursive traditions than either Olcott or Blavatsky. Olcott had been a colonel in the Union Army during the Civil War. After the war, he, like so many others, had taken an interest in spiritualism, a belief in conversations with the "spirits" of physically dead persons. Spiritualism had begun in upstate New York in 1848 and had since spread through the United States and Europe. On a trip to Vermont in 1874 to visit the Eddy family, known to have been remarkably successful in their communications with spirits, Olcott met Madame Blavatsky, a German-Russian who had escaped her husband, vice-governor of Yerevan in the Caucasus. Like the Eddy family she could converse with spirits, but, more than that, she could command the spirits and, even more extraordinary, communicate with the Masters who ruled the universe. In her life story, as she herself told it, her most singular event had been her meeting with "Himalayan Masters" while traveling in Tibet. That she had even been to Tibet is, of course, highly unlikely. Her claim has to be understood not only in terms of the contemporary construction of Tibet as the nowhereland of Shangri-La, but also in terms of the geopolitical struggle between Britain and Russia for Central Asian hegemony. But Madame Blavatsky was Russian, after all, and contemporary fantasies about Russia only added to her powers.

Olcott's and Blavatsky's experiments with spiritualism had very little to do with Hinduism as such, but Blavatsky made the brilliant move to connect spiritualism, the communication with spirits, with spirituality, the unbounded tradition of mysticism. According to Theosophy, both the major spirits (the "Masters of the Universe") and spiritual thought originated in "the East" and, since one could not go to Tibet, colonized India and Sri Lanka replaced it for all practical purposes. Indian civilization had, at least since Schopenhauer, captured the Orientalist imagination of being the cradle of spiritual thought, so that the Theosophists' choice to live among the Hindus in India should not surprise us.

It is also no surprise that a Hindu with an "authentic" religious pedigree like Dayananda was somewhat taken aback when he found out what his new followers from the West were actually up to. Communicating with spirits of the dead (*bhut, pret, jinnat*) is certainly part of Hindu beliefs and practices, but the intermediaries are not highly regarded. In fact, they are seen as impure and inauspicious, tainted by their contact with the dead, and often they are of low caste. Another well-known Hindu practice is possession by gods or goddesses, but that practice can only find its meaning within a particular discursive framework of devotional religion. It is precisely these beliefs, concerned as they were with spirits and devotional religion, that Dayananda, following particular Brahmanical discursive traditions, wanted to get rid of in his rationalist strivings. He could also make little sense of the "Masters of the Universe" with whom Madame Blavatsky was in frequent contact. They were definitely not part of the Vedic religion he was trying to spread in India.

Crucial to both Theosophists and Hindus was the issue of authenticity, of genuine religion as against "fake," unauthentic religion. Theosophists had to defend themselves constantly against the charge that they were inauthentic frauds, but many Hindus as well did not accept Dayananda as authentic. He was painted as a reformist with dangerous, modern ideas that threatened ancient Hinduism. In fact, his opponents were seen as defending the caste system as well as *Sanatana Dharma*, authentic, unchanging "eternal religion." This opposition was organized by the nineteenth-century precursor of the present-day Viswa Hindu Parishad, the Bharat Dharma Mahamandal, founded in 1887 by Din Dayalu Sharma. It is worth noting that one of the founding members of this stronghold of Hindu orthodoxy was Colonel Olcott, the Theosophist. So the question of who stands for "authentic Hinduism," when comparing the Arya Samaj and Theosophy, is not so straightforward after all. Or, more to the point, the ground for deciding authenticity and orthodoxy had drastically changed in the nineteenth century under conditions of modernity.

The politics of authenticity concerning Theosophy's understanding of Hinduism cannot be addressed without examining Theosophy's role in Britain. Theosophy turned out to be quite successful for a time in India and Sri Lanka, but also in Britain. Its success followed upon a remarkable interest in spiritualism that hit Britain in the mid-nineteenth century.

. . . . .

In this chapter I examine the appeal of spiritualism in these two sites of empire. In the case of Theosophy, which is a worldwide movement, one might have to take a global perspective, but it is not so much Theosophy I wish to explore as the peculiarities of colonial relations. I argue that spiritualism, and Theosophy in particular, played a significant role in the development of radical, anticolonial politics both in Britain and India. Second, that in doing so it enunciated an anti-Christian rationality, available in both spiritualism and secularism, that provided an opportunity to participate in scientific experimentation to those who did not belong to the elite circles of Victorian intellectual aristocracy, as described in Stefan Collini's *Public Moralists*.[2] While Theosophists were often recruited from relatively elite backgrounds, they were marginal in relation to the moral state, as described in the previous chapter, and carried some of the radical messages that characterized spiritualist movements. Spiritualists were largely plebeian autodidacts, but the category included women as well as the colonized elites of India. An important element in the plebeian appropriation of science is its anti-Christian, antiestablishment nature. It is from this background that the career of someone like Annie Besant, which seems so contradictory at first, comes to be understood. Third, I suggest that a comparison with the colonized world religions, such as Hinduism and Buddhism, which seem sufficiently different from colonizing Christianity, is an important element in anti-Christian rhetoric. Such a comparison is predicated upon an opposition between "spirituality" and "materialism." The construction of "spirituality" rests partly on the findings of Orientalist science and produces, in turn, innovative understandings of "science," both in the metropole and in the colony.

I first describe the political and social field Theosophy entered in Britain and the place of India and Hinduism in that field. Then I take a look at India and Sri Lanka and try to illuminate the reasons for Theosophy's success there. Finally, I show how the enthusiasms in India, Sri Lanka, and Britain feed into one another in the construction of Eastern spirituality and anticolonialism.

British Spirits

What did the religious scene in Britain look like when spiritualism and later Theosophy made their appearance in the second half of the nineteenth century? In the first half of that century, evangelical Christianity captured the national imaginary and, by the same token, became more inclusive. It created an imperial and missionary nationalism: a nation with a mission. In the 1860s and 1870s this vision of a moral nation-state gradually came to be characterized by the superior qualities of a ruling race, when the realities of empire became simultaneously more definite and all-embracing as well as insecure. The benchmark events signaling this shift are the Indian mutiny of 1857 and the debate about the behavior of Governor Eyre in the Morant Bay affair of 1865. The Indian mutiny shocked the British out of their complacent belief that they were allied with the Indian people in trying to reform Indian society. In this period of great anxiety about the loss of control over India, many stories were circulated in Britain about the inhumanity of the Indians who massacred innocent women and children. This, and the successful suppression of the revolt, not only confirmed the religious and racial superiority of the British but also strengthened a lingering doubt that the Indians were capable of becoming civilized. The moral optimism that had characterized the triumph of the abolition of slavery and the Reform Act of 1832 had gradually given way to a more racialized pessimism about the prospects of universal progress, which surfaced in public opinion most prominently in the debate about the behavior of Governor Eyre who had violently suppressed riots in Jamaica among the freed slaves. Thomas Carlyle and John Stuart Mill found themselves on opposite ends of that debate. Without question, Thomas Carlyle got the upper hand in the struggle over public opinion with, as Catherine Hall argues, his strongly masculine, racist notion of a white, English middle class ruling over women, blacks, and the lower classes in the empire.[3] What I suggest is that in the second half of the nineteenth century Britain, as a Christian nation, comes to be characterized by a muscular Christianity, based on a gendered notion of racial superiority.

The above forms the background against which the ascendancy of spiritualism and later Theosophy in Britain has to be seen. Britain was a deeply religious, Christian nation, led by a bourgeoisie whose ideas became increasingly racialized in the second half of the nineteenth century. Evangelicalism had succeeded largely in bridging the gap between Nonconformism or Dissent and the Anglican state church, between church and chapel. Although it had had a radical, mass-political agenda concerning abolition, conversion, and anti-Catholicism in the first half of the nineteenth century, it gradually became part of Gladstone's moral state, as I argued in the previous chapter. The essential point is that, first, it is false to see liberalism and evangelicalism as deadly foes. In many ways they actually joined forces in the construction of the moral state. Second, evangelicalism loses much of its social radicalism in the second half of the nineteenth century. This leads us to the question of where to locate the opposition to the development of the moral state. I suggest that we have to look to anti-Christian atheism and secularism, which originate not so much in the liberal Enlightenment but in radical comparisons with other world religions, and to radical Christianity.

Silvia Berti has recently argued that "in writing its own history, secular ideology started gradually to think itself as independent of the religious context from which it had emerged."[4] Berti makes a strong case for the importance of the Jewish tradition of anti-Christian polemics for the development of deism in England in the seventeenth century. It is through a comparative examination of Judaism and Christianity that deists like John Toland and Anthony Collins in the early eighteenth century conclude that Christianity is in fact "reformed Judaism" and that the Christianity of the church has no foundation. The comparison of Christianity with other religions and civilizations is an important feature in the work of Hume and Adam Ferguson in the Scottish Enlightenment, as well as in the work of Voltaire, Montesquieu, and Diderot in the French Enlightenment. A shared feature of these widely divergent interpretations of the "Other"—found in China, India, or Persia—is that they were used to critique the intolerance, violence, and hypocrisy of Christianity. Criticism of one's own society by means of comparing it to another is continued in the nineteenth century in the evolutionary theories of Marx and Engels. Contrary to what is often surmised, it is not the dichotomy of civilized versus barbaric that is the central feature of much of the "othering" going on in Western thought but rather the critique of specific European—and often Christian—practices either by showing these practices to be prevalent in "Oriental despotism," as in Montesquieu, or by showing them to be absent in other societies, as in Voltaire. Important in that critique is an insistence on the universality of religion, which makes Christianity only one among many religions, as well as an insistence on the comparative intolerance of Christianity.

While comparative religion is one source for criticism of Christianity, radical mysticism is another. Radical mysticism can be traced, if one wishes, to neo-Platonism, but also to Jewish Cabbalism. In the eighteenth century English-speaking world one can discern the influence of Jacob Boehme and Emanuel Swedenborg (1688–1778). Forms of religion, inspired by radical mysticism, are an important presence on the British scene from the seventeenth to the twentieth century. Even the Muggletonians, a radical sect founded in 1651, at least in E. P. Thompson's romantic view, continued into the twentieth century in order to enable Thompson to receive their archive from the last Muggletonian and to call himself, in the midst of the 1968 campus revolts, a "Muggletonian Marxist." While the rebellious Levellers, Diggers, and Ranters were defeated in the seventeenth century, a tradition of what might be called antinomianism remained salient in the eighteenth century, and, as I will argue, in the nineteenth century as well. Antinomianism can be seen as a broad current, found in a number of sectarian tendencies, to attack moral law as it is embodied by the state and the church. As E. P. Thompson explains, in his beautiful book on William Blake:

> Antinomian doctrine was expressive of a profound distrust of the "reasons" of the genteel and comfortable, and of ecclesiastical and academic institutions, not so much because they produced false knowledge but because they offered specious apologetics ("serpent reasonings") for a rotten social order based, in the last resort, on violence and material self-interest. In short, the antinomian stance was not against knowledge but against the ideological assumptions which pretended to be knowledge and the ideological contamination of the rest.[5]

What we are dealing with here is a subaltern, antihegemonic undercurrent of radical Christianity and millenarianism in British history, carried by autodidacts of artisan, tradesman, and shopkeeper backgrounds, such as William Blake. I suggest that this undercurrent was not entirely taken over or encapsulated by the antislavery and conversionist moralism of the evangelicals, though some of it certainly was. At the same time, I distance myself somewhat from E. P. Thompson's emphasis on the exclusively plebeian nature of radical mysticism. In my view class background does not determine people's interest in one crucial area that is engaged by radical mysticism, namely, the area of healing and medicine. It is in this field that animal magnetism or mesmerism, herbalism, crystal-ball gazing, and astrology enjoyed great popularity among all classes. The ideas behind these practices belonged to radical mysticism in one form or another. A further example of how class interests were sometimes transcended in radical mysticism is exemplified by the Utopian socialism of Robert Owen and the Owenites.

Owen (1771–1858), a successful cotton magnate, was also a millenarian radical. In a typical antinomian fashion, he argued, in his *New Religion* of 1830, "that the religion of the world is the sole cause now of all the disunion, hatred, uncharitableness, and crime, which pervade the population of the earth; and that, as long as this ignorant and worldly religion shall be taught to mankind, it will be utterly impracticable to train men to love one another, or to have common charity for each other."[6] All this anti-church rhetoric was buttressed by a strong appeal to reason and science without losing any of its millenarian appeal. Perhaps one might call it a kind of plebeian, antinomian deism, but one has to underline its reworkings of current materialist science and its political radicalism. A man like Owen thought he could have a key to all truth, and that key was not to be found in the Christian churches and chapels. His ideas were anti-Christian, not anti-Christ. He would have endorsed William Blake's saying that "Christ died as an Unbeliever." It is perhaps difficult for our contemporary society to understand this deeply religious "infidelity," or secularism as it was renamed in the 1850s, but that is what it was.

By 1850 Owen was in his eighties, and Owenism had faded but had not disappeared entirely.[7] It was more or less revitalized by Owen's discovery of spiritualism. Spiritualism had taken its first step toward becoming a mass movement on March 31, 1848, in Hydesville, near Rochester, when the Fox sisters discovered they had acted as mediums for mysterious raps that occurred in their cottage. Their discovery brought huge publicity and crowds to Hydesville, and spiritualism started its march to the rest of the world. In the early 1850s Robert Owen became a spiritualist under the guidance of a Mrs. Hayden, who was among the first to bring spiritualism from the United States to Britain. Owen contacted the spirits of Jefferson, Franklin, and Shelley (note their elitist character) and became convinced that the millennium would begin in 1855, "to be effected through the agency of departed spirits of good and superior men and women." Spiritualism proved to be a great success in the higher circles of society, but perhaps as impressive was the substantial interest taken by working- or lower-middle-class secularists. These were autodidacts with a radical and sometimes antinomian background wanting to experiment for themselves. For these seances, it is important to note, one could simply get together in a private home and "do it yourself," which circumvented the intermediary authority of both church and chapel.

Logie Barrow records the career of Richmond, a British craftsman who had been in America since 1842, a Shaker since 1846, a teetotaler since 1836, and a vegetarian since 1841. Richmond had visited the Fox sisters and brought spiritualism to Britain, when he returned in 1853. His first meeting was in his native town of Darlington "by invitation of secularistic teetotallers. At Keighley was the next Secularistic Society who listened to [his] Gospel, and embraced spiritualism. London was the next Secular Society, as the City Road Rooms [the then H.Q. of London secularists, where he argued with their current leader Holyoake, and their future one, Bradlaugh] and also at the Secularist Rooms in Whitechapel, and afterwards at Middlesboro by invitation of the Secularists."[8] Holyoake, of course, had coined the term *secularism* and had been imprisoned in the

1840s for suggesting that God, like a retired officer, should be placed on half-pay. Although he did not convert to spiritualism, he wrote a column in a spiritualist journal, and his movement remained open to spiritualists.[9] It is quite remarkable how often the London meeting place of the secularists, the Hall of Science, had spiritualist speakers. Spiritualism offered a mix of rationalism, experimentation, and anti-Christian secularism, which turned out to be tremendously attractive to secularist working men. Moreover, it dealt with death and the dead in ways that were far more satisfying than the very dry rationalism of secularist societies. It was also close to healing practices such as mesmerism and herbalism, which enjoyed a considerable plebeian appeal. Contrary to what one might expect, therefore, secularism turned out to be a fertile ground for the development of spiritualism among the working class.

This provides an essential background for an understanding of the remarkable career of Annie Besant (1847–1933). Part of her long life seems to have been scripted along the stereotypical lines of Victorian melodrama. She was born in a middle-class family which, after the death of her father, suffered financial hardship. She was then brought up and educated by an evangelical lady who had adopted her. Much of her later high-minded idealism and conversionist preacherism can be traced to this upbringing. When she was twenty she married an Anglican clergyman, Frank Besant, had two children, and lost her belief in Christ. Partly this loss came about through theological thinking, but the more important motive seems to have been a radical rejection of the cold, bourgeois values of her husband. In 1873 she refused to take communion in her husband's church and separated from him.

Besant's move from domesticity to independence exemplifies a perhaps less well-known Victorian narrative, in which a number of independence-minded women left their husbands and became spiritualist mediums.[10] Besant, however, took up spiritualism in the form of Theosophy much later, after being active in the secularist, socialist cause. In 1874 she met Charles Bradlaugh, Holyoake's rival and successor as leader of the secularists. Bradlaugh was a working-class atheist who had left his wife. He and Besant became very close friends and companions in a common cause. Besant took up the editorship of Bradlaugh's journal, *The National Reformer*. Together they were tried for publishing a book on contraception that the authorities had deemed pornographic. After that, Besant wrote her own pamphlet on contraception entitled *The Law of Population* which sold 90,000 copies in Britain and 110.000 in the United States, and was translated into Swedish, Danish, Dutch, French, German, and Italian.

Bradlaugh, meanwhile, was engaged in socialist battles. In 1880 he won the election in Northampton but was forcibly prevented from taking his seat in the House of Commons because he did not want to affirm or swear on the Bible. Part of the melodrama of Bradlaugh's death scene in 1891 was that, while he was dying, this action of the House was expunged from the records with cheers and the support of Gladstone. It signified the public recognition of "unbelief" in the political arena. Bradlaugh's funeral was a grand affair with thousands of people attending. Among them was a small group of Indian students, including the twenty-one-year-old Mohandas K. Gandhi.[11] Bradlaugh's popularity among these Indian students was the result of his open anticolonial stance. He had been interested in Indian affairs for quite some time. In 1876 he and Besant had organized a mass petition to Parliament protesting a trip to India by the Prince of Wales and Disraeli's proclamation of Queen Victoria as Empress of India.[12] After that, Bradlaugh had continued to be an advocate of Indian causes and, in 1889, he participated in the annual meeting of the National Congress at Bombay.

Besant was at the forefront of radical activism in Britain concerning women's rights, birth control, trade unionism, socialism, and secularism during the 1870s. She had also a great interest in science and enrolled as the first woman at London University to study for a Bachelor of Science degree. Her interest in education was apparent also when she got herself elected to the London School Board. This is not the place to summarize Annie Besant's career, and it is hardly a feasible enterprise anyway. However, I want to argue against an opposition often made in the literature between her socialist activism and her conversion to Theosophy. I suggest that Theosophy contained, among other things, a radical anticolonial and anticlerical universalism that opposed the Christian and racial notions of superiority which informed the prevalent British sense of being a "nation with a mission." This universalism, however, carried its own contradictions. As Gauri Viswanathan has pointed out, Besant's thinking is very much influenced by the prevalent racial evolutionism of the time. Like many people of her time (Karl Marx, for instance) Besant combined anticolonialism with a sense that colonization of one race by another is a necessary step in the realization of what she calls "universal brotherhood."[13] The genealogy of such a notion of universal brotherhood, produced by miscegenation of people and ideas, can be traced to conflicting arguments about colonialism in the eighteenth century by thinkers ranging from Diderot to Herder.[14] In Besant's time, racial evolutionism, the most important scientific paradigm, added a particular direction to this line of thought. It is almost impossible to penetrate the way in which Madame Blavatsky appropriated racial evolutionism in convoluted notions of root races and sub-races, but it enabled Besant to combine a strong resistance to colonial racism with the racially informed support of Hindu anticolonial nationalism in India. Her notion of "universal brotherhood" does not borrow from the French Revolution, in which equality is central, but is one of hierarchy and evolutionism, thanks to which the imperial encounter of East and West can produce a superior race.

As we have already seen, there was a strong interest in spiritualism and in Eastern non-Christian religions in the radical circles in which Besant moved. Although she is not known to have been involved with plebeian spiritualism, she developed an interest in Theosophy from the angle of an anti-Christian comparative religion. Max Müller at the time was editing *The Sacred Books of the East*, and, in 1879, Edwin Arnold published his immensely popular *Light of Asia*. Orientalist scholarship was considered to be among the highest scientific achievements of the time, and there was a widely shared interest in it. Besant reviewed Max Müller and other authors on the religions of the East, which were in her view far superior to Christianity. In 1889 she reviewed Madame Blavatsky's *Secret Doctrine* for the *Pall Mall Gazette*, one of the journals of the great nineteenth-century journalist W. T. Stead with whom she had organized the Law and Liberty League to help workers who had been arrested during a prohibited meeting at Trafalgar Square. She was impressed with the book and, in the company of her friend, the socialist leader Burrows, traveled to London to meet Madame Blavatsky. Both joined the Theosophical Society. Theosophy became the enduring enthusiasm of Besant's life. Her step from socialist radicalism to Theosophy can be understood if we acknowledge how the radical anticlerical and anticolonial stance of British spiritualism had been inherited by Theosophy. As we have seen, spiritualism and secular socialism had been in close association in a number of radical circles in this period. This is not to say that spiritualism and secular socialism are the same or that Theosophy and plebeian spiritualism drew the same audiences. The secular socialist Bradlaugh had very little time for spiritualism, and Blavatsky, with her quasi-intellectualism, was more interested in an elite following that could support her than in socialist causes. It should be clear, however, that the distinctions made today between spiritualism, secularism, elites, and masses are not of much help in understanding the moves made by Annie Besant and some of her contemporaries. Nevertheless, Bernard Shaw, to whom Besant was romantically attached, and Charles Bradlaugh were shocked. When Shaw saw that

Annie Besant had signed an article headed "Sic Itur ad Astra; or, Why I Became a Theosophist," he expressed his surprise as follows:

> Staggered by this unprepared blow, which meant to me the loss of a powerful colleague and of a friendship which had become part of my daily life, I rushed round to her office in Fleet Street, and there delivered myself of an unbounded denunciation of Theosophy in general, of female inconstancy, and in particular of H. P. Blavatsky, one of whose books—I forget whether it was "The Secret Doctrine" or "Isis Unveiled"—had done all the mischief."[15]

In 1891 both Bradlaugh and Madame Blavatsky died, and in 1893 Annie Besant left for the "spiritual teacher of the world," India, where she rapidly took over the leadership of the Theosophical Society, first together with Olcott and, after his death, alone. While doing this, she did not abandon her anticolonialism nor her interest in mass education.

India's Spiritual Heritage

> Nothing less is demanded of us Englishmen, to whose charge the Almighty has committed the souls and bodies of two hundred and forty millions of His creatures, than that every man among us, whether clerical or lay, should strive to be a missionary according to the standard set up by the first great Missionary-Christ Himself. Let no lower standard of our duty satisfy us. So will the good time arrive when not only every ear shall have the good news of the reconciliation of man to his Maker, but every tongue also of every native of India—from Cape Comorin to the Himalaya mountains—shall confess that Jesus Christ is Lord, to the glory of God the Father.[16]

This is not taken, as one might think, from some minor speech by an Evangelist preacher at the beginning of the nineteenth century, but from a major text on Hinduism by Monier-Williams, the Boden Professor of Sanskrit at Balliol College, Oxford, in 1877. The impact of the colonial state on Indian society in the nineteenth century has not escaped anyone's attention. A great deal of work has been done to show that colonial rule was based on a colonial sociology of India and the ways in which this knowledge was constructed. But it has not been sufficiently realized that the nature of the colonial project was profoundly Christian. To some extent this failure can be explained by the fact that the missionary effort to convert Indians to Christianity was executed by voluntary, missionary organizations that did not depend formally on the government of India. However, as I argue in an earlier chapter, it is very difficult to demarcate the boundaries of the modern state. Certainly Indians confronted with the colonial project saw it as a Christian one, no matter whether it was executed by missionary societies or by government officials.

There were at least three possible intellectual responses to the Christian attack on Hinduism. One was to see Christianity as one instance of universal religion and to combine elements of Christianity and Hinduism into a common, rational religion with strong deist tendencies. This was, as we have seen in previous chapters, the approach taken by Rammohan Roy and the early Brahmo Samaj. The following extensive quote from a letter sent by Rammohan Roy, in 1833, to Robert Dale Owen, the son of the Freethinker Robert Owen, is illuminating:

> It is not necessary, either in England or in America, to oppose Religion in promoting the social, domestic, and political welfare of their Inhabitants, particularly a system of Religion which inculcates the doctrine of Universal love and Charity. Did such Philanthropists as Locke & Newton oppose Religion? No! They rather tried to remove the perversions gradually introduced in religion. Admitting for a moment that the Truths of the Divinity of Religion cannot be established to the satisfaction of a Freethinker, but from an impartial inquiry I presume we may feel persuaded to believe that a system of Religion (Christianity) which consists in Love and Charity is capable of furthering our happiness, facilitating our reciprocal transactions and curbing our obnoxious passions and feelings, I grieve to observe that by opposing Religion your most benevolent Father has hitherto impeded his success. He, I firmly believe, is a follower of Christianity in the above sense though he is not being aware of being so. Allow me to send Hamiltons East Indies (1st Vol) in which you will find, page 35 line 3rd, that more than two thousand years ago the wise and pious Brahmans of India entertained almost the same opinions which your Father now offers though they by no means were destitute of religion.(Transcription of Roy's letter to Robert Dale Owen, sent from 48 Bedford Square, London, on April 19, 1833)[17]

This letter is fascinating in its appeal to a universal morality (love and charity) as a standard to judge religions, be they Christianity or Brahmanism. Roy opposes real religion to perverted religion. In doing so he circumvents secularism. It is a discourse that could be used for antinomian purposes both in Britain (against the state church) and in India (against Christian colonialism). An example of such a critique of Christian colonialism by referring to true Christian values can be found in a speech by Keshabchandra Sen (1838–1884), the leader of the Brahmo Samaj thirty years after Roy:

> I regard every European settler in India as a missionary of Christ, and I have a right to demand that he should always remember and act up to his high responsibilities. But alas! owing to the reckless conduct of a number of pseudo-Christians, Christianity has failed to produce any wholesome moral influence on my countrymen. Yes, their muscular Christianity has led many a Native to identify the religion of Jesus with the power and privilege of inflicting blows and kicks with impunity. And thus has Jesus been dishonoured in India. (May 5, 1866)[18]

A second approach was much more aggressive by repudiating Christianity and showing the failures and problems of Christian thought, preferably in the Bible itself. Swami Dayananda, for instance, devoted chapter 13 of his major work on Aryan religion, *Satyartha Prakash*, to a devastating critique of Christian ideas. Incidentally, as Barbara Metcalf has observed, he objected precisely to those elements in Christianity that could also be found in Islam, typically attacking both in one stroke.[19]

A third possibility perhaps was developed by Narendranath Datta or Swami Vivekananda (1863–1902) who argued that Christianity was simply a lesser form of the universal spirituality found in all religions, but at the highest level only in Vedantic Hinduism. Christianity had been much corrupted by materialism, indeed to the extent that it had lost its spiritual value. It could only be redeemed by exposure to the ancient spirituality of the Hindus. This became the official creed, as it were, of Hindu nationalism of all shades and hues, from the militant right-wing Rashtriya Swayamsevak Sangh to Gandhi. It is interesting to note here that this universalizing strategy of Vivekananda found its counterpart in the fulfillment theology of Christian missionaries such as J. N. Farquhar who suggested in 1913, in a famous book, that "Christ was the Crown of Hinduism."[20] This notion of Christianity as the fulfillment of Hinduism is a far cry from Monier-Williams's perspective on Hinduism and the Christian mission with which I began this section.

These three responses have quite different consequences. For instance, the Arya Samaj challenged notions of caste in marriage and in religious practice. The Brahmo Samaj and Vivekananda's Ramakrishna Mission were much less demanding in those areas of social life. Nevertheless, they converge at the discursive level in the appropriation of scientific rationality and social activism, features also found in the secularist and spiritualist movements in Britain discussed in the previous section. Both the Indian and British movements are anti-Christian, but whereas the British movements are rooted in a Christianity they want to repudiate, the Indian movements are rooted in a Hinduism they want to reform. The convergence of these Indian and British movements are best demonstrated by examining the construction of the concept of "spirituality." I would argue that a master concept like "spirituality" is not epiphenomenal to "real history" but rather productive of historical change.[21]

In all these movements, both British and Indian, the term *spirituality* plays a central role. First, it is a Western term and has a variety of meanings depending on the context. In the comparison of East and West, the East is often called the home of spirituality as a criticism of Western materialism. In his recent book on Indian nationalism, Partha Chatterjee argues that,

> anticolonial nationalism creates its own domain of sovereignty within colonial society well before it begins its political battle with the imperial power. It does this by dividing the world of social institutions and practices into two domains—the material and the spiritual. The material is the domain of the "outside," of the economy and of statecraft, of science and technology, a domain where the West had proved its superiority and the East had succumbed. . . . The spiritual, on the other hand, is an "inner" domain bearing the "essential" marks of cultural identity. The greater one's success in imitating Western skills in the material domain, therefore, the greater the need to preserve the distinctness of one's spiritual culture.[22]

This is an elegant formulation, but too simple. Chatterjee does not account for the fact that the notion of "the spiritual" also operates in the West to criticize certain aspects of Christian society. As I argue above, in spiritualism there is an access to a world of spirits, transcending death, that is not under the control of Ecclesiastical authorities. The ideas and practices of spiritualism are, in the second half of the nineteenth century, reinterpreted in terms of an Orientalist reading of Eastern spirituality, in which one discovers a variety of gods and powers with whom one can communicate. These ideas about spiritualism and spirituality are not opposed to materialist science at all. In fact, inherent in these ideas is a strong materialist, rationalist, and indeed scientific reasoning. What they oppose is the domination and control over knowledge by polite, Christian society and its materialist (that is, utilitarian) morality.

Western discourse on "Eastern spirituality" is reappropriated by the Indian religious movements of this period. I would not quite know how to translate "spirituality" into Sanskrit, but it is a fact that Hindu religious discourses are now captured under the term *spirituality*. It is significant that Ashok Singhal, the leader of the Hindu nationalist Vishva Hindu Parishad, uses the English term *spirituality* when he explains in Hindi to Lise McKean that "of all nations, India alone has spirituality."[23] *Spirituality* is a comparative, polemical term used against Christian colonialism, and, contrary to what Chatterjee claims, it does not leave an "outer" domain of science, etcetera, to Western dominance. In fact, as in Britain itself, it contests the very colonial domination of scientific knowledge by showing that there are either earlier or alternative forms of science available in Hinduism.

To be useful in the contestation of Christian colonialism, the translation of Hindu discursive traditions into "spirituality" meant a significant transformation of these traditions. This process can be closely followed by examining the way Vivekananda made a sanitized version of the religious ideas and practices of Ramakrishna for a modernizing, middle class in Calcutta. Partha Chatterjee devotes a chapter of his *Nation and Its Fragments* on a social-historical interpretation of the *Ramkrsna kathamrta*, a text dealing with Ramakrishna's life. His aim in this chapter is to explore middle-class religion and its fears and anxieties. Fortunately, this text has also been the subject of a recent book-length study by Jeffrey Kripal that allows us to probe somewhat deeper in issues Chatterjee chooses to ignore.[24]

Ramakrishna (1836–1886) was an illiterate priest in a Kali temple who became successful among Brahmo literati in middle-class Calcutta, thanks to his charismatic personality. He indeed was a medium, but not of a spirit that would have given him only a low-caste status and a particular priestly function but of the Mother Goddess Kali. Ramakrishna's ideas and practices were based on a specific, highly eroticized tradition of Tantra, a fact that is easily forgotten when reading Chatterjee's analysis of the *kathamrta*. Kripal circumscribes Tantra with five direct quotations from the *kathamrta*:

> 1. "That about which in the Vedas and the Puranas it is said, 'Don't do this, this shouldn't be done,' in the Tantras is called good." This shows the extent to which the Tantras are radically heterodox and transgressive of Brahmanical norms.
> 2. "They practice according to the views of the Tantras. They practice the Five M's." The Five M's are *madya* (wine), *mamsa* (meat), *matsya* (fish), *mudra* (parched grain), and *maithuna* (sexual intercourse).

3. "In the first state there is form, in the second state there is the formless, and, after that, there is the state beyond form and the formless." This metaphysical statement is glossed by Kripal as saying that there is no dualistic opposition between *bhukti* (enjoyment) and *mukti* (liberation), but that they are dialectically related in the sexual union.

4. "Everything about a Tantrika is secret." An exasperating element of Tantric texts is that they hide their transgressive nature in a secret language (*sandhabhasha*), which makes it very difficult to interpret them without a guru's guidance.

5. "Shame, disgust, and fear—these three must not remain." In Kripal's reading, fear has very much to do with the transgressive and dark side of sexuality. In Chatterjee's analysis, however, fear refers to something quite different: "A mortal fear of the Englishman and of the world over which he dominated was a constituent element in the consciousness of the Calcutta middle class."[25] One could argue perhaps that in Tantra one was engaged in a hidden ritual world that transgressed both the oppressive world of Brahmanical norms and that of colonial domination. Tantrikas could derive considerable power and fearlessness from this engagement, which escaped surveillance from authorities.

6. "The Saktas follow the views of the Tantras." In Ramakrishna's tradition, Tantrikas are the same as Shaktas, that is, worshipers of Shakti or Power, which is Mother Kali.[26]

Much can be said about Ramakrishna's Tantric tradition that would avoid both the sociological reductionism of Chatterjee and the psychological reductionism of Kripal. That is not the subject here, but I would point out that even though we have considerable hagiographic data on Ramakrishna that are exceptional, Ramakrishna himself was not an exceptional figure. One must recognize that Ramakrishna was not some kind of isolated phenomenon but rather a particularly gifted guru in a tradition that was available in many versions throughout Hindu India. One need only look at Jonathan Parry's (1994) work on Kina Ram in Benares, or my own (1988) on the Ramanandis, or Morinis's (1984) on Bengali pilgrimage to see how many of the themes in the *kathamrta* are reflected elsewhere in North Indian Hinduism.[27] Ramakrishna belonged to a tradition that was and still is very strong in Bengal, much stronger than Brahmanism has ever been, and also among the so-called middle class. "Every Bengali is half Vaishnava and half Shakta," the saying goes.[28] If there is an antinomian tradition in Hindu India it is definitely Shaktism, but it is less anti-state than anti-Brahmanism, and its message has primarily to do with gender and sexuality. For our purpose, its main interest lies in the fact that it is so unpalatable for the Victorian Age.

Whatever the possibilities of Vivekananda's discourse, there was no way he could even begin to translate the beliefs and practices of Ramakrishna into a Hindu universalism. The Goddess Kali, with her protruding tongue and her necklace of skulls dancing on the corpse of Siva, stood perhaps for everything a Victorian Britisher would find abhorrent in Hinduism and thus could not easily be adopted in a Brahmo religion meant to mediate the worlds of the colonizers and colonized. Ramakrishna was outrageous. When he would go into a trance, he would place his foot on the genitals of one of his young boy disciples, whom he called "pure pots" that could hold the "milk" of his divine love.[29] Kripal shows convincingly that Tantra allowed Ramakrishna to enact his homosexuality, a sexual inclination deeply frowned upon both in India and Britain. Ramakrishna's aversion toward women cannot only be explained by the tradition of renouncing the world as Chatterjee does but also has to do with homosexual tendencies within that tradition.[30]

Whereas we can still interpret most of Ramakrishna's beliefs and practices in terms of Hindu discursive traditions, with Vivekananda we enter the terrain of colonial translation. Vivekananda is the peculiar and unusual figure here. He was entirely devoted to Ramakrishna, on the one hand, but, on the other, he decided to create a Hindu religious system that sanitized everything characterizing Ramakrishna's beliefs and practices. Undoubtedly Vivekananda was totally swept off his feet by his encounter with Ramakrishna and became an ardent disciple. Nevertheless, his education in Western philosophy and his engagement with Brahmo religion prevented him from accepting Ramakrishna's Shaktism. Vivekananda removed Tantric Shaktism and the awesome Kali from sight. Vivekananda's Vedanta was a logocentric, masculine form of Hinduism, unlike Ramakrishna's feminized form of mad possession. Ramakrishna's highly eroticized meditation on Kali as Mother and Lover, on Kali on top of Shiva, on Kali's tongue were edited out of Vivekananda's message to the world. Kali was replaced by Mother India, as Tantrism was by nationalism. Tantric enjoyment was replaced by ascetic dedication to the nation.

Vivekananda's translation of Ramakrishna's message in terms of "spirituality" was literally transferred to the West during his trip to the United States after Ramakrishna's death. In 1893 he visited the World Parliament of Religions in Chicago, a sideshow of the Columbian Exposition, celebrating the four-hundredth anniversary of Columbus's voyage to the New World but, more important perhaps, Chicago's recovery from the Great

Fire of 1871. Religions represented in this show, or religious universalism, included Hinduism, Buddhism, Judaism, Roman Catholicism, Eastern Orthodoxy, Protestantism, Islam, Shinto, Confucianism, Taoism, Jainism, and others.[31] But the show was stolen by the representative of Hinduism, Swami Vivekananda. In his speech to the Parliament, Vivekananda claimed that "he was proud to belong to a religion which had taught the world both tolerance and universal acceptance."[32] Vivekananda's spirituality was not modest or meek; it was forceful, polemical, and proud. As indicated by the response in the Parliament and the reaction to his later lecture tours in the United States, this was a message that resonated powerfully among American audiences. His writings in English often compare the lack of spirituality in the West to its abundance in India. Vivekananda is probably the first major Indian advocate of a "Hindu spirituality," largely created by Orientalism and adopted in the anticlerical and anticolonial rhetorics of Theosophy.[33]

A major achievement was Vivekananda's creation of yoga as the Indian science of supraconsciousness. *Yoga* is a Sanskrit word that can be translated as "discipline." It has a complex history with a number of disparate traditions, but the classical text is Patanjali's *Yoga-sutras* which was probably composed around the fifth century A.D.[34] Yoga was now made into the unifying sign of the Indian nation—and not only for national consumption but for consumption by the entire world. This is a new doctrine, although Vivekananda emphasized that it was ancient "wisdom." Especially the body exercises of hatha yoga, underpinned by a metaphysics of mind-body unity, continues to be a major entity in the health industry, especially in the United States. What I find important in Vivekananda's construction of yoga as the core of Hindu "spirituality" is that it is devoid of any specific devotional content that would involve, for example, temple worship and thus a theological and ritual position in sectarian debates. Vivekananda is, first and foremost, interested in Hindu unity:

> Here am I, not to find difference that exists among us, but to find where we agree. Here I am trying to understand on what ground we may always remain brothers, upon what foundations the voice that has spoken from eternity may become stronger and stronger as it grows. . . . National union in India must be a gathering up of its scattered spiritual forces. A nation in India must be a union of those whose hearts beat to the same spiritual tune. There have been sects in this country. There are sects enough in the future, because this has been the peculiarity of our religion that in abstract principles so much latitude has been given that, although afterwards so much

detail has been worked out, all these details are the working out of principles, broad as the skies above our heads, eternal as nature itself. Sects must exist here, but what need not exist is sectarian quarrel. Sects must be but sectarianism need not.[35]

This lack of religious specificity together with the claim to be scientific is crucial for the nationalist appeal of Vivekananda's message. From Vivekananda's viewpoint, religion is based on reason, not belief. Yoga is legitimized as a scientific tradition in terms of rational criteria. An offshoot of this is that health issues could be addressed in terms of a national science of yoga. I suggest that Vivekananda has developed a translation of Hindu traditions in terms remarkably similar to what is cobbled together in Theosophy and its later outgrowth, Steiner's Anthroposophy.

Vivekananda's construction of "spirituality" and its relation with nationalism has had an enormous impact on a whole range of thinkers and movements. While it has influenced thinkers on India as different as Savarkar, Aurobindo, Gandhi, and Nehru, it has also impacted a great variety of Western spiritual movements, including the current New Age movement. As I argue elsewhere, it is a construction crucial to the notion that one can be a renouncer and still be active in political and social causes. Hindu nationalism could hardly exist without such a notion. Lise McKean has shown the extent to which the idea of spirituality is even used in promoting national products, such as Indian handlooms and handicrafts.[36] There seems to be no escape today from the relentless marketing of India's spirituality.

Vivekananda's peculiar hybridity was the result of his mediation of Ramakrishna's world and the colonial world. He found an authentic religious authority in Ramakrishna but had to translate his ideas beyond recognition to allow them to make sense in the colonial world he inhabited. It is Vivekananda's social reformism and anticolonial, anti-Christian radicalism that connects him to the spiritualists in Britain. Although the same word—*spirituality*—was used in English, the unifying language of the empire, it had very different meanings where it stood in relation to Christian traditions in the metropole and to Hindu traditions in the colony. The point here is that these divergences did not stand in the way of a shared antinomian radicalism against the state in Britain and the colonial state in India.

It is against this background that Indian enthusiasm for the Theosophists has to be seen. Here colonized Indians encountered Westerners who declared that Hinduism and Buddhism were far superior to Christianity precisely in terms of scientific rationality and moral values. Gananath Obeyesekere has demonstrated the importance of the Theosophists in the creation of Buddhist nationalism in Sri Lanka. Like Indian Hindus, Sri Lankan Buddhists organized themselves against attacks by Christian missionary societies in the 1860s and received unexpected support from the West. Reginald Copleston, Bishop of Colombo, noted in 1879 that the secretary of "an obscure society" was corresponding with monks, "hailing them as brothers in the march of intellect" and praising them for their spirited antimissionary and anti-Christian challenges. "This nonsense had a good deal of effect, I think, on the common people, while the more educated, having really become free thinkers, welcome the extravagant encomiums passed on the true, original Buddhism by European writers."[37]

The "obscure society" was, of course, the Theosophical Society, and the secretary Colonel Olcott. In May 1880 he and Madame Blavatsky arrived in Sri Lanka and were enthusiastically welcomed by Buddhist monks. Both even became Buddhists in a ceremony one week after their arrival, although they also continued to be Theosophists. Olcott's foremost contribution to modern Buddhism was his *Buddhist Cathechism* written in 1881. This was a major step toward what Obeyesekere has called "the laicization of Buddhism" and even "Protestant Buddhism." The book was based on Olcott's reading of contemporary Orientalist scholarship on Buddhism. In it Olcott rejected all forms of popular religion (which included, ironically, spirit religion) and argued that purified Buddhism was entirely compatible with modern science. The Sinhala translation of the *Catechism* is used till the present day in Sri Lanka. Olcott made another major contribution to modern Buddhism when, in 1884, he initiated the later Buddhist reformer Anagarika Dharmapala (1864–1933) in the Theosophical Society. While Vivekananda represented Hinduism in the World's Parliament of Religions in Chicago in 1893, Dharmapala represented Buddhism. The role that Vivekananda played in developing a discourse for Hindu nationalism was played by Dharmapala for Buddhist nationalism in Sri Lanka. Incidentally, the Theosophical Society had been represented in Chicago by Annie Besant and Gyanendranath Chakravarti, a Brahman professor of mathematics at Allahabad University.

The role of Olcott and the Theosophical Society in the creation of a particular anticolonial Hindu nationalism was minor compared to their role in creating Buddhist nationalism. Indeed, there is no recorded influence of Theosophy on Vivekananda, and the relationship with Dayananda soon turned sour, as we have seen. Nevertheless, there was considerable enthusiasm in India for Theosophy which coincided largely with an upsurge of nationalist, anticolonial feelings. In 1881 the Theosophical Society had set up a branch in Tinnevelly in South India, and in 1882 moved its headquarters from Bombay to Adyar in Madras, where they are still located today. Its open anti-Christian character was an especially great hit in the South. Moreover, Olcott had discovered in 1882 in Sri Lanka that he had healing powers, and this in itself created a large following. These people did not often become official members of the Theosophical Society, but their exposure to Theosophical lectures helped them in creating a public sphere of voluntary associations, debating clubs, and the like, which was highly critical of both the colonial government and Christianity.[38] There is also little doubt that Theosophists did much to revitalize and transform what might be called the "Hindu national heritage" of classical art, such as Bharatanatyam dance. Rukmini Devi, the wife of George Arundale, who later became president of the Theosophical Society, became not only the leader of the Kalakshetra school of art but also India's most important propagandist of Bharatanatyam.

When Annie Besant entered India in 1893 she stepped into a field of social, political, and religious activism that had been spurred by Olcott and Blavatsky. It may not have been her intention to become politically active, but, as we have seen, there was no escape from the spirit of the age, nationalism. Her first social activity in India was very much in line with what she had been doing in London, the building of an educational program in schools and colleges. In 1898 she founded the Central Hindu College and in 1911 worked with Pandit Madan Mohan Malaviya to transform it into the Benares Hindu University. Incidentally, this transformation implied that all Theosophical teachings were removed from the curriculum. Two important matters are evinced here. First, Theosophy typically played a crucial role in initiating change but was then left behind as soon as the enterprise gained momentum. Second, just as Blavatsky and Olcott began to think of themselves as Buddhists in Sri Lanka, Besant began to regard herself as a Hindu. There was a clear and undisguised connection between her racial evolutionism, with the importance it placed on the Aryan race, and Hindu nationalist claims to superiority, based on racial and spiritual grounds. In her, British and Indian Aryanism came together. Quite striking is that she initiated the Hindu response to the founding of a Muslim university at Aligarh by creating Benares Hindu University. The Hindu nature of her spirituality has been recognized in the 1980s by the Hindu nationalist Vishva Hindu Parishad by enshrining her image (with that of Sister Nivedita, the Irish follower of Vivekananda) in the nationalist Bharat Mata temple in Hardwar.[39] Spirituality was not so universal after all. It tended to leave out Christianity and by the same token Islam, while being very partial to Hinduism and Buddhism, the wisdom of the East.

In the second decade of the twentieth century Besant had fully entered Indian nationalist politics. Members of the nationalist elite, such as Motilal Nehru and his son, Jawaharlal Nehru, all were members of the Theosophical Society, at least for a while. Annie Besant was in constant communication with the leader of the "moderate" faction of the Congress, Gopal Krishna Gokhale, and with the leader of the "radicals," Bal Gangadhar Tilak. During the First World War she created, almost at the same time as Tilak, a Home Rule League, which brought her into sharp conflict with the colonial government which, in 1917, decided to intern her. This internment made her very popular in nationalist circles. After her release she became president of the Indian National Congress in 1917. This was the height of her political career in India; soon after, however, her position as mediator between the "extremist" and "moderate" factions in the Congress movement became impossible, and a new leader with his own brand of universal spirituality emerged: Mohandas K. Gandhi. Ironically the Theosophists were always on the lookout for what they called "Mahatmas" to guide the world, but the very rise of Mahatma Gandhi led to the virtual eclipse of the Theosophical Society from Indian politics.

CONCLUDING REMARKS

A century later the Zeitgeist of the Victorian period is already difficult to understand. Spiritualism and Theosophy seem so irrational and escapist. Ramakrishna's Tantrism seems the same but under the sign of difference, that is, irrationality and escapism in the culture of "the Other," easily essentialized as the perfect opposite of an essentialized Western culture. The thrust of this chapter has been to problematize these views. I have argued that spiritualism and Theosophy have played a crucial role in the development of radical antiestablishment and anticolonial politics, both in Britain and India. Early socialism, feminism, democratic science, and anticolonialism were the social causes for which Annie Besant, the Theosophist, fought. A defining element in these battles was an anti-Christian rhetoric, fed by an Orientalist comparison with "Eastern spirituality." This spirituality was not constructed as antiscientific or antirational. On the contrary, compared to Christianity it was scientific and rational. Nietzsche, the great polemicist against Christian morality in the German-speaking world, clearly expresses his admiration for the Vedanta:

> The newer philosophy, as a form of epistemological skepticism, is, hidden or openly, anti-Christian; however, for more subtle ears, by no means anti-religious . . . Kant wanted essentially to show that one could not prove the subject on the basis of the subject—nor indeed the object; the possibility of an illusionary existence of the subject, or the "soul," will not have been alien to him, since it is an idea that has been present on earth already with tremendous power as Vedanta-philosophy.[40]

Nietzsche (following Schopenhauer) argues that Kant's modern philosophy, which he sees as anti-Christian but not antireligious, was prefigured in Indian Vedanta. This is obviously not literally true, since Kant was much less influenced by Indian philosophy than were the great philosophers of German romanticism: Schlegel, Schopenhauer, and Schelling; still, Nietzsche has an intuition here that is worth pursuing. As Peter van Rooden has pointed out, Kant's view of universal, enlightened religion, which is the source of morality, locates religion in the interior life of the individual and not in social institutions, such as the church. This makes it possible for the German romantics to interpret Kant's enlightenment not as a secular rationalism but, in a somewhat perverse way, as a mystical enlightenment. Perhaps it should not surprise us that Kant's *Kritik der Reinen Vernunft* was translated into English by the greatest interpreter of Indian traditions in nineteenth-century Britain, the Indologist (Friedrich) Max Müller, also the translator of the Rg-Veda. As the founder of *Religionswissenschaft*, Science of Religion, Müller argued, in Kantian fashion, that there is Religion, transcendental Truth, and historical religions (in the plural), including Christianity, which all contain elements of Religion as Truth. Science of Religion enables one to discover Religion by studying religions. For Müller, the Vedanta clearly expressed this Universal Truth. That Max Müller could put Christianity at the same level as other historical religions in his Science of Religion (far more explicit and daring than Kant) while teaching in an academic institution like Oxford, which was part of the clerical establishment, is an important sign of the shifting location of religion in nineteenth-century Britain. Müller could make such a radical argument without losing touch with the political elites, among whom he was generally very popular, or even without having to fear that his argument would be taken as an attack on the state. Where Kant constantly affirms his support of institutional religion and of the state and narrowly defines the limits of enlightened debate, Müller can make similar arguments a century later without all these precautions. Vedanta philosophy, which is so extraordinarily praised by Nietzsche and Müller, is used by Vivekananda to translate Ramakrishna's discourse and practice into the imperial language of anti-Christian and anticolonial "spirituality."

Madame Blavatsky stood in a tradition of popular beliefs and practices that seems the very opposite of Kantian enlightenment. Nevertheless, there is some common ground in the rejection of the established church as the site of true religion, although with very different political consequences. While Kant and his latter-day follower, Müller, continue to see the state as guaranteeing Reason and Progress, Blavatsky and Besant are openly critical of the state and colonialism as impediments to Reason and Progress.

There can be no doubt that spirits, spiritualism, and spirituality have different meanings in the Indian and British contexts in the late nineteenth century. The importance of Theosophy was to connect them and create a universal language-game in which they came to be connected to radical politics both in Britain and India. I suggest that at least three aspects of this radicalism need further exploration, namely, the representation of absence in spiritualism, the negotiation of science and rationality, and the role of gender and sexuality.

Regarding the representation of absence, one must ask what exactly is being represented in spirit seances. In my view it is crucial to see what kind of spirits are summoned. First, there are spirits that belong to the circles of family and friends. Colonel Olcott had been an important officer in the American Civil War. Spiritualism emerged in the wake of the carnage of that war, and, similarly, it enjoyed great success after the Great War in Britain. The reason was the same: The bereft wanted to stay in touch with those who had been killed in the war. There is a "do-it-yourself" quality to seances that is democratic and deflects the authority of Christian institutions and the class distinctions related to them. Spiritualism offers direct access to an afterworld without the theological baggage of Christianity.

On the other hand, and quite striking, is that voices of authority were often made present in the circles of spiritualist leaders. The Theosophical Society developed an entire hierarchy of Masters of the Universe and, of course, of those able to represent them in life. Indeed, one could view the summoning of spirits and invisible masters as an attempt to represent the authority of the modern, bureaucratic state in order to deflect its mecha-

79

nisms of control. In a penetrating and amusing analysis of Theosophist A. P. Sinnett's *Mahatma Letters to A. P. Sinnett: From the Mahatmas M. and K.H.* (1923), Gauri Viswanathan observes that the spirits reflect the bureaucratic style of the colonial administration in India.[41] They give voice to what we can never see but which has power over our lives. This reminds me most of Kafka's *Trial* in which Josef K. tries to find out what "the authorities" want from him. The Mystery of Power continues to elude him, since the state remains hidden. The theater of spirit seances consists of an elaborate negotiation and display of power. Freud speaks extensively in his *Traumdeutung* (The interpretation of dreams) about spirits. In his view they represent the ambivalence of the living toward the dead, partly the guilt about the happiness we feel that they are dead and we are living, partly the denial of their death. I suggest, however, that Freud's interpretation of spirits as the individual's psychological problem is why communication with spirits came to be classified as "madness" to be treated by state institutions. This development demolished the capacity spiritualism had had in the nineteenth century to develop radical, antinomian politics.

The second problem I want to address is the negotiation of science and rationality in spiritualism and spirituality. British spiritualism and Indian spirituality were both anti-Christian and pro-science. Scientific naturalism and rational explanation were crucial to Besant, Dayananda, and Vivekananda. They asserted that spiritualism and Indian spirituality were entirely consistent with current scientific arguments and discoveries. In spiritualism there was a strong emphasis on the experimental nature of spirit seances. When phenomena could not be explained in terms of existing natural law, this only meant that some important workings of the universe had not yet been discovered. This was the age of discovery, and spiritualism's claims to experimental truth were more or less accepted by a wide variety of people, foremost among them working-class autodidacts. One should not forget that spiritualism, like earlier Mesmerism, was considered to be entirely within the realm of science in the third quarter of the nineteenth century. For instance, Alfred Russel Wallace, coauthor with Charles Darwin of the principle of natural selection, was a fervent follower of spiritualism. He and others were particularly convinced of the reality of spiritual phenomena by the fact that photographs could be made of them.[42] This obviously raises the question of the changing realm of the visual in the period of photography, spectroscopy, and the early motion picture. Making the invisible visible was something experimented on widely in this period. It is also remarkable how influential

Theosophy was on the painters of modern life, on the Symbolists of course, and, perhaps more important, on pioneers of abstraction such as Piet Mondrian and Wassily Kandinsky.

Oriental philology, comparative religion, and anthropology as well were all seen as a part of science in this period. Results from these disciplines could be and were used against Christian claims of superiority. Similarly, the debate about spirituality can be seen as an intervention in the discussion of race and biology. These issues and disciplines are interconnected in a number of ways. Indian leaders, such as Dayananda and Vivekananda, found it important to stress that the scientific discoveries of the West were already "hidden" or "prefigured" in the great texts of Hinduism and Buddhism, especially the Vedas. One of the discursive moves made here is that it was important to use these discoveries to enlighten mankind and not to suppress them by means of colonialism. What we see here is a nationalization of science and a series of appropriations, in which science goes native. Yoga is definitely seen as a national, experimental science and continues to be viewed as such today by the Indian government.

Finally, an important element in the radical politics of spiritualism is gender. In spiritualism British women escaped the restrictive domestic role Victorian society tried to impose on them. This gender construction was partly based on women's "difference," their "innate," "natural" capacity for the spiritual. This, in effect, enabled women to become spirit mediums and to use that role precisely to go beyond the restrictions of Victorian domesticity. Both Madame Blavatsky and Annie Besant had left their husbands and were independent women. In my view their spirituality and the power derived from it has to be seen in connection with the struggle for women's rights and the tensions and contradictions involved in that struggle.

The Indian situation appears to be just the opposite of this. The leaders of nationalist spirituality in India were all men. As I argue elsewhere, within Hindu discursive traditions men acquire spiritual powers by realizing their own feminine side.[43] Power (*shakti*) is definitely feminine in Hindu discursive traditions, but, to acquire it, "real existing women" are not needed. In fact, Hindu monks I have spoken to in earlier research all stressed that women were too weak to engage in monastic practices.

The spirit of the age was nationalism. The struggle in both the metropole and the colony was about who would participate in the political process, and indeed in the national society through education and public debate. The spirits of spiritualism and spirituality were involved in that everyday struggle that connected these two sites of empire. Contrary to what we might think, secularism as an ideological movement was much less antireligious than anti-Christian, as Nietzsche understood so well. That is why secularism is closer to spiritualism and spirituality than expected, and perhaps also why it is far more effective in Britain than in India.

Moral Muscle: Masculinity and Its Religious Uses

GENDER IS A WAY of signifying relationships of power. An important transformation in these relationships in the nineteenth century is the rise of the gendered distinction between public and private. This distinction is crucial to the development of a modern ideology of the family, domesticity, and the moral order. Studies of the Victorian period point at the emergence of a bourgeois ideal of the domesticated housewife, the "angel in the house." As Catherine Hall has shown, this ideal had strong religious overtones in Britain.[1] It is important to see that religious discourse not only provided symbols for the expression of power relations external to it but that it also shaped considerably the public sphere itself and its cultural praxis. Evangelicalism played a major role in the creation of an ideology of female domesticity and male activism. Practical Christianity—as the evangelical Wilberforce called it—depended on moral firmness in a corrupt society. The centerpiece of that firmness was family life, the religious household run by women who kept their distance from the public sphere. The role of men was located neither in leisure nor in hard work for its own sake but in spreading the word of God in the world. Obviously such gendered ideologies could never be entirely clear-cut and self-explanatory. If they were to be effective, some tension between femininity and masculinity had to be retained. One could argue, for example, that the masculine strength required for social activism in evangelicalism was compromised by a sense of total dependence on God. Evangelicalism was sometimes characterized by strong emotional outbursts of devotional surrender to God. Showing one's emotions was common in evangelical circles and was regarded as a sign of femininity. This continued to be a tension in the way evangelicalism buttressed the gendered distinction of public and private till the rise of "muscular Christianity" in the second part of the nineteenth century.

In this chapter we are concerned with the ways gender signified colonial relationships. Religion (Christianity, Hinduism, Islam) provided a gendered language to deal with the new realities of the imperial nation-state and of the colony. Symbols of masculinity and femininity were crucial to the development of imperial attitudes both in the metropole and the colony, but not enough attention has been paid to the ways they were embedded in new conceptions of religiosity and secularity. The sites of the construction of gendered, religious mentalities were manifold, but foremost among them were the family, the school, and leisure activities.

This chapter focuses on the role of Christianity in the construction of the "manly" Englishman and its counterpart, the "effeminate" Hindu, as well as on the role of Hinduism in the construction of the "manly" Hindu. A great number of studies have already begun to explore the colonial world from the perspective of gender by examining the "woman's question" and the development of domesticity. The great nineteenth-century debates on widow burning, child marriages, prostitution, separation of the sexes, and female education have all been the subject of thorough research. Still understudied, however, is the construction of masculinity both in Britain and India and especially the importance of the connection of these two sites for that construction.

This topic is taken up in Ashis Nandy's *Intimate Enemy*, which offers a broad insight in colonial psychology.[2] More recently it has been studied by Mrnalini Sinha in her excellent *Colonial Masculinity*.[3] Sinha analyzes a number of well-known controversies in colonial Bengal, such as the Ilbert Bill controversy and the age-of-consent controversy, in terms of the construction of masculinity both in Britain and India. She wants to complicate "notions of Modern Western masculinity or of traditional Indian conceptions of masculinity as discrete or mutually exclusive categories by a recognition of their mutual implication in imperial politics."[4] From a similar perspective I want to address the role of religion in the construction of colonizing and colonized masculinities.

The propagation of manly virtues, such as willpower, honor, and courage, has been crucial to identity formation in a great variety of historical and cultural conditions. What needs to be understood here is how they have been harnessed to national and imperial projects, and have been transformed by them. While the fascination with the male body is a well-known feature of radical politics, be it fascist or communist, the connection with religion in Britain and India is often puzzling to observers. My argument here is that men of religion had to come to grips with new conceptions of manhood, generated by the emergent conditions of leisure and education. They do so in a number of ways, making use of existing vocabularies to express new social practices. The nationalization of religion in Britain and India involves these new conceptions in the articulation of masculine assertiveness in a newly constructed public sphere. This chapter focuses on "muscular Christianity" and "muscular Hinduism" by looking at the public sites in which these masculine forms of religion were produced: schools, sports, and boys' movements.

MUSCULAR CHRISTIANITY

The Victorians were given to nationalist hero worship. Britain's ascendancy as a power that "rules the waves" was celebrated by worshiping Nelson. Its defeat of its arch-enemy France in the Napoleonic wars was captured by worshiping the hero of Waterloo, the Duke of Wellington. Nonconformist Christians, however, felt a considerable ambivalence toward this heroism of war since it did not show the required humility in the face of God's punishments for the nation's sins and, at the same time, kept an undesirable social order in place. Evangelicals often tried to steer clear from the celebration of war and to argue that evangelicalism abroad and at home would make the world a place where peace would reign. Such pacifistic sentiments were especially expressed in the period of the French Revolution and led to accusations of disloyalty. Nevertheless, there was a strong sense among evangelicals that the fate of the nation was tied to its moral condition and to Providence. War was a calamity inflicted on the British to show them God's displeasure with their immorality. There was nothing heroic or commendable in it.

For the evangelical, the heroic was situated in the spread of the Gospel. As such, it was directly related to the imperialist project, understood as a pacification and civilizing of barbaric, heathen populations by propagating Christian values. Of course, missionaries were heroes, and Livingstone was probably the best example of pioneering, Christian heroism. In the course of the nineteenth century, however, evangelicals gradually changed their minds. Like the rest of the British nation, they came to see warfare as a kind of police action, to quell unrest, to prevent injustice. The pacifism of the Napoleonic period and the moral condemnation of warfare gave way to a celebration of Christian heroism in the Crimean War and the Indian Mutiny. The latter especially provided imperialism with the imagery of the brave Christian soldier, particularly in the figure of General Henry Havelock.

India was of great importance to evangelical Christians. It was the largest missionary field for the British. It was also regarded as an exceedingly difficult field, and the ultimate goal of conversion continued to appear unreachable. The Mutiny dealt a great blow to any hope the British had to Christianize the Indians. The Christian response to it shows how the earlier view of war as punishment for British sins was combined with a new view of war as rightful action for a just cause. One response to it in a way typified the earlier view, namely, the wish for atonement. All Anglican churches held services on October 7, 1857, called by royal proclamation a "day of national humiliation."[5] The main argument in the sermons of that day was that Britain had not done enough to promote the gospel in India and that the Mutiny was God's retribution for that sinful negligence.[6] However, no one believed that the suppression of the Mutiny was a deplorable war from which righteous Christians had to keep their distance. The Mutiny was regarded as a satanic, murderous uprising against the forces of justice. Pacifistic sentiments seem not to have been present or thoroughly marginalized.

The evangelical response was to celebrate the Christian heroes of the Mutiny: Edwardes, the two brothers John and Henry Lawrence, and, of course, Havelock were all devout evangelical Christians. Havelock contributed British victory to the excellence of its artillery and "to the blessing of Almighty God on a most righteous cause, the cause of justice, humanity, truth, and good government in India,"[7] The suppression of the Mutiny was brutal and very much an act of revenge by the British. Still, the vast majority of Christians saw the Mutiny's suppression as entirely justified. The British public was outraged and called for cruel and bloody revenge. This paved the way for hanging prisoners or blowing them from the mouths of cannons without trial. All this was viewed as just revenge, with lone dissenting voices emerging only long after the fact. One such dissenter was the missionary Edward Thompson, the historian E. P. Thompson's father, who, in *The Other Side of the Medal* (1925), protested against the British misrepresentation of the Mutiny.

The Mutiny triggered great anxieties about the imperial project in Britain. The British realized more than ever their vulnerability in governing huge expanses of territory with large populations. Despite the evangelical and Utilitarian efforts to civilize them, the natives of India proved to be as heathen and barbaric as before. Their immoral nature showed itself especially in the atrocities inflicted on defenseless, British women. It was their sexual violation of the "purity" of the Victorian "angel in the house" that unleashed a hysterical, sexualized, and racialized hatred against the Indian natives. For Flora Annie Steel, the author of *On the Face of the Waters* (1896), an immensely popular novel about the Mutiny, the cruel suppression was "the epic of the British race."[8] The main emotion expressed in the novel was the urge for revenge of the "senseless" murder of fair Englishwomen by the dark races of Hindus and Muslims. Sexualized fear became an enduring framework for interpreting the relationship with India, although the evidence even available at the time made it clear that British women had not been sexually violated.[9]

Some fifty novels were written about the Mutiny before 1900, and at least thirty more before the Second World War.[10] Nothing captivated the imperial imagination more than the Mutiny. Most of these novels focus on "the well at Cawnpore," where the mutilated bodies of British wives and children were thrown after they had been killed despite a promise of safe passage from the rebellious town. In the Mutiny novels, the melodrama often focused on the desire of the mutineers to capture British women for their harem. The harem was a stock image of the lack of manly restraint among Orientals. When Oriental desire to add a white woman to the collection failed, the fury, unleashed by frustration, was tremendous and led to atrocious killings. The "treacherous" massacre of Kanpur, more than anything less, was again the sign of the opponent's unmanly character.

Violence in India was always—and continues to be—represented as base and senseless. That the massacre at Kanpur probably had been a retaliation after much larger massacres by the British in other places in North India was not even noticed in the British coverage of the Mutiny. It was the representation of the Mutiny that provided the strongest legitimation for British rule in the period of High Imperialism. The killing of British women and children, often represented in a sadistic way, was the clearest sign that even when Indians revolted violently they did so not as honest soldiers, as real men, but as cruel beasts.

This interpretive framework also justified Governor Eyre's brutal actions in the suppression of the Morant Bay uprising of 1865 in Jamaica. Thomas Carlyle came to the governor's defense when John Stuart Mill set up a committee asking Parliament to prosecute him. For Carlyle, Eyre embodied all the true masculine virtues of the English. As Eyre had already argued in his "Occasional Discourse on the Negro Question" (1849), blacks were simply not equal to whites nor were they potentially equal.[11] Eyre was a hero for preventing Jamaica from being plunged in black anarchy and for thus saving white women.

Carlyle was the national expert on heroism after the publication of his lectures *On Heroes, Hero-Worship, and the Heroic in History* (1844). He was one of the main influences behind the creation of "muscular Christianity."[12] Carlyle discovered the importance of heroic savior-men in history (such as Oliver Cromwell) who were "the embodiment of the Divine Idea and the purposes of God."[13] This view was taken over by Christian writers, such as Charles Kingsley and Thomas Hughes, celebrators of the manly virtues of Christianity and founders of what was called at the time, in a slightly pejorative manner, "Muscular Christianity." The models for this form of Christian masculinity were the Christian heroes of the missionary movement and of the military actions in India, the Sudan, and the Crimea. The sites for its propagation were sports, schools, and boys' movements.

While Kingsley supported Carlyle's Eyre Defense Committee, Thomas Hughes did not. Muscular Christianity did not have to be jingoist or racist; it only demanded a strong activist commitment to the worldly affairs of the empire. Undoubtedly this implied an imperialist attitude, but it could also support Christian socialism.[14] Kingsley contributed to the Christian Socialist weekly, *Politics for the People*, and was greatly influenced by its founder, F. D. Maurice.[15] The great desire of the Christian Socialists was to civilize the working class not by repressing their legitimate demands but by channeling them into a controlled Christian manliness. Their reasoning was that by putting oneself into the service of the larger social body, the nation and empire, one would become a full man. To some extent, this can be interpreted as an antirevolutionary tactic to prevent the working class from organizing itself politically. It advances an organic view of the nation as a whole to prevent the chaotic violence of class struggle; at the same time, however, it acknowledges the inequities in society and the necessity to remove them through Christian education and leisure activities.

Kingsley was a clergyman-novelist who tried to Christianize the emerging secular fields of education, leisure, and empire. He loved nature and was interested in accommodating the new scientific findings of Darwin and Huxley within a Christian-romantic nature worship, inspired by Coleridge. The main point in his muscular Christianity was that he wrote from a moral perspective about topics for which Christianity appeared to be irrelevant. New fields of activity were developed, and their relationship with organized Christianity was still unstable and vague. Muscular Christianity was developed to allow Christians to participate, for instance, in sports, which therefore should not be condemned as "worldly" and un-Christian. Christian sportsmanship was greatly helped in 1884 when the "Cambridge Seven," famous cricketers, went to work with the China Inland Mission. The battle, of course, shifted in the twentieth century to sports on Sundays. The most famous episode in that battle was the refusal of the celebrated Scottish athlete Eric Liddle to run on Sunday in the one-hundred-meter dash at the 1924 Paris Olympics. He shifted to the four-hundred-meter run on another day and won the gold medal. He was the subject of the popular film *Chariots of Fire* and the greatest hero of muscular Christianity, especially when he followed the example of the "Cambridge Seven" and departed for missionary work in China.[16]

Not only sports were Christianized through muscular Christianity. Other leisure activities, belonging to a popular culture of drinking, visiting pubs, and especially engaging in the sexual dangers of the Victorian city, came under the assault of a muscular Christianity that focused on the urban underclass. General William Booth's Salvation Army tried to attack the delights of the city with military discipline. The Salvation Army not only disciplined working-class men into leading a life of Christian respectability but also organized working-class women in public activities such as preaching and Evangelizing in the streets. In this way it definitely transcended the gendered distinction between private and public which was part of bourgeois religiosity. Female preachers, called "Hallelujah Lasses" or "Happy Elizas" by the public, drew even more attention than the Salvation Army's brass bands and music-hall songs.[17] During the 1880s they were centrally involved in the battle against child prostitution and the trafficking of girls. They were also major actors in the agitation against the Contagious Diseases Act, which regulated prostitution and was suspended in 1883, and in the movement in favor of the Age of Consent Act of 1885.

In the second half of the nineteenth century, muscular Christianity also became a crucial element in Christian thinking about leisure for the middle class. One of its offshoots was the Boys' Brigade, founded by William Alexander Smith in Glasgow in 1883. Smith had been associated with the Young Men's Christian Association (YMCA), the famous evangelical organization set up in 1848 to organize Christian leisure activities for young men. Adding weekly drill parades to Bible classes, it provided an attractive alternative to the run-of-the mill Sunday School.[18] It was the Anglican predecessor of Baden-Powell's Boy Scouts, an organization no longer affiliated with any church, though suffused with Christian moralism.

In 1904 Baden-Powell attended the Annual Drill and Review of the Boys' Brigade in Glasgow and was asked by Smith to revise the booklet, *Aids to Scouting*, which Baden-Powell had made for the army, for use by the boys of the Brigade.[19] Like Smith, Baden-Powell was a military man whose career had brought him to India and later to South Africa. His role in the siege of Mafeking had made him a hero comparable to Havelock, the Christian hero of the Mutiny. The guiding idea in his *Scouting for Boys* (1908), written at Smith's request, was that a healthy mind in a healthy body was the basis of both nation and empire. The subtitle of the handbook he wrote together with his sister, Agnes, in 1912, *The Handbook for Girl Guides; or, How Girls Can Help Build the Empire* tells it all. His success was apparent when, in 1922, the Prince of Wales returned from an imperial tour wearing a Scout uniform and was welcomed by sixty thousand Scouts.[20]

Baden-Powell was the son of a clergyman, but his interests focused more on national fitness than on theological morality as the bulwark against world corruption. His principal concern was the deterioration of the British race. To be able to rule the empire and fight the Germans, not only did the middle and upper classes have to be physically and morally fit but so, too, did the working classes. Baden-Powell was greatly influenced by Elliott Mills's anonymously published pamphlet *The Decline and Fall of the British Empire: Appointed for Use in the National Schools of Japan, Tokio 2005* (1905). Mills's pamphlet was based on the conceit that it instructed the next great empire, Japan, on how to avoid the decadence of Britain.[21] Baden-Powell's explicit aim for the Boy Scout movement was to assist "race-regeneration" and patriotism: "Country first, self second," as it is expressed in *Scouting for Boys.*

The success of the Boys Scout movement was astounding, and after the World War it became more and more international. In 1929, at the World Jamboree, Scouts from forty-two nations were assembled outside Birkenhead, England.[22] The movement's very success, however, created its own difficulties. In the first edition of *Scouting for Boys*, Baden-Powell could still, without hesitation, express his British imperialist attitudes. In the book he celebrates the heroism of John Nicholson, one of the British generals during the Indian Mutiny. An example of British pluck may be seen in the following anecdote Baden-Powell related about Nicholson. When an Indian chief does not remove his shoes to show respect to Nicholson, Nicholson orders him to do so:

> Thou camest here to show contempt for me, who represent your Queen. But you forget that you are dealing with a Briton—one of that band who never brooks an insult even from an equal, much less from a native of this land. Were I a common soldier it would be the same; a Briton, even though alone amongst a thousand of your kind, shall be respected, though it brought about his death. That's how we hold the world.[23]

This illustration of British fairness and pluck was omitted from subsequent editions, but Baden-Powell's imperialist and sometimes racist attitudes did not disappear overnight.

The problem with the Boy Scout movement's triumph was not only that it was successful among the colonizers but it also thrived among the colonized. One difficulty was that in South Africa blacks and Indians wanted to join the movement, which, in principle, was open to all regardless of race. This issue bothered the organization until, in 1936, it created three parallel associations under the supervision of the original white Boy Scout movement: the Pathfinder Boy Scouts for blacks, the Indian Boy Scouts for Indians, and the Colored Boy Scouts for half-castes.[24] In India the government tried to prevent the spread of the movement to the native population. This policy led to a proliferation of alternative scouting movements outside government control, including one founded by the Theosophist Annie Besant. The colonial government regarded this an even greater danger and changed its tactics in 1921 by forming, and giving full support to, the All-India Council for Scouts, with the Viceroy as the Chief Scout of India.

Besides leisure activities, another emerging field of social endeavor that featured in muscular Christianity was education. Sunday was not only a day of worship but also of education. Perhaps the most important element in the evangelical transformation of British society in the nineteenth century was Sunday school, a central feature of working-class life. Religious instruction in reading and writing for several hours each Sunday profoundly influenced large numbers of people. Thus, by creating mass literacy, Sunday schools, perhaps more than anything else, were responsible for producing a Christian nation. First, they made the Bible accessible, placing it at the heart of daily religious experience. Children came to be seen as agents of the moral regeneration of lower-class family life.[25] Sunday schools provided a Christian alternative to the worldly leisure activities of the street. Education not only took up much of the leisure time, but it also gave people alternative ways of spending their time in a civilized manner, primarily by reading but also, for example, by attending science lectures in the Halls of Science (see chapter 3). The great evil was drink and the pub, the focus of much working-class recreation.[26] Sunday schools provided special outings to counter attractions, such as fairs, which, ironically, were occasions for heavy drinking.[27]

Besides Sunday school, which continued to be important for working-class children who worked on weekdays, the nineteenth century saw the emergence of the new public school for the middle and upper classes. The classical text here is Thomas Hughes's immensely popular novel, *Tom Brown's Schooldays* (1857). It is the account of how sports, education, and Christian morality were brought together in the educational program at Rugby, Thomas Arnold's public school. The boys at Rugby, the society they formed, represented the nation as a whole in Arnold's conception. They also symbolized the ethereal body of the ideal Christian, as Dennis Allen has argued.[28] At the same time, the emergence of public school as a national institution signified the growing importance of the middle class as the guardian of public morality.[29]

Thomas Arnold, Matthew Arnold's father, became headmaster of Rugby in 1827. He was a Christian moralist who insisted that education was essential to the physical and moral improvement of the British nation. By combining the functions of headmaster and pastor, he could deliver a sermon every Sunday in the Rugby chapel. In these sermons he stressed the connections between morality, physicality, and intellectual growth in education. Arnold's influence on the emergence of the English school system cannot be overestimated. He organized the public school as a total pedagogic institution of discipline and surveillance, as if it were a monastery. He established a system of "fagging," in which pupils in the lower grades were required to "fag," or act as servant, for the pupils in the final grade, who acquired responsibility for the younger boys. This hierarchical system, with its emphasis on the moral relationships among the pupils themselves, was adopted by other founding public schools in Britain. The choice of the word *fag* was intentional, implying that this morality also served to regulate the element of forbidden homosexuality, ever present in public schools. As Lytton Strachey put it in his biographical essay on Arnold: "This was the means by which Dr. Arnold hoped to turn Rugby into 'a place of real Christian salvation.' The boys were to work out their own salvation, like the human race. He himself, involved in awful grandeur, ruled remotely, through his chosen instruments, from an inaccessible heaven."[30]

Thomas Hughes popularized Arnold's ideas about Christian righteousness and self-reliant masculinity in his novel. It describes the life of Tom Brown from birth through graduation from Rugby. Pluck and moral strength carry the day, both in sports and life in general. Tom Brown is rescued from moral laxity and religious indifference by the wonderful combination of cricket and Christianity. There is a strong emphasis on selfless work for the common good, an idea that inspires Thomas Hughes's Christian socialism: "Hughes's muscular Christian is, ultimately, a middle-class Christian who stands as the signifier of a universal brotherhood."[31]

"Once the Empire was established, the public schools sustained it,' as J. A. Mangan puts it.[32] Not only did they spread imperial values, but they also bred imperial officials. A headmaster like Edmond Warre of Eton (1884–1905) saw his school primarily as a foundation stone of the empire.[33] In the Victorian era the headmanship was firmly in the hands of the clergy. H. H. Almond, headmaster of Loretto School, was a strong believer in the Christian mission: "Loretto is a humble attempt to carry out, in one particular line, the Christian idea of the establishment of a Kingdom of Heaven upon Earth. That kingdom must be a great many things beside being rational, but it must be also rational."[34] The Reverend J.E.C. Welldon, headmaster of Harrow School from 1881 to 1895, believed that God had endowed the British "with a world-wide Empire, an Empire transcending all imperial systems, not for their own aggrandisement but that they may be executants of his sovereign purpose in the world."[35] His God was not merely Christian but specifically Protestant, since he thought that "wherever there was a country that was stationary and retrogressive it was Catholic, wherever there was a people that was progressive and Imperial it was Protestant."[36]

Cricket, right along with Christianity, carried the imperial mission. Cricket became a political metaphor: "The greatest game in the world is played wherever the Union Jack is unfurled, and it has no small place in cementing the ties that bond together every part of the Empire . . . On the cricket grounds of the Empire is fostered the spirit of never knowing when you are beaten, of playing for your side and not for yourself, and of never giving up a game as lost. This is as invaluable in Imperial matters as cricket."[37] Cricket and Christianity were building stones of the imperial character: the stiff upper lip, the fair play, the incorruptibility of the British imperial officer, all hovering above the hidden underworld of sexual desire and military violence.

These ideals of "imperial masculine character" were conveyed in an interesting way in perhaps the most famous book on imperial boyhood: Rudyard Kipling's *Kim*. More than anything else, it is a book about imperial masculinity. Of course, Kim is not a middle-class British boy like Tom Brown, educated in a public school, destined to become a clergyman. Kim is a hybrid character, the son of an Irishman in India, brought up by a half-caste Indian woman: "a poor white of the very poorest." That gives him the capacity to cross boundaries to be Indian with the Indians, to speak their dialects without actually belonging to them. It is the imperial fantasy of disguise that affords crucial knowledge of the natives and their ways of thinking without ever losing sight of the Great Game, as imperialism in the context of the purely male world of the North-Western Frontier is called in the novel. Kim is educated in the disciplinary practices of the empire by Colonial Creighton, the ultimate authority figure in the novel. Another central character is Mahbub Ali the horse trader, a Pathan (tribesman from the frontier) with concepts of honor, courage, and loyalty similar to those inculcated in the public schools. The Muslims of the Frontier were "real men" who needed to be controlled by superior, imperial power but could also be respected as men and were thus different from the "effeminate" Bengali Hindus.[38] Kipling's narrative definitely belongs to the genre of adventure writing, but of the imperial sort. As Edward Said points out, Baden-Powell, Kipling's contemporary, was greatly influenced by Kipling's work. They agreed that "boys ultimately should conceive of life and empire as governed by unbreakable Laws, and that service is more enjoyable when thought of as similar less to a story—linear, continuous, temporal—than to a playing field—many dimensional, discontinuous, and spatial."[39] *Kim* is an imperial fantasy played out in India, where the natives, when they have good intentions, are favorably inclined toward imperial rule. What is totally elided in Kipling's narrative is the other story, that of native nationalism and its own fantasies of religiously inflected masculinity.

HINDUSTANI HONOR

In 1937 the Indian Boy Scouts movement went through a crisis on an issue of crucial significance for our discussion of how British masculinity was constructed by simultaneously feminizing the colonized Indians. As we will see, this imperialist construction of muscular Christianity was answered by an Indian nationalist construction of muscular Hinduism. According to Baden-Powell, there was no word in Hindustani that could fully translate the notion of honor that was central to the building of character in the Boy Scout movement: "When in India I asked one or two Scouters what word they used for 'Honour' in teaching their boys character and they said 'Izzut.' I asked 2 or 3 other men what was the Hindustani for 'Honour' and they could only suggest 'Izzut.' But Izzut does not convey the idea of Honour. I allow we have not the exact equivalent in English for Izzut and have to borrow from the French—

'Prestige.'"[40] The Indians took this as a straightforward insult, implying that Indians did not have "honour." When Baden-Powell refused to change his position in this matter, the Boy Scout Association of India declared its independence from the mother organization.

By denying the translatability of the English "honour" into Hindustani, Baden-Powell effectively denied the masculinity of the colonized Indians. That "Izzut" was the central concept in Indian masculinity could not have escaped him in the years he had been an officer in the colonial army in India. This denial of the masculinity of the colonized was a central theme in British colonialism. Indians were seen as effeminate and weak in character. The Bengalis especially were examples of deficient masculinity. Thomas Babington Macaulay was most eloquent on this point in an essay on Warren Hastings:

> The physical organization of the Bengalee is feeble even to effeminacy. He lives in a constant vapour bath. His pursuits are sedentary, his limbs delicate, his movements languid. During many ages he has been trampled upon by men of bolder and more hardy breeds. Courage, independence, veracity are qualities to which his constitution and his situation are equally unfavourable (1843).[41]

Ironically, it was precisely Macaulay's educational ideal, the brown gentleman, thoroughly Anglicized, who came in for severe criticism of being effete. A large proportion of the Westernized bureaucrats through whom India was ruled were Bengal clerks or *babus*. They formed the prime example of effeminacy.

There was already an older tradition of gendering the Orient as feminine. According to this tradition in Western philosophy, Hinduism lacked masculine, world-ordering rationality. Hindus were guided by feminine fantasies and imagination rather than by masculine reason according to Hegel.[42] Their dependence on priests and idolatry was also seen as a deficient male autonomy. These older images were connected with the very fact of colonial submission, and even precolonial submission. Hindus were weak. They were conquered first by Muslim tribesmen and later by the British. Their very history of submission made them an effeminate race.

Not all Indians were captured in this gendered stereotype, not even all Hindus. Muslims were exempted because of their long history of dominance in India and their history of world expansion. They were often also identified with the tribesmen of the frontier, the sturdy and masculine Pathans. Sikhs were also exempted because of their valiant resistance in

95

the Anglo-Sikh Wars against the British. Their martial traditions and worship of the sword were unambiguous signs of masculinity. Similarly, among the Hindus it was the so-called martial races, such as the Rajputs, that somehow escaped the stigma of effeminacy that was so easily applied to Bengalis. Also the Gurkhas from Nepal, being hillsmen, were seen as martial, real men despite their Hinduism. All these groups suited the romantic image of the masculine life of the hills as opposed to the effeminate ways of city people. They exemplified the chivalric code of manly behavior that was so important both in the novels of Sir Walter Scott and the travel stories of Richard Burton. Burton fashioned himself after the manly image of the Pathan to spy on Mecca and Sindh in disguise, prefiguring Kipling's *Kim*.[43]

All these groups of real men among the colonized were put to the test of English "honour," however—and honor in British India basically meant loyalty to the empire. Real men, like Sikhs and Gurkhas, whose loyalty was beyond doubt, had that special masculine quality of trustworthiness that was so essential for Baden-Powell. Lying, dishonesty, treacherous behavior, these qualities could be found among martial men who were the enemy of the empire, and especially among Muslims, whose allegiance to a "pan-Islamic" community was always seen by the British as a potential conspiracy against their rule. Submission without loyalty to colonial rule was therefore a sign of effeminacy. Resistance and opposition against it, however, were also not quite the real thing. It is this imagery of barbarism and disloyalty that made Baden-Powell, half a century after the Mutiny, so tenacious in his denial of the possibility of translating English honor into Hindustani Izzut.

The masculinity of the Hindus was also put into doubt in legal reform. One of the great legal battles in which masculinity was negotiated both in the metropole and the colony concerned the age of consent. In 1891 the Age of Consent Act was signed, raising the age of consent for sexual intercourse for Indian girls from ten to twelve years. The new law was, in fact, hardly ever implemented because of the controversy it caused in India. There is no instance of colonial legislation in the nineteenth century that mobilized Indian public opinion to the extent that the Age of Consent Act did. Much has been written about it and Mrnalini Sinha has ably summarized the issues. Antireformist groups argued that the new law was an unacceptable interference with Hindu religion and custom, while reformist groups tried to show that the law was entirely within the spirit of Hinduism. The former group can be considered victorious, since the law was never truly implemented. The law's real effect was a reassertion of Hindu patriarchal control over the domestic sphere as a nationalist cause.

The reformists were branded as Westernized, outside the national culture. This particular strategy made it easier to define religion as the terrain on which the controversy had to be debated. The reformists were forced to concede this point and therefore lost the possibility to show the arbitrary nature of religious arguments in this issue.

The British linked early sexual intercourse in India to effeminacy. A number of vices, such as masturbation, and diseases, such as diabetes, were the result.[44] One of the guiding notions behind the bill, therefore, was a eugenic one, namely, to improve the Indian race. The protest against it could not have surprised anyone among the British who had the idea that the Hindus were effeminate. The opponents of the bill, however, turned the tables by linking the proposed reform to a deliberate British policy to emasculate Hindu men. Especially the marital rape clause in the bill, which argued that sexual intercourse without the wife's consent was rape, created strong resistance, all the more since it differed from legislation in Britain where the matrimonial contract gave lawful access to the wife always. Sinha shows that even reformist nationalists saw this as a blatant attack on the honor of the Indian man.[45]

Before the colonial authorities introduced the Age of Consent Act in India, Britain had just seen similar debates relating to its own Age of Consent Act. Here, perhaps more explicitly than in the Indian case, the issue was linked to child prostitution and the dangerous vices of the Victorian city. As Judith Walkowitz shows in her brilliant analysis of the narratives of sexual danger in late Victorian London, it was the journalist W. T. Stead, editor of the *Pall Mall Gazette*, who engineered a highly publicized campaign against child prostitution ending in a huge demonstration in Hyde Park, which forced the passage of age-of-consent legislation in Parliament.[46] The Criminal Law Amendment of 1885 raised the age of consent for girls from thirteen to sixteen. As in India, however, national public opinion was formed around the issue of sexual danger and social purity. This became the basis of a number of movements against pornography, prostitution, and the like. An important difference with the developments in India was that, according to Walkowitz,[47] the age-of-consent controversy in Britain allowed women to speak for themselves as well as permitting middle-class women to speak for working-class women on issues of sexual crime and to protest Victorian patriarchy. In India, however, it was men speaking for men about the threat to Hindu patriarchy posed by colonial regulations of sexual access to women.

The similarities between the British and Indian controversies around the age-of-consent legislations are as striking as their differences. The main and deciding difference was the relatively secure place of masculinity in the self-perception of the British elite that ruled an empire and the much more endangered masculinity of the Indian elite that served under an increasingly racist colonial regime. The Indians felt emasculated by their position and thus increased their efforts to stay at least masters in the home. The British stereotype of the effete Hindu had left an impression especially on the Bengali elite who sought ways to redress this humiliation by supporting martial arts and physical culture. As Bankim Chandra Chatterjee put it: "Why are not Bengalis courageous? The reason is simple: the physical is the father of the moral man" (1874).[48] He and others expressed a general feeling that the Bengali race was in a process of physical degeneration, from which it had to be saved.

It is paradoxical that both the colonizing British and the colonized Bengalis saw "Westernization" as a main cause for this emasculation. Nevertheless, the British were firmly committed to promote British education in India. Much of the educational field was in the hands of Christian missionaries whose ultimate aim obviously was not to strengthen the Hindu race but to convert their pupils to a superior religion, Christianity. The response to this was predictable. Hindus, Sikhs, and Muslims started their own educational institutions that included their own religious education within a highly Anglicized curriculum. Educational reformers in these communities shared the British view of education as the cultivation of "character."[49] Instead of Christianity, Hinduism or Islam or Sikhism were seen as the wellsprings of such "good character." Sports were generally taken to belong to the accepted British scheme of cultivating manly character. The improvement of physical culture followed, in part, the same trajectory in India as in Britain. Gymnastics and sports were added to the curriculum with the support of the colonial government. Indians also mastered Western sports, such as hockey, football, and cricket. Indian teams started to play football in the 1880s. The team of Mohan Bagan was the best native team and was allowed to compete with British army teams. It succeeded in defeating the East Yorkshire Regiment team and ultimately winning the final of the Indian Football Association Shield in Calcutta in 1911, an event that is remembered with patriotic pride to the present day.[50] Soon Indian teams showed their masculine qualities in hockey and cricket as well. More than any other sport, cricket, as we have seen, was the ultimate public school sport. Arjun Appadurai summarizes the Victorian values expressed by cricket as follows: "Cricket was a quintessentially masculine activity and expressed the codes that were expected to govern all masculine behavior: sportsmanship, a sense of fair play, thorough control over the expression of

strong sentiments by players on the field, subordination of personal sentiments and interests to those of the side, unquestioned loyalty to the
team."[51] He shows that Indian princes especially became the main pa-
trons of the sport and sometimes important cricketers themselves, like
the prince of Nawanagar in West India, Ranjitsinhji (1872–1933). While
more often than not the princes were fully loyal to the crown and perceived cricket as a thoroughly "English" game, others soon began to
indigenize it as a truly Indian national sport.

Certainly, equal in importance to the introduction of British physical
culture was the transformation of religious martiality into sports in the
service of an emerging nationalist masculinity. During my fieldwork on
pilgrimage in Ayodhya I encountered a living tradition of ascetic wrestling
and martial arts.[52] This tradition was found among so-called *nagas*, or
"naked ascetics." This term is used exclusively for a section of Hindu
ascetics who are "fighting ascetics." They are organized into armies and
regiments, live in fortified temples, and are trained in wrestling and fighting with hand weapons. Westerners often find it difficult to accept that
this tradition is part of Hinduism, which they believe to be nonviolent.
Ahimsa, often translated as "nonviolence," is indeed a religious value
among these ascetics, but it refers to nonviolence toward animals, not to
violence between men. In fact, asceticism and organized violence is a long-
standing historical combination. Traditionally ascetics were mercenaries
as well as traders and moneylenders. They dominated trade and money-
lending in North India in the second part of the eighteenth century, just
before British colonial expansion. Ascetics of different persuasions—Vish-
nuite, Shivaite, Sikh, or Muslim—constantly clashed, especially during
the great Hindu bathing festivals. They roamed the countryside, trading
in horses and camels, and soliciting alms from the laity.

This world of migrant ascetic trader-soldiers who serviced a network
of pilgrimage centers that doubled as trading centers was destroyed by
the Pax Britannica at the end of the eighteenth century during the so-
called Sannyasi Rebellion, a protracted struggle between 1770 and 1800.
Soldiering acquired a different form in the Bengal army till the Mutiny
led the British to disband these large native regiments and replaced them
with more manageable regiments of loyal troops of Gurkhas and Sikhs.
Long-distance trade was transformed completely with the introduction of
metal highways and railways. It is in this period, the first half of the nineteenth century, that militant asceticism was "laicized" into martial arts
and wrestling. The transformation is easily recognizable in the shifting
meaning of the word *akhara*, which is defined originally as a camp of

ascetics, then a fortified temple of fighting ascetics, and finally a gymnasium where wrestlers meet.

The traditions of the akhara, as we encounter them today in cities and the countryside, continue many of the religious ideas and practices of asceticism. Young men train under the guidance of a guru who teaches them not only how to wrestle but also how to eat, sleep, and, in short, control their bodily functions. Joseph Alter has given us an ethnography of wrestling among Hindu men in North India.[53] The extent to which these lay wrestlers follow the religious practices and ideas of fighting ascetics is striking. A good example is their devotion to Hanuman, the Hindu monkey-god. The identity of both fighting ascetic and wrestler, exemplified in the figure of Hanuman, is based on a connection between divine power (*shakti*) and physical strength (*bal*). The source of Hanuman's divine power is his extreme devotion to the god Rama and his wife Sita, the chief protagonists in the religious epic *Ramayana* in which Hanuman also plays a significant role. As I argue elsewhere, *shakti* is gendered as a feminine power that men can acquire through celibacy.[54] Both fighting ascetics and wrestlers are celibate, and celibacy is seen as the source of their strength. Through the disciplines of celibacy and wrestling, men acquire self-control and realize the feminine power within themselves. This also allows them to develop fully another feminine capacity: selfless devotion. With Hanuman, this is a selfless devotion to the divine couple, but this devotion can, for fighting ascetics and wrestlers, be transformed through nationalist discourse into a selfless devotion to the cause of the nation.

As Alter points out, wrestlers feel a direct connection between their somatic discipline and nationalist ethos.[55] As in Britain, there is a constant bemoaning of national degeneration. More than in Britain, however, this is couched in a language of the body, bodily fluids, and food intake. In Britain, the language of health foods, homeopathic medicine, and gymnastics exists at a subcultural level, whereas in India it is part of the dominant culture. Wrestlers are especially finicky about their food, and their attitudes are underpinned by a theory that character, emotions, and moral behavior are intimately connected to the kinds of food one eats. From the wrestlers' point of view, the degeneration of the Indian people has everything to do with Westernization and the decline of India's "ancient" martial arts. This lament is heard continuously from the mid-nineteenth century to the 1980s when Alter did his fieldwork. The following quotation from a wrestling aficionado is typical:

There was a time when every village had an akhara . . . This sport, which costs nothing, has made India great in terms of strength and fitness . . . Not until every man in India has spent ten to twelve years in the earth of an akhara can we hope to regain our national strength . . . Our energy should be spent building strength and wisdom. In this way we can prevent the wastage of our national wealth. The health of the nation will increase. The character of the nation will grow strong.[56]

How much this Hindu emphasis on sports, physical health, and moral regeneration resembles the imperial language discussed above is striking.

The Hindu response to the imperialist construction of Christian masculinity and Hindu femininity had a feature of mimicry. First, there was the imitation of British physical culture in sports like cricket and of all the features of British education. Second, there was the imitation of the Carlylean theme of historical heroes. These heroes were found in the Aryan race's past, as in Rajanikanta Gupta's *Aryakirti*, "the fame of the Aryans"(1887), which was basically a retelling of the lore of Rajput valor. They were also found in the Bengali present, as in the amusing story of the Bengali colonel, Suresh Biswas (1861–1902), who traveled first to England and then to Brazil to serve as an officer there. He was a typical Bengali, "frail of frame," but according to his biography a strong and courageous man. And as Indira Chowdhury-Sengupta remarks in her discussion of this biography, the mere existence of a Bengali colonel was already a refutation of the colonial stereotype.[57]

Besides this feature of mimicry there was, of course, the transformation in nationalist terms of longue duree religious discourses and practices. The connection between physicality and morality already existed in precolonial India, and the emergence of nationalism under colonial conditions implied a transformation of this connection in ways familiar to us from European history. It is especially the articulation of notions of gender and sexuality with notions of race that strikes me as typical of this period. In the early twentieth century the articulation of physicality and morality under the aegis of nationalism develops into fascist forms of xenophobia both in Europe and India.

THE INTERNAL ENEMY

Where British discourse on masculinity and national regeneration emphasized the burdens of empire and later the threat of German expansionism,

Hindu discourse on masculinity immediately focused on the threat Muslims posed to Mother India ("the rape of the motherland"). Hindu discourse portrayed Muslims as excessively masculine and militant. The possibility of Muslim men marrying four wives was seen as an excessive enjoyment that is regarded with masculine envy. It is also regarded as the source of Muslim fertility and numerical proliferation in face of Hindu stagnation or decline. The theme of "Muslim lust" and the threat it posed to Hindu women was exacerbated by the threat to Hindu male control over female sexuality, posed in the age-of-consent controversies of the last decade of the nineteenth century. Stories of abduction of Hindu women during riots belonged to the standard repertory of Hindu nationalism. An enormously influential book in this regard was U. N. Mukherjee's *Hindus: A Dying Race*, published in Bengal in 1909. Here a numerical obsession, originating in the colonial census operations, was combined with the fear of emasculation. As P. K. Datta argues in his analysis of Mukherjee's text, much of this has become part of Hindu common sense in the first decades of the twentieth century. He also sees as its subtext the notion that the threatened Hindu male body had to be trained in order to prevent their becoming a "dying race."[58]

A crucial element in this paranoid nationalism was a discourse on race. As I explore further in chapter 6, Hindu ideologues took up the popular European theme of the "Aryan race" to racialize the Hindu community and make the religious difference between them and Muslims into an immutable, racial one. The militant Aryans were masculine to the extreme, and the ideological message behind that view was the usual call for national regeneration. The notion of common Hindu race came to play the role of national unifier in a society extremely divided by regional, linguistic, and caste identities. As in Germany and Britain we find in India in the 1920s the combination of an ideal masculinity and a racial superiority connected to a heightened nationalism and an extreme fear of a minority within the population.[59] One crucial difference should be noted, however. In Britain and Germany such a combination became increasingly divorced from religious identities through a displacement of religion by race, whereas in India religion continued to be the foremost signifier.

The best example of the connection between youth, masculinity, and militant nationalism in India is perhaps the Rashtriya Swayamsevak Sangh (RSS), the National Volunteer Corps founded in 1925 by K. B. Hedgewar. This is Hindu India's most violent youth organization with an ultra-nationalist and strongly anti-Muslim message. Former RSS members were the assassins of the nationalist leader Mahatma Gandhi after India's independence, and the organization was subsequently forbidden by the Indian state for a number of years. In the context of our discussion, it is interesting to note that Nathuram Godse, Gandhi's murderer, in his statement for the court in 1947, explicitly referred to his fear that Gandhi's ideas "would ultimately result in the emasculation of the Hindu community."[60]

The RSS propagates the development of physical strength through quasi-military drill and exercise. The members of a local RSS branch meet for one hour every day for physical exercise, military drill, and ideological training. In the words of Hedgewar's successor, M. S. Golwarkar:

> The first thing is invincible physical strength. We have to be so strong that none in the world will be able to overawe and subdue us. For that we require strong and healthy bodies . . . [but] character is more important. Strength without character will only make a brute of man. Purity of character as well as the national standpoint is the real life-breath of national glory and greatness.[61]

Like with the wrestlers and fighting ascetics, the RSS also embodies a religious emphasis on masculine celibacy and on Hanuman as the paradigm of selfless devotion and physical strength. A crucial difference, however, is that the RSS is a centralized organization that has an explicit political purpose, namely, the total remaking of multicultural India into Hindu India.

The language of masculinity as a counterpoint to colonial emasculation has been crucial not only to the RSS but to all radical Hindu movements, starting with Bengali anticolonial "terrorists" such as Aurobindo Ghosh (1872–1950), the later philosopher-saint of Pondicherry. After having been trained in philology at Cambridge, he returned to India and became active in organized militant youth groups in Bengal between 1898 and 1910. These groups formed a loosely organized network called Anusilan Samiti. Anusilan referred to the fullest development of mental and physical faculties.[62] The groups trained themselves to fight with sticks (*lathi*), but they also took religious vows, such as that of celibacy (*brahmacarya*). Some of them became involved in attacks on the British. In that connection, Aurobindo was arrested by the British and fled from his prison to the French colony Pondicherry. He withdrew from politics and started a religious center (*ashram*), which, after his death, was led by a French disciple called "the Mother." Still today the center emphasizes yoga and military drill for boys. The teaching is obviously mystical but also nationalistic.

In Maharashtra, West India, we also find an emphasis on physical culture: youthful masculinity in incipient Hindu nationalism. This is already evident, in an ideological form, among nineteenth-century reformers such as Bal Gangadhar Tilak. It clearly shows itself in the writings of Veer ("strong hero") Savarkar (1882–1966), who, in 1907, founded the right-wing political party Hindu Mahasabha. In 1908 Savarkar published his immensely influential interpretation of the Mutiny, entitled, typically, *Indian War of Independence, 1857*. The book's tone is quite militant, and the book was immediately forbidden. In 1910 Savarkar was arrested for conspiracy against the British. From 1910 to 1922 he was imprisoned in the Andaman Islands, and from 1922 to 1937 he was confined in Ratnagiri district in Maharashtra. The British viewed him as one of the most dangerous revolutionaries of his time, almost equal to his opponent Mahatma Gandhi. His writings and political ideas became the basis of the ideology of the RSS, an organization that originated in Maharashtra and whose militant masculinity is discussed above. In Savarkar's major nationalist treatise, *Hindutva: Who Is a Hindu?* (1923), he connects Aryan race and Aryan territory in the definition of the Hindu. Savarkar felt a strong attraction to European fascism and admired Hitler.

All this continues to be relevant today. The battle against the British has been gradually replaced (long before the Partition of 1947) by a battle against Muslims. In his analysis of Hindu nationalism, Thomas Blom Hansen argues that recuperation of masculinity continues to be a common, deep-running theme in Hindu nationalist discourses and organizations.[63] As argued above, the fear of effeminization not only relates to the colonial experience but also typically to the often violent competition with "the enemy within," the Muslims. The myth that Hindus lost their masculinity "under foreign occupation" first by Muslims and later by the British underlies much of Hindu nationalist discourse. Hansen argues that both the hedonistic Westerner (the excessive, intoxicated, and immoral consumer) and the lustful, wily, and hedonistic Muslim are stereotypical Hindu images of excess projected onto the Other. They are fantasies produced by a lack of self-esteem. This "lack" can, according to Hindu ideology, be redeemed by promoting self-discipline and control.

CONCLUDING REMARKS

Muscular religion developed in both sites of the colonial encounter in response to similar challenges. Modern life produced new conditions of leisure and education and new conceptions of manhood. Public schools in Britain and in India developed curricula in which physical exercise became expressive of moral pluck. Empire provided a "Great Game" in which both British and Indian conceptions of honor and loyalty could be tested. While boys' movements on the British side culminated in Baden-Powell's secularized Boy Scouts, in which race took precedence over religion as a marker of identity, they became in India more and more communalized as part of Hindu-Muslim competition in the struggle for nationhood.

The sexualization of imperial and communal relations became the enduring frame of interpreting violence after the Mutiny. The British not only differentiated Hindus and Muslims in terms of masculine martiality but also Rajputs, Pathans, Gurkhas, and Bengalis. Against this variety the British imagined that they themselves typified the superior masculinity of the ruling race. They were never certain of this, however, as the responses to the Mutiny and to feminism at home clearly show. The reactions to the introduction of age-of-consent legislation on both the Indian and British sides show sexual anxieties that are crucial in the production of masculinities, inflected by discourses of religion, nation, and empire. Demographic statistics and discourses of eugenics and health, both bodily and morally, also come to play an increasingly important role in both Indian and British perceptions of the embattled nature of nation and empire. Sexuality and gendered identities, perhaps more than any other area of social life, show the ambivalences and contradictions, and thus the instability, of colonial encounters.

Monumental Texts: Orientalism and the Critical Edition of India's National Heritage

"THE FACT THAT Max Müller was German by birth and spent his early life in Germany has quite unnecessarily fixed the idea that he was a German scholar writing in German. Actually, he was naturalized in England and always wrote in English with complete mastery of the language, except when he employed German for a special purpose in a book, article, or his correspondence." Nirad C. Chaudhuri, the famous Bengali writer and Anglophile, has this "important note" precede his biography of (Friedrich) Max Müller (1823–1900). Chaudhuri recalls how, as a child, he came to know about Müller:

> My father was not a highly educated man in the formal sense, for he had received only a school education and that too in the backwaters of East Bengal and not in Calcutta, the centre of modern Bengali culture. None the less, it was he who explained to me how Max Müller had established that our languages and the European languages belonged to the same family; that our words, *pita, mata, duhita*, etc., were the same as the English words, "father," "mother," "daughter," etc.; that Sanskrit *Dyaus Pitr* and the Greek *Zeus Pater* were identical; and that we Hindus and the Europeans were both peoples descended from the same original stock.[1]

It is remarkable that a discovery made by Sir William Jones (1746–1794), Justice at the Calcutta High Court, half a century before Müller's lifetime was attributed, by Chaudhuri's father, to Müller, who, in India but nowhere else, is still seen today as one of the greatest Western men of science of all times. One of the reasons for that misattribution lies in the simple fact that Jones was a British colonizer and Müller was a German "outsider." At least he is consistently regarded as such in India, which explains why Chaudhuri wrote his "important note" at the opening of his biography.

Müller's German birth was not only significant for his Indian admirers but also for the British. While he was recognized as one of the great lights of Oxford in his time, his status was always ambiguous. He was seen as a pedantic German, an outsider, and was often fiercely attacked for his views on Christianity and, indeed, for his championship of comparative philology as a foundational discipline in making any argument about language and race. In short, he was regarded as "un-English," both in the metropole and in the colony. Such an identification of a famous scholar who lived and worked for most of his life in Oxford cannot be understood in terms of birth alone. Müller's German origin underlined the fact that his science, Orientalist philology, was a "foreign" one, a German *Wissenschaft*, if indeed there was any. One of the ironies of Edward Said's trenchant critique of Orientalism, the scientific study of the Orient, is that it does not deal at all with the German provenance of the bulk of Orientalist writing in the nineteenth century. Orientalist writing on Indian texts was largely done in Germany, where every university appeared to have a chair in Sanskrit. Though this kind of work was also done in Britain, it was certainly much more contested than in Germany, and, what is more, it did not occupy a central place in the British formulation of imperial policy after the 1830s. The relationship between the production of Orientalist knowledge and the imperialist project is therefore much more twisted and complex than one would gather from Said's study.

hm, seems direct in France?

In this chapter I examine Max Müller's work on the science of language and the science of religion in order to understand the critical role of Orientalist philology in the analysis of the triangle of religion-nation-empire both in Britain and in India. My argument is that while in Britain philology became marginalized when it was rejected as an instrument of imperial rule, in India it became an authoritative science for the transformation and translation of Hindu traditions. Orientalism in the second half of the nineteenth century played a significant role in new understandings of the place of religion in defining nation and empire, both in the metropole and the colony.

Müller's Science

On October 27, 1868, Friedrich Max Müller gave his inaugural lecture as professor of comparative philology at the University of Oxford. He began by pointing out that this new branch of scientific research had gained recognition at Oxford much later than in France and Germany. He continued by lamenting, page after page, that Oxford and Cambridge were basically institutions for undergraduate teaching and were not research universities as were their counterparts on the continent. He called for a fundamental reform of Oxford from a clerical institution to a secular university, in which *Wissenschaft* was a *"Berufung"* (a calling), to use Max Weber's famous phrase. The first half of his lecture was quite polemical, especially when he criticized the British tendency to look down on "knowledge for its own sake, and a chivalrous devotion to studies which command no price in the fair of the world, and lead to no places of emolument in church or state."[2] The second half of the lecture ventured to illustrate the importance of comparative philology, based on a sound knowledge of Sanskrit, for research on grammar and etymology, and for the study of classical and modern languages generally.

Müller's plea for the transformation of Oxford was really a German one. Prussia's greatest contribution to world culture was the founding of the University of Berlin which became the model for all research universities, first in Germany and later in the rest of the world. Central to that university was Humboldt's idea of *Wissenschaft*, which consisted of three elements: first, continuous research (not simply handing down what is known); second, the notion that each discipline contributes to the understanding of the world and life as a whole; and third, the notion that it had no goal outside itself, that practical utility is secondary.[3] The success of Humboldt's idea has been astounding. German *Wissenschaft* gained international importance, and the notion of international reputation instead of local, collegial support became the principle of professorial selection. The center of German *Wissenschaft* was philosophy cum philology, practiced entirely free of the state but fully supported by the state. The German professor was (and is) a state official, and, according to idealist philosophy (especially that of Hegel) his research would discover the higher purposes of the state. It is not difficult to see how much Müller embodied this ideal of the German professor in the very different context of an imperial state.

The reason for Müller's polemical tone can be found in the controversies leading to the creation of this new chair in comparative philology.[4] Müller had been Taylorian Professor of modern European languages at Oxford since 1854 and a Fellow of All Souls since 1858. In 1860, however, a much better position with a considerable endowment opened up: the Boden Professorship of Sanskrit. The Taylorian Professorship brought a salary of five hundred pounds, and the Boden Professor's salary was between nine hundred and one thousand pounds a year. The Professorship had been endowed by a retired East India Company officer, Joseph Boden, "being of the opinion that a more general knowledge and critical knowledge of the Sanskrit language will be a means of enabling his countrymen to proceed in the conversion of the Natives of India to the Christian Religion, by disseminating a knowledge of the sacred scriptures amongst them, more effectually than all means whatever." In 1832 Horace Hayman Wilson was appointed to the post, and after his death in 1860 the chair became vacant. There were two competitors, Monier Monier-Williams and Max Müller. Müller was undoubtedly the greater Orientalist of the two, but, to Müller's immense disappointment, Monier-Williams was elected to the chair. The reasons for Müller's rejection were complex, but two stand out: first, he was regarded as a pedantic German, and, second, he was not considered the right person to carry out the intentions of the chair's founder. Monier-Williams had argued forcefully that he had the right Christian credentials for the missionary purposes of the chair, and his arguments carried the day. A few years later, Oxford acknowledged Müller's status as one of the leading scholars of his time by creating a new chair for him in comparative philology. Despite all the opposition, there was a clear awareness of Müller's stature at Oxford. He and his Oxford colleague, Sir Henry Maine, author of the foundational *Ancient Law*, were the principal spokesmen for the comparative method, not only in the study of language and religion but also in other fields such as law, politics, and history.[5] Knowledge of the "Aryan institutions" of ancient India, and Sanskrit as the medium to gain access to them, were considered essential in the comparative method. The results were not only produced in part by the imperial experience, but they were also instrumental in ruling the empire, as, for example, Maine's notion of the "village community."

Monier-Williams was not one of the leaders in this emerging field of comparative "Aryan" studies, but he was correct in claiming to be the right man to carry out the intentions of the Boden chair. Like his predecessor, Wilson, Monier-Williams had an Evangelical zeal that is clearly evident in his textbook on Hinduism (see chapter 3). Monier-Williams's point of view was in line with the Evangelical views of the preceding half-century that had inspired Joseph Boden to endow the chair. Sanskrit could be used for Evangelical purposes: "Such, indeed, is the exuberance and flexibility of this language and its power of compounding words, that when it has been, so to speak, baptized, and thoroughly penetrated with the spirit of Christianity, it will probably be found to be, next to Hebrew and Greek, the most expressive vehicle of Christian truth."[6]

Müller's views had much more in common with the eighteenth-century Orientalist views that had inspired Sir William Jones but were defeated by the Anglicist arguments of the early nineteenth century. His views, however, were not mere survivals of an earlier period; they also expressed new understandings of a universal Christian religion. This new point of view would become dominant in the twentieth century as a result of the success of nationalist movements in the colonized world.

Müller's views on the Christian missionary effort were expressed most clearly in a controversial lecture he delivered in the nave of Westminster Abbey on December 3, 1873. In this lecture he argued that "among the six religions of the Aryan and Semitic World, there are three that are opposed to all missionary enterprise—Judaism, Brahmanism, and Zoroastrianism; and three that have a missionary character from their very beginning—Buddhism, Mohammedanism, and Christianity."[7] The difference between the two was that the missionary religions were alive, had "the spirit of truth," wanted to convince and conquer, whereas the other religions were dying or dead. Between the missionary religions "the decisive battle for the dominion of the world will have to be fought" (252). Müller acknowledged that it was not very likely that a person belonging to one of the missionary religions would be converted to another, but he still saw a purpose in a continuing missionary effort, even when the world was divided between the three missionary religions. This was a "kind of missionary activity, which has produced the most important results, and through which alone, I believe, the final victory will be gained" (255). This was the direct influence the missionaries had on those who would not convert but would be reformed. Müller argued that religious reform movements in Hinduism were the most enduring result of the missionary effort in India. In his view, "true Christianity lives, not in our belief, but in our love—*in our love of God, in our love of man, founded on our love of God.* That is the whole Law and the Prophets, that is the religion to be preached to the whole world, that is the Gospel which will conquer all other religions—even Buddhism and Mohammedanism—which will win the hearts of all men" (264).

Müller's lecture caused, to use his own words, "great excitement at the time" (296). The gist of his argument was indeed striking, since it went against the Evangelical spirit that had inspired the rise of missionary movements for almost a century. Basically he argued that there was an essential message of Love hidden in the religions of mankind that would be uncovered by the efforts of Christian missionaries without any need to "transplant, if possible, Christianity in its full integrity from England to India, as we might need to transplant a full-grown tree" (261). There appears to be a contradiction in his idea that, on the one hand, Brahmanism was dead or dying, while, on the other, Hindu reform revitalized

Hinduism under the influence of Christian missionaries. The contradiction can be solved if we recognize that Müller propagated a universal morality, based on Humanism and Natural Religion, that replaced all previously existing religions, while retaining some distinctive characteristics of its predecessors in the various national traditions. This notion of Unity in Diversity inspired a number of modernist religious movements in this period. It was also the guiding idea behind the World Parliament of Religions, held in Chicago in 1893. In a lecture given at Oxford in 1894, Müller compared *The Sacred Books of the East*, the famous series of fifty volumes he edited, to the Chicago events as both being "parliaments of religion."[8] Müller's religion was not Christianity in a narrow sense but universal religion, and the science of religion he helped to establish was an integral part of that conception.

Müller is a full member of the historicist school in his belief that the history of religion is the true science of religion.[9] History shows "how the human mind, unassisted by what is called special revelation, gradually found its way from the lowest perception of something material and visible to the highest conception of a supreme and invisible God.[10] This is what Müller calls "the natural revelation," that is, the perception of natural phenomena that leads to the conception of the God-Creator. Another element of the science of religion is the comparative method. Obviously the critical and contested issue here is the comparison of Christianity with other religions. Müller argues that Christians should not be afraid of such a comparison, since Christian truths only gain in power when they are also found in other religions that are independent of Christian influence.[11] The implication of that argument is that Christianity contains universal truth, but does not possess it exclusively. Also implicit is that Christianity has to be studied with the same historical and comparative method as the other religions. The assumption is that Christianity is the highest religious form in an evolutionary sense, although a contrary assumption is that one must get to the original source to find the truest religion devoid of later blemishes.[12] Both the evolutionary, progressivist notion and the romantic notion of decay and decline are simultaneously at work here. This also implies that one must "distinguish between the Christianity of the nineteenth century and the religion of Christ."[13] The upshot of all this is that there is Religion, transcendental Truth, but there are also historical religions that all contain some elements of Religion. The science of religion will enable one to discover Religion by studying religions. The truly radical move is to include Christianity among the religions and gain support from the state to do this kind of work in institutions like Oxford and

111

Cambridge which are part of the clerical establishment. That this move could be made was an important sign of the shifting location of religion in nineteenth-century Britain.

The science of religion follows the model of the science of language. Comparative philology had enabled scientists to discover the root elements of language and the principles of their combination in the historical growth of language.[14] Similarly, the science of religion will discover the essential elements of religion and the principles of historical change in religions. Müller does not argue this in the rigorous way Levi-Strauss does, when half a century later the latter applies the principles of structural linguistics to the analysis of myth and ritual, but the two scholars share the search for universalia with the help of a language model. The great difference is, of course, that Müller writes in the heyday of historical philology before the Saussurian revolution in linguistics. Müller wants to study the foundational, sacred texts of the major religious traditions with the help of philological methods in order to grasp the essence of natural religion. In that sense he is closer to Marcel Mauss, another great Sanskritist who used the comparative method to understand the essence of sacrifice and gift giving. Mauss's work, again, is informed by Durkheim's sociological method, which is much more rigorous and successful than Müller's moralistic speculations about Love, Charity, and One God. Müller's strength lies in the philological handiwork of critical editions, etymology, and historical grammar. He uses these skills to provide his universalist, religious arguments a scientific underpinning. For that purpose he had prepared a critical edition of the foundation of Indian Brahmanical tradition, the Rg-Veda, his major scholarly achievement. And also for that purpose he went on to edit his series *The Sacred Books of the East*. It is the prestige of German philology that allows Müller to embark on his radical comparisons of all religions. And it is this prestige that convinces the directors of the East India Company to subsidize Müller's edition of the Rg-Veda and also persuades the Prince of Wales to take several copies of it with him to India as presents for Indian rajas.[15] To understand the status awarded German philology, it is important to analyze the possibilities and limits of the science of language in the British context.

The founder of comparative philology was British. Sir William Jones (1746–1794), founder and first president of the Asiatic Society, was already a formidable scholar in Persian before he went to India to become a judge in the Calcutta Court. A famous achievement was his 1789 translation of Kalidasa's Sanskrit play *Shakuntala*, which influenced Goethe's

Faust. Together with Wilkins's translation of the *Bhagavadgita* of 1785, this work promoted in Europe a sizable interest for Hindu thought and literature. To say that the British were driven in their work on these matters by pure Orientalist curiosity would be an exaggeration. They became leaders in the newly emerging field of Orientalist scholarship, "la Renaissance Orientale," as Raymond Schwab has called it, thanks to their colonizing presence in India. In order to colonize India the British had to acquire empirical knowledge about India's population, geography, history, languages, and customs. In a number of important publications, Bernard Cohn has shown that this colonial documentation project constructed a large body of authoritative knowledge to which everything that came to be said about India had to refer.[16] An encyclopedic library of reports, statistics, censuses, gazetteers, histories, and ethnographies was produced out of utilitarian motives no doubt, but, more important, out of a far-reaching desire for scientific, empirical knowledge.[17]

The most significant contribution of Orientalism to this documentation project that provided the British with their instruments of rule was the "discovery" of indigenous law. The capacity to assess taxes was, of course, intimately linked to knowledge about property rights and legal procedures. Instead of outright imposition of British law on India, the East India Company, under Warren Hastings, persuaded "eleven of the most respectable pandits of Bengal" to compile a code from Sanskrit sources on Hindu law that could be translated into English for use by the newly appointed judges. This Sanskrit compilation was first translated into Persian since no European at the time knew Sanskrit, and then from Persian into English. The English translation by Halhed was published in 1776 in London under the title *A Code of Gentoo Laws.* This code was used until the early nineteenth century. Another important treatise on Hindu law was translated by Henri Thomas Colebrooke in 1798 under the title *A Digest of Hindu Law on Contracts and Successions.* In his Judicial Plan of 1772 Warren Hastings decided that "in all suits regarding inheritance, marriage, caste, and other religious usages, or institutions, the laws of the Koran with respect to Mahometans and those of the *Shaster* with respect to gentoos shall be invariably adhered to."[18] An important element in this line of thought was not only to apply native law but to locate this law in religious books, not in local customs. Native law could be divided into Hindu and Muslim law, and the canonical texts of these religious traditions provided its sources. As Bernard Cohn has shown, however, the end result was in fact that "Hindu Law" was turned into a form of English case law.[19]

113

Sir William Jones did not trust the compilation and began to learn Sanskrit in order to gain direct access to that fixed body of legal knowledge that was Hindu law, locked up in the heads and texts of pandits, Hindu religious specialists. Instead of relying on the fragmented and constantly disputed knowledge of individual native specialists, an authoritative Urtext had to be reconstructed. The search for the oldest text was supposed to yield the most authoritative and authentic statement. The empiricist desire to go back to the Ur-text was, in the case of the colonial lawyers, immediately related to a perceived need to transcend the internal disputes among native specialists.[20] It was also propelled by Enlightenment notions of a search for the "lost origins" of a common civilization, characterized by "natural light," tolerance, and purity. Of course colonial India only showed decay and corruption of these higher ideals, but by going back to the origins one could retrieve this remarkable civilization.

Jones's most famous contribution to Orientalist scholarship was his "discovery" of the affinity in lexicon and grammar between Sanskrit, Latin, Greek, Gothic, Celtic, and old Persian. This became the foundation of what Max Müller was to call "Indo-Aryan" comparative philology. This discipline, however, rapidly came to be dominated by German scholars, especially after Franz Bopp's publication, in 1816, of a comparative study of the system of conjugation in Sanskrit, Greek, Persian, and German, followed by Jacob Grimm's famous study of the German language using the insights of comparative philology with an unprecedented success. The reason for the eclipse of British preeminence in the field of Orientalism lies in the fact that the British had to rule India, which meant that they had to reform the Indians, had to educate them. The Orientalist position that Hindus had a great civilization whose achievements could be compared to the highest ones of classical antiquity led them to argue that the East India Company had to support the natives to pursue studies in their native classical tradition, just as the British did back home. This viewpoint came under increasing attack from Evangelical missionaries and Utilitarian administrators in the first decades of the nineteenth century. The opponents of the Orientalists, called "Anglicists," argued that the Indians had to be educated in the achievements of English culture. After his death Jones became the bête noire for both missionaries and Utilitarians, and the prime target of James Mill's *History of British India* (1817), the foundational text of the British colonial project in the nineteenth century. We can only appreciate how iconoclastic those attacks on Jones were at the time when we look at the grand statue of Jones in St Paul's Cathedral, erected in his memory by the East India Company.[21]

Although the iconoclasm was successful enough to relegate British Orientalism to a secondary status in the nineteenth century, clearly Orientalist arguments continued to have an impact in Britain, as witnessed by the career of Max Müller but also by the avatar of Orientalist love of India, the anticolonial discourse of the Theosophists (see chapter 3). The battle between the Anglicists and the Orientalists was decisively won by the former when Thomas Babington Macaulay, Utilitarian administrator and son of a leader of the Evangelical Clapham Sect, wrote his *Minute on Indian Education* (1835). This set the educational agenda for the rest of the colonial era and deemphasized, for administrators, knowledge of India's classical tradition.

The French, to some extent, but especially the Germans took over leadership from the British in the emerging field of comparative philology. The German romantic philosophers, beginning with Herder and ending perhaps with Nietzsche, developed a great interest in philology as a method of uncovering the origins of the German people and thereby its essence. Significantly, it was August Wilhelm von Schlegel, the brother of the famous romantic philosopher Friedrich Schlegel, who held the first chair for Sanskrit in Germany, at the University of Bonn (1818). The Germans were not hindered by the exigencies of colonial rule, such as the need to educate the Indians. They saw language as the key to the *Geist*, the Spirit, of the German people. Historical and comparative philology was an instrument to gain access to the "wordview" of the German people. Herder's emphasis on language and culture as defining characteristics of the German nation is well known, but perhaps as important was the linguistic philosophy of Humboldt, Hegel, and Grimm, claiming that language was the system through which a particular people could understand the world. This philosophy not only influenced Müller but was to have a lasting effect on American anthropology in the twentieth century, thanks to its German founder, Franz Boas.

The nature of Indology as a science emerged most clearly perhaps in comparative Indo-European linguistics where "laws" were discovered that govern the mutations from language to language and by which, ultimately, a hypothetical original Indo-European language was reconstructed. There is a strong connection between this linguistic enterprise and the text-critical project in which philological scholarship reconstructs original texts (ur-text). One can say, perhaps, that comparative linguistics gave philology its scientific status. To accomplish "scientific objectivity," the philologist had to circumvent further any dependence on the messiness of localized, native interpretation. As we have seen above, it was the con-

115

struction of Hindu law that already had shown that the establishment of Ur-texts could perform this function perfectly.

As Sheldon Pollock has argued. the colonizing project turned itself inward in the German case to produce an "internal Orientalism" in which a master race was distinguished from slave peoples.[22] Sanskrit was essential to the construction of an essentialized dichotomy between "Indo-German" and "Semite." This racist ideology was given philological legitimation through the appropriation of the Brahmanical opposition between the Aryan master and the Shudra slave. Pollock's argument, though focusing on the much later national-socialist period of the 1930s and 1940s, shows the extent to which Orientalist discourse was deployed in the construction of German nationalism. The point here is that Orientalist scholarship played a very different role in Germany, where it became central to linguistic and ethnic nationalism legitimized by *Wissenschaft*, than in Britain, where nationalism came to be connected to racist imperialism, legitimized by biological science. Max Müller, the German in Britain, continued the universalist tradition of early British Orientalism and used the theory of the linguistic and racial unity of the Aryans not against the Jews but to rescue "the brotherhood" of Indians and British from the rise of racist imperialism in late Victorian Britain.[23] It is interesting to note in this connection that Müller bypasses the German romantic philosophers of the nineteenth century to return to the universalist, rational enlightenment of Kant, whose *Kritik der Reinen Vernunft* he translated into English.[24]

India's Adoption of German *Wissenschaft*

Müller never went to India, but in his recollections, *Auld Lang Syne*, he remembers his meetings with several Indians. As a young man in Paris he met Dwarkanath Tagore, the father of Debendranath Tagore, the leader of the Brahmo Samaj. Dwarkanath lived in an expensive suite in one of Paris's best hotels and was primarily interested in Italian and French music. When Müller's teacher, Eugene Burnouf, presented him with a copy of his edition of the Bhagavata Purana—with the Sanskrit text on one side and the French translation on the other—Dwarkanath said that he would have loved to have a better knowledge of French but had no interest in learning Sanskrit. Nevertheless, when he was introduced to this young German who declared that he wanted to edit the Rg-Veda, he took interest in him and brought him into contact with his Brahmo son, who, at the time, had sent Brahmans, at his expense, from Calcutta to Benares to gain proper knowledge of the Vedas.

Müller's edition of the Rg-Veda was of great importance for Hindus who consider it the source of all sacred knowledge. The Vedas, of which the Rg-Veda is the most important, were transmitted orally with the help of scattered manuscripts. They are known as *shruti*, "that which is heard" from someone who knows a part of the Veda, a Brahmin *vaidika*. In other words, a centralized knowledge of the entire Rg-Veda was unavailable in India. Brahman boys memorized parts of it, inscribing the knowledge through mnemonic techniques on their body. Clearly knowledge of the Veda was truly embodied knowledge. Vedic recitation is a part of many Hindu practices still today, and the verses are not so much subject of theological debate as of devotional practice.

So despite the notion, accepted by all Hindus, that everything in Hinduism finds its authorization in the Vedas, there was no central text nor central authority to whom one might refer. This changed, however, with Max Müller's pioneering edition of the Rg-Veda and the later edition of other Vedas by his colleagues in Germany. Müller describes the shock felt by what he calls the "orthodox party" in India when they found out what this European barbarian (*mleccha*) was doing.[25] He sees it as a necessary crisis that will support the cause of the reformists in India. He has a clear preference for the Brahmo Samaj over Dayananand's Arya Samaj. The Brahmos were much closer to Müller's own "rational religion," whereas Dayanand took the search for the origin of pure Hinduism in the Vedas very seriously and thus conflicted with Müller's own understanding of the Vedas. Müller attributes Dayanand's "wild ideas" to his ignorance of English, which "deprived him of much that would have been helpful to him and would have kept him from some of his wild ideas about the Veda."[26] Certainly Müller is correct in claiming that philology played a central role in Hindu reform, but he does not quite realize that philology also served a nationalist purpose, as it had in Germany. This becomes most evident when we take a close look at the way Indian scholars adopt German *Wissenschaft* to edit their national heritage.

In their editions of Sanskrit texts the Germans followed a methodology, developed in the philological study of European antiquity, now known as the Lachmann method. This method reconstructs an author's original text based on the genealogical classification of manuscript exemplars into groupings known as families. The idea is that the genealogical tree will provide an objective means of eliminating erroneous readings introduced into the author's text and reconstructing the lost original. It is, as David

117

Hult states, "a mechanistic, scientific approach to method that is governed, ultimately, by a deceptive measure of subjectivity."[27] One of the gestures used by the editor who employs this method is to attribute authenticity to the *lectio difficilior*. So, what is more difficult and less common is more likely to be the original text, but of course it should not be too difficult since it would then start to become incomprehensible. It is interesting to note here that scribes of later manuscripts who have tried to emendate the text they received are corrected by the (final?) editor who replaces their emendations with a more difficult reading, but who, in other instances, emendates what is otherwise too difficult to understand.

Let us now turn to the critical editions of the Indian text. The major text to be edited, both in terms of length and canonical status, was the Mahabharata. This was done in the Bhandarkar Oriental Research Institute in Poona, founded in 1918 by Sripad Krishna Belvalkar, a professor of Sanskrit in Deccan College. The ruler of Aundh would first bestow a gift of one lakh of rupees, then other gifts would follow. The critical edition of the Mahabharata was originally planned by the German Indologist Moritz Winternitz in 1897 and funds were earmarked for that purpose by the Academies of Berlin and Vienna in 1904. To further the project, the Indologist Heinrich Luders of the University of Berlin prepared a specimen of a critical edition in 1908 with funds from the Königliche Gesellschaft der Wissenschaften in Göttingen. The First World War (or, as it is called in India, the First European War) intervened and the Bhandarkar Institute took over.

Vishnu Sitaram Sukthankar (1887–1943), a Gauda Sarasvat Brahman from Bombay, was to be the editor in chief of this immense project in 1925. Sukthankar studied mathematics in Cambridge and went on to do his Sanskrit dissertation under Luders in Berlin in 1914. He had a methodical, scientific mind, which was exactly what was needed to accomplish this project. To appreciate the immensity of the project, one need only look at the first book (*adiparvan*) of a text that consists of eighteen books (*parvan*), reaching a total of seventy thousand to one hundred thousand stanzas. Sukthankar states that 235 manuscripts of this book were known to him, 107 of which were in the Devanagari script.[28] Of these 107, Sukthankar collated about 70. The oldest manuscripts were from the sixteenth century. There were two main recensions, one northern and one southern. As Sukthankar notes, this fact already gave rise to acrimonious debates in India. An earlier edition (1883–96) by Protap Chandra Roy, based largely on the northern manuscripts, led to attacks, in 1885, in the South Indian newspaper *The Hindu*. Sukthankar quotes from Roy's reply:

"I know of no method except that of taking that only as undoubtedly genuine which occurs in all the manuscripts of the East, the North, the West, and the South."[29] Sukthankar agrees with this statement, but beneath it we may glimpse the nationalist gesture.

Sukthankar's starting point is that of German classical philology, but he is well aware that, in this case, this model can only be applied in a limited sense. As he says, in the Mahabharata we have a text with more or less a dozen independent versions whose extreme types differ, in extent, by about twenty-six thousand lines. Moreover, one cannot decide the dates of the rival recensions. Then he comes to the crucial point: The northern and southern recensions are independent copies of an orally transmitted text.[30] This is therefore an oral tradition, in which manuscripts are only to be used as partial support for that tradition. Nevertheless, Sukthankar continues to believe in creating "the oldest form of the text which it is possible to reach, on the basis of the manuscript material available"—that is, not the Ur-text but the oldest version possible.[31]

The chief difficulty in editing the Mahabharata, as Sukthankar observed, was that the Mahabharata tradition was mainly transmitted orally. Nevertheless, Orientalist scholars wanted to have texts on which to base their translations and interpretations. The East had to be textually represented in correct texts and correct translations as in Max Müller's *Sacred Books of the East*. This Orientalist desire was intimately connected to the desire among Hindu scholars to have scriptures, like Christianity and Islam. That Islam made a crucial distinction between *ahl-i-kitab*, people with a book, and Hindus, people without a book, was already known in India from the advent of Islam, but a Hindu response to that distinction had not been very forthcoming. The colonial, textualizing project of modernity, however, elicited a stronger reaction. It provided a sufficient motivation to prepare a critical edition of the Mahabharata and, later, the Ramayana and the Puranas, since Indian scholars wanted to represent their tradition in a manner equal to how other civilizations represented their traditions.

As Sukthankar stated: "Great Britain is a small nation, a young nation, compared to India. And our love of knowledge, love of literature, love of scriptures, is greater. We are the inheritors of the great book, this "book of books" composed at a time when Great Britain was not yet entered on the map of civilized nations."[32] Echoes of Müller's arguments resound here. As is often the case, the religious and civilizational become completely entangled. Writing has come to be seen in Modern Europe as a sign of "being civilized." Until only recently, it was common in anthropology to mark the absence of writing as a criterion to distinguish the primitive from the civilized. Prehistory and history is also divided by the presence or absence of writing. A similar argument about literacy, made famous by the anthropologist Jack Goody, is that there is a connection between literacy, critical inquiry, and planned change.[33]

As we have seen, however, manuscripts of the epics were available, and writing was indeed present in Indian civilization. I suggest that it was the unwieldy, hybrid nature of Hindu traditions—partly written, partly oral—that Hindu nationalists considered a problem. These traditions had to be made more compact, unified, homogenized in order to be able to print them as authoritative texts. It is this need for printed texts that provides the final push to the production of critical editions. As Benedict Anderson has forcefully argued, an important connection exists between print capitalism and nationalism.[34] One cannot imagine the modern nation without the collective simultaneity of the private act of reading, made possible by print capitalism. It is not so much writing but print textuality that is privileged in Anderson's theory to carry the nationalist imagination. It is important to see that Anderson's theory does not deal with what is at least of equal importance in the nationalisms of colonized Asia, namely, collective action in public arenas and the oral performance of sacred texts.[35] Nevertheless, despite the marginality of the printed word in nineteenth-century India, it is the privileged connection between printed scripture and nation that is not only adopted by Anderson in his recent theory but also by the ideologues of Hindu nationalism.

If "history" and "nation" are only possible in the presence of the written/printed word, then it is quite understandable that the orality of Hindu traditions was a "national" embarrassment for Indian scholars who were confronted with the comparison with the West. Here one should note that the high value attributed to writing in Europe is not present in Hindu traditions.[36] On the contrary, the sacrality of the Vedic mantras depends on speaking and listening. In fact, writing these mantras down is explicitly forbidden. This prohibition has also to do with the secret power of these sounds that should only be known by the higher castes and certainly not by the lower castes and women. The Vedas were transmitted orally and were only transcribed into written texts by the nineteenth-century Orientalists, starting with Max Müller's six-volume edition of the Rg-Veda.

The Mahabharata, Ramayana, and Puranas are regarded as second in authority to the Vedas. They are called "remembered" (*smrti*) traditions. In their case as well, however, the preferred mode of transmission is oral recitation. An important way to sacralize a specific occasion, such as a birth or the building of a house in North India, is the "unbroken recitation" (*akhand-path*) of the Ramayana, but in Hindi, not Sanskrit. Regarding both the Ramayana and the Mahabharata, as well as other traditions, the dramatic enactment of the text in popular plays is a major mode of keeping the oral tradition alive. These performative traditions can only be understood in their local or regional contexts. They are even more diverse than the numerous manuscripts Sukthankar consulted.

As an illustration, let us look at the performative elaboration of the Mahabharata lore in the context of the Tamil Draupadi cult. Whereas the Sanskrit Mahabharata's composition is conventionally dated between 500 B.C. and A.D. 400, we find Tamil versions already in the first centuries A.D. This immediately raises the question of why, in the critical edition, Sanskrit manuscripts are privileged over the Tamil contemporary ones. This only makes sense in a search for a foundational Sanskrit Ur-text from which every other "regional" text is derived. There are a great many Draupadi temples and festivals in Tamil Nadu, whereas hardly any attention is paid to Draupadi in many other parts of India. Thus there is great unevenness in the importance attached to the Mahabharata lore in different parts of the country. It is not the Brahmans that dominate the Draupadi cult but some major peasant castes such as the Velalars. Elements of possession, which are abhorred in Brahmanical ideology, are crucial in the performance of the Draupadi cult, which is largely in the hands of itinerant professionals. What we find in South India is a cult which, in the words of Alf Hiltebeitel, is "an adroit and compelling multileveled interpretation of a living Mahabharata."[37] The performances are articulated with complex regional traditions in a variety of political and social contexts. The attempt to produce a critical edition of these traditions is almost against their very nature.

I use the word *almost* deliberately, since one element in the management of Hindu traditions at least appears to have something in common with modern philology. This is the Brahmanical division between authoritative, transcendent knowledge (*shastrik*) and contextual, immanent knowledge (*laukik*). The Vedas are, of course, the main source of authoritative knowledge and that is why religious innovation has to be legitimized by reference to the Vedas. This is already true for precolonial reform movements, but in the case of a nineteenth-century reform movement such as the Arya Samaj, it is connected with an Orientalist empiricistic attempt not only to refer vaguely to a hoary tradition but to recuperate the Vedas and to establish the facts of the connection. Orientalism adds an empiricist element to the search for originary authority. It is the attempt to transcend historical referentiality and to "Vedicize" whatever "remembered" tradition by calling it "one of the Vedas" which characterized the earlier establishment of authoritative discourse. The Mahabharata is, for example, sometimes called the "fifth Veda." In the modern, colonial period, this Brahmanical need to ground authoritative discourse in what the Vedic rishis have "heard" in the time of origins is linked to the Orientalist search for the golden age of Indo-European civilization in Sanskrit Ur-texts. Together they provide the intellectual context for the critical edition of the Mahabharata. This ideological link between Brahmanism and Orientalism is perfectly illustrated by the fact that in the last quarter of the seventeenth century Nilakantha, a Brahman scholar of Maharashtra, had already written a commentary on the Mahabharata for which he had consulted a number of copies, collected from different parts of India, to determine the best reading.[38] In some respects, Orientalist philology was simply the successor of Brahmanical philology. The final element needed for the articulation of Brahmanical and Orientalist discourse is to be found in the urge to nationalize the past by editing and printing it. Anderson's print capitalism gets used for the dissemination of religious texts in the context of Hindu nationalism.

TEXTS AND THE NATIONALIST IMAGINAIRE

Anderson and others see the novel as the literary expression of the nationalist imagination. In the Indian context, however, classical epics seem more important for nationalism than novels.[39] If one tries to find the literary sources of the Hindu nationalist imaginaire, one first has to look at the Mahabharata and the Ramayana. But there is a circular element here, since the unification of Mahabharata traditions for the production of a unified, canonical text is certainly novel and finds its origin precisely in the nationalist imaginaire. The Ramayana differs somewhat in important respects. A unified, canonical rendition of its story in Hindi has already been made in the precolonial period.

The Mahabharata, even in its critical edition, remains too lengthy and unwieldy to be appropriated as a hegemonic text of nationalism in its entirety. The story deals with the struggle between two clans of one tribe that traces itself to one ancestor, Bharata. Thus it is a family drama and the nationalist fiction is that the Indian nation traces itself back to this Aryan tribe whose habitat was India (Bharatvarsh). Perhaps one might even imagine that the length and unwieldiness of the Mahabharata reflects that old cliché about the vastness and variety of India and its population.

Besides this notion that the nation's complex past is told in the Mahabharata, a very important and useful episode can be separated from the body of the text. This is the Bhagavadgita, which has become the classical text of Hindu nationalism. The important Maratha Hindu nationalist Bal Gangadhar Tilak (1856–1920) wrote an extensive commentary on the Bhagavadgita entitled "The Hindu Philosophy of Life, Ethics, and Religion," which was inspired by the thirteenth-century *Jnanesvari*, the Marathi commentary on the Bhagavadgita. Tilak tried to make a convincing argument for the racial and cultural superiority of the Aryans and their immediate heirs, the Indian nation. In his commentary, he responded to Christian arguments that the Gita had adopted certain ideas from Christianity. He argued in his conclusion that "there is a very strong probability, and almost a certainty, that the principles of Self-Identification, Renunciation, Non-Enmity, and Devotion, to be found in the New Testament of the Bible, must have been taken into the Christian religion from Buddhism, and therefore, indirectly from the Vedic religion; and that, Indians had no need to look to other people for finding these religious principles."[40]

Tilak was definitely the major figure in Hindu nationalism in Maharashtra, and he was very much in favor of scientific approaches to Indian material. His father had been a friend of the prominent Sanskrit professor and social reformer R. G. Bhandarkar (1837–1925), who would give his name to the institute where the critical edition was to be prepared. At one point Tilak himself became involved in a famous quarrel with Bhandarkar about the Age of Consent Act of 1891, in which Tilak took the side of Brahmanical orthodoxy. It is worth noting that the interpretation of Hindu law was the chosen site for this important political dispute. Later, the two set aside their differences and worked together for the combined cause of reformism and nationalism. Between 1914 and 1920 Belvalkar, the founder of the Bhandarkar Oriental Research Institute, met with Tilak regularly, and Tilak donated one thousand rupees toward the founding of the Bhandarkar Institute. Tilak also wrote a contribution for the volume commemorating Bhandarkar's eightieth birthday, which was published in 1917 on the occasion of the founding of the institute. On the first anniversary of Tilak's death in 1921, Belvalkar constituted a Lokamanya Memorial Fund in Deccan College to commemorate the great nationalist.

Neo-Hindu ideologues like Tilak and Vivekananda made the Bhagavadgita into a canonical text. Its centrality to religious nationalism was underlined by the fact that Gandhi chose it as the foundational text of his political philosophy. Gandhi transformed the old ritual injunction to avoid killing sacrificial victims (*ahimsa*) into a positive ethics of nonviolent political action. His notion of the necessity of acting in the world (*karma-yoga*) is ultimately based on his interpretation of the Bhagavadgita. Finally, the philosopher (and later president of India) Sarvepalli Radhakrishnan completed the project of making the Bhagavadgita the representation of Hindu thought, Hindu civilization, and the Hindu nation.

Certainly to make the Mahabharata the national text did not require a critical edition of the Mahabharata. But the fact that the Mahabharata lent itself to nationalist appropriation explains why there was wide support for the idea that a critical edition of the Mahabharata was in the national interest. A similar conclusion may be drawn from the fact that it was C. Rajagopalachari's English summary of the Mahabharata that was the first book printed in the so-called Book University, published by the Bharatiya Vidya Bhavan in Bombay. The latter was an initiative for the "integration of the Indian culture in the light of modern knowledge and to suit present-day needs and the resuscitation of its fundamental values in their pristine vigour," an initiative taken by the well-known Gujarati nationalist K. M. Munshi who, incidentally, was one of the speakers at the presentation of the Sukthankar memorial edition of the Mahabharata in 1944.

To those involved in the production of the critical edition of the Mahabharata, the significance of the project for the Indian nation was without question. In the foreword of the critical edition of the first book of the Mahabharata, its editor, V. S. Sukthankar, states:

> I may be permitted to remark that the renown of the Bharatavarsha, of its Princes and its People, is for all time inseparably linked with the Mahabharata, which is, in more sense than one the greatest epic the world has produced. It must be manifest to anyone who bestows a thought on the subject that the monumental work of preparing the first critical edition of this colossal encyclopedia of ancient India could be carried on and completed by the young Institute by which it has been undertaken only if it can count upon substantial aid from other sources and upon co-operation on a much wider scale. If the Princes and the People of India were to associate themselves with this imposing enterprise, they would indeed be supporting a *national* work. On behalf of the Institute which I represent, I appeal to all true Indians to ally themselves with the Institute in supporting the publica-

tion of a work which is in a unique manner bound up with the history of the Indian people and the prestige of Indian scholarship.[41]

While one may disregard this as fund-raising rhetoric, the nationalist gesture is expressed even more clearly in the last public speech Sukthankar gave before his death in 1943, on the occasion of presenting another Book of the Mahabharata to the principal donor, the Raja of Aundh:

> The question may occur to you. Is it worth all this expenditure? Whether we realize it or not, we still stand under the spell of the Mahabharata. Amid the deepest strands that are woven in the thread of our civilization, there is more than one that is drawn originally from Bharatavarsha and from Sanskrit literature. And well in the centre of this vast mass of literature, there stands this deathless, traditional book of divine inspiration, unapproachable and far removed from possibilities of human competition. There is a danger that in our pseudo-scientific mood, we may be tempted to discard this great book, thinking that we have outgrown it. That would be a capital blunder! That would in fact mean nothing but an indication of our will to commit suicide, national suicide, the signal of our national extinction. For never was truer word spoken than when the late German Indologist Hermann Oldenberg said that "in the Mahabharata breathe the united soul of India, and the individual souls of her people." And why is that? Because the Mahabharata is the national saga of India. It is, in other words, the content of our collective consciousness. And just for that reason it refuses to be discarded. We must therefore grasp this great book with both hands and face it squarely. Then we shall recognize that it is our past which has prolonged itself into the present. *We are it*: I mean the real WE! Shall we be guilty of strangling our own soul? NEVER![42]

The strong echo of Herder in Oldenberg's and Sukthankar's words is striking.

While the Mahabharata is the national text of Hindu nationalism, the Ramayana is its religious text. Following the example of Poona's edition of the Mahabharata, the Oriental Institute in Baroda, between 1960 and 1975, produced a critical edition of the Ramayana. Again, the orality of the poem is beyond doubt, but the text is much shorter and far more coherent, which has led to a strong thesis that the poem had been produced by a single author, Valmiki. The method used for the critical edition of the Ramayana is the same as that applied to the Mahabharata: eliminate interpolations. The astounding result is an edition that omits 25 percent of the major, southern recension.[43] Again, there are considerable performative traditions (*Ram Lilas*) that can only be interpreted in their regional, historical, and political contexts. In fact, in large parts of India, Valmiki's Ramayana has been eclipsed by renditions of the story in many other languages, not to mention the sixteenth-century Hindi rendition of the poem by Tulsidas.[44] It is this rendition that is the most significant in the contemporary Rama cult, a major strand in modern Hinduism, although the Sanskrit archetype is the one put under philological scrutiny.

It is in the language of Tulsidas that Mahatma Gandhi tried to communicate his political ideal of Ramraj, the ideal social order of Lord Rama in Ayodhya. Gandhi continuously quoted the Ramayana to bolster his political views, as did a great many literate Hindus. If Indians could live according to the high ideals of this text, they would be able to overcome poverty, untouchability, and foreign rule. At least in North India, his constant reference to Rama and Rama's just rule, Ramraj, had an almost millenarian impact on the Hindu population.[45] Clearly it was also an appeal that totally ignored and alienated the "Muslim other" in India. While Gandhi gave his usual "inclusivist" interpretation of the Ramayana, Hindu radicals were prone to use the devotional message for "anti-demonic" purposes. The struggle between Rama, the Good, and Ravana, the Bad, could easily be appropriated as a conceptual framework to understand and legitimize the struggle between Hindus and Muslims.

The effort here is to recover India's national past through a philological project of editing Hindu texts. It is a construction of a Sanskrit canon that privileges a "classical age" before A.D. 1200 and marginalizes or ignores not only the literatures written in modern Indian languages, such as Tamil, Bengali, or Urdu, but even the Sanskrit literature that preceded the nineteenth century by almost a millennium. This construction is one of the foundational elements in the periodization of Indian history in a Hindu, a Muslim, and a British period, as was already seen in James Mill's *History of British India* (1817). The construction of the Sanskrit canon as the foundation of Indian (= Hindu) civilization took the Muslim invasions as the end of the Hindu period. The Muslim presence was effectively occluded from the Indian past. Since Orientalism constructed the archive of India's past, this occlusion remained a striking feature of nationalist historiography of the nation-state which the constitution calls "India, that is Bharat." Bharat is an abbreviation of the Sanskrit Bharatavarsha, the land of the Bharata clan, the subject of the Hindu epos, the Mahabharata.

As Partha Chatterjee has argued, nationalist history, as it started to be written in the nineteenth century, only mentioned Muslims as a cause of the corruption and decadence of Hindu society. The Hindu nation had been subjected by Muslims, and the nation's regeneration had only become possible after the British had abolished Muslim rule. Muslims were merely mentioned as aggressive murderers, plunderers, destroyers of India's Hindu culture. Above all they were outsiders, foreigners in the nationalist imaginaire. In this narrative Hindus were weak because of their tolerance and corrupted practices, but nevertheless they constantly resisted Muslim oppression. The glories of ancient Hindu India were extolled in the same manner as the Orientalist had been doing. The conclusion of nineteenth-century writing is clear: Reform Hindu society, revive the true ideals enshrined in the ancient Sanskrit texts, and, by that token, take one's political destiny in one's own (that is, Hindu) hands. To quote Chatterjee: "The idea of the singularity of national history has inevitably led to a single source of Indian tradition, viz. ancient Hindu civilization. Islam here is either the history of foreign conquest or a domesticated element of everyday popular life. The classical heritage of Islam remains external to Indian history."[46]

Hindu nationalist projects attempt to use the Ramayana and the Mahabharata (especially the Bhagavadgita) to project a kind of ideal Hindu state that is thought to have existed "before the Muslim invasions." In my view this includes not only the recent campaign of the Hindu nationalist extremists to destroy the mosque in Ayodhya but also Gandhi's multiculturalist project. These undertakings combine a "classicist" view of the "golden age," very much part of elite nationalism, with a populist utopia of God Rama intervening to make life more just. The critical edition of the text, showing their scientific apparatus on every page, did not produce these imaginations, since the story of the Ramayana was well known, but it provided it with a presence in an elitist arena of scholarly debate on the national past. Certainly critical editions of the Mahabharata and the Ramayana are not necessary in the nationalist project. Indeed, they are empowered by it rather than the other way around. Nevertheless, the very empiricism of the philological endeavor provides a realistic aura of authenticity and facticity to the nationalist imagination that is quite essential to it.

In religious nationalism a major object of worship is "facts," "historical referentiality." They are no longer irrelevant *sub specie aeternitatis*, as in prenationalist religious discourse, but are important evidence of the eternal existence of the nation. The Orientalist master-narrative of the necessity of colonial rule has been replaced by the nationalist teleology of the nation's ultimate victory. The emphasis on "facts" implies a "literal," "historical" reading of religious sources, enabled by German philology.

127

It also implies a combination of historical study of literary sources and archaeological research on material remains, that is, "hard facts." But all these "facts" have to fit the predetermined narrative.

Archaeological excavations were performed at sites, described in the epics Mahabharata and Ramayana. Pottery, called "painted gray ware," was found at the Mahabharata sites and used to date events and dynasties mentioned in this epic. Contrary to religious tradition, excavations at Ramayana sites, such as Ayodhya, show these sites to be younger than Mahabharata sites. As one might expect, other traditions can be found to support the archaeological discovery that Rama of the Ramayana is later than Krishna of the Mahabharata. Nevertheless, in the main, these findings conflict with a tradition almost universally accepted by Hindus that Rama should come before Krishna, but, as one archaeologist observes, "we will strive and strive with success to make Archaeology and Tradition about Rama and Krishna meet on the same plane of time."[47] Meanwhile, however, this is a case in which the regime of archaeological facts forces researchers to reject part of the religious discourse but without challenging this discourse as such. It remains a technical matter for specialists and does not enter the public arena; nor does it challenge authoritative arguments in that arena. Nevertheless, it gratifies the notion among archaeologists and historians that they are not simply following religious dogmata but are in pursuit of pure scientific knowledge. B. B. Lal, a former director-general of the Indian Archaeological Survey, thus sees his project on the historicity of the Hindu epics as a "test on the touchstone of archaeology."[48]

The metaphor often used by archaeologists is that they deal with the *terra firma*, firm ground. However, as Romila Thapar argues, there is nothing firm here:

> In the absence of contemporary written records or deciphered scripts, any attempt to co-relate archaeological material with traditional accounts of the past becomes a venture into speculation. This is particularly so as the literary sources represent accretions over a period of many centuries and the archaeological evidence is partial, supported more by exploration than excavation and ultimately based on vertical rather than horizontal excavation.[49]

Thapar pleads for more intensive excavation before attempting to "co-relate" the information with the historical tradition. The practice of a project like B. B. Lal's goes against the grain of such a plea, however. The sites are chosen on the basis of the literary tradition, and the narrative frame of the tradition is accepted and filled up with archaeological findings. Moreover, the point Thapar makes about "accretions" is highly significant. The epic and puranic literary traditions are not unified, homogeneous texts but compilations of disparate, often conflicting, regionally diverse oral and written traditions, in which one version often presupposes another.[50] The entire notion of a homogeneous literary tradition is the result of hard, Orientalist labor in the production of "critical editions." The critical editions of the Mahabharata and Ramayana, as well as the ongoing Purana projects, are apt symbols of the process of selection and unification essential to the nationalist project. Archaeology and textual research play a crucial role in the nationalist appropriation of history.

SPEAKING, WRITING, WATCHING

In comments on Levi-Strauss's anthropology, Jacques Derrida questions the sharp distinction often made between "societies without writing" and "societies with writing."[51] Here, and in his *Of Grammatology,* he demonstrates that Western philosophy (at least from Aristotle on) has always seen speech as preceding writing and thus as closer to reality.[52] Similarly, writing has been portrayed as a derivative, phonetic transcription of speech. In this privileging of speech Derrida sees a nostalgia of origins, of pure presence. Indian society is obviously not a "society without writing," but a large segment of the population has always been illiterate to the present day. Orality thus plays a significant role in Indian culture. But this should not lead us to the romantic notion that orality provides direct access to, for instance, "subaltern consciousness." Oral traditions are often the site of a struggle for domination between groups and individuals. They are certainly not the unmediated speech of an undifferentiated "folk" making their own history "from below."

We should be equally wary of an interpretation of the Orientalist archive as marking a total transition from self-identifying, authentic speech to imperialist textuality. This is, of course, a highly complex issue. There are hegemonic, elitist projects with their own archives of the past in place, when the British begin to colonize India, but they are drastically transformed under the conditions of colonial rule. This is not to say that they become totally encapsulated by the colonial archive; rather, the colonial archive itself becomes the site of a struggle that is conducted increasingly in terms initiated by the European Enlightenment. Nationalism is definitely a struggle against colonial domination, and, as such, it partakes

129

very much in Orientalist discourse with at least some signs reversed. However, it is also a historical product of other projects, such as those of Brahmanical elites or monastic orders, that were already on their way before the onset of colonial rule.

Both the Mahabharata and the Ramayana traditions have, for a millennium or so, combined different mediums of transmission, such as orality, writing, and theatrical/ritual performance. The place of written manuscripts in these traditions is historically contingent. Written texts have a certain "consultability," but they do not fixate a tradition entirely. Rather than assuming what their function is and thereby essentializing writing, one may do better to inquire what reading of texts amounts to in different historical settings.[53] "Reading" the Ramayana or the Mahabharata is generally not a solitary practice in India as it is for Western scholars; instead, it is "reading out loud," reciting (*path*) in a social space, as a collective practice. Often it is not a simple, individual choice but is prompted by an occasion at which the reading is customary. Thus reading is directly linked to speaking or reciting, and, although listeners need not be present, they often are. Lutgendorf distinguishes three genres: simple recitation (performer and audience are the same), recitation plus exposition, and full dramatic enactment.[54]

As a social performance, recitation is a political event. This was brought home to me most clearly during my fieldwork in Ayodhya. In November 1984 I attended three different gatherings (*melas*) in which the Ramayana was recited. One was an international Ramayana Conference, held in the huge Valmiki Bhavan, the marble walls of which are covered with texts from the Ramayana. This conference was staged by a foundation supported by the Indian government. Participants came from the Soviet Union, Trinidad, Canada, the United States, Britain, the Netherlands, Mauritius, Singapore, Thailand, and India. The contributors' speeches on aspects of the Ramayana were broadcast on Lucknow television. The purpose of the conference was to convey the message of brotherhood and unity between people worldwide, as "preached in the Ramayana." For Indians, the Ramayana provided the bridge between regions in India as well as between the overseas Indian communities and the motherland. This unifying message had, at that moment, a specific political significance owing to the recent murder of Mrs. Gandhi, India's prime minister, by Sikh extremists. The speeches emphasized that the late Mrs. Gandhi was known to have been a great lover of the Ramayana and a preacher of its universal message.

130

At the same time two other Ramayana *melas* were held in Ayodhya. One was organized by the state government of Uttar Pradesh to which some regionally known reciters as well as a few abbots who were supporters of the Congress Party, led by Indira Gandhi, were invited. The other was organized by an abbot who was one of the local leaders in the campaign to destroy the Babari Mosque. The latter was explicitly organized as a protest against the two progovernment gatherings. The settings of recitation were quite different, and the larger context totally politicized. The meaning of what was recited was not stable and fixed but was established through the performance itself. Clearly, who speaks, who listens, and who sponsors the gathering is just as important as which selections are chosen from the text.

The Mahabharata and Ramayana traditions have not only been written down but have been transmitted through every available modern medium, be it printing, audio recordings, television, or film. What is noteworthy here is that these modern media do not destroy, let alone marginalize, speaking and watching. They also have not produced the solitary reader or watcher. However, they do have a unifying tendency in that they make more people hear and watch the same thing. That is not to say, however, that everyone *sees* the same thing. Indeed, the spectators actively produce different meanings, as Purnima Mankekar has recently shown in an interpretation of spectators' reactions to the serialization of the Mahabharata on Indian television.[55] She emphasizes, though, that the spectators are not simply free to choose these meanings; rather, they are produced in discursive frameworks, such as that of nationalism.

CONCLUDING REMARKS

India has, of course, many languages and many literatures in these languages. Moreover, still today, much of the literary production is in the oral and performative mode. To explore the category of Indian literature is thus fraught with great conceptual difficulties.[56] It is almost inescapable to look for homogenizing principles, to pose the civilizational or national question or both. Certainly one may go about this in a great many ways, but one important approach developed in the colonial period was to canonize the Sanskrit classics, to see them as the basis of Hindu civilization (*sanskriti*). A crucial corollary of this approach was to equate Hindu with Indian. "Hindoo literature" was broadly conceived by eighteenth- and nineteenth-century Orientalists as all Sanskrit texts, including science, grammar, and law. This totalizing conception of literature was not found among the Sanskrit theorists themselves, who made a whole series of distinctions between history, science, poetry, and so on.[57] The conception of literature the Orientalists applied was a new and radical product of eighteenth-century European thought. However, they also placed this "literature" under the sign of "Hinduism," and by this token produced a Sanskrit (Hindu) literature that came to be conceived as *Nationalliteratur*, in Herder's sense. This discursive move set the agenda for Indological philology, which continues to be influential in India today.

It was Aurobindo's idea, in his *Foundations of Indian Culture*, that the Mahabharata and the Ramayana constitute the essence of Indian literature. This Orientalist notion was foundational for the Hindu nationalization of Indian civilization. Not only were Islamic and other cultures excluded from the canon, but, even more important, the canon was partly about their very exclusion. Most striking in all this is that a civilization incessantly talked about in terms of the spiritual and metaphysical is taken to be factual and realistic. Orientalist empiricism has bred nationalist realism. The critical editions of the major epics have had a specific role in making this relation, as has television. I have argued that it is not the critical editions that have pushed the regional, performative traditions to the margins. Despite all the centralization and homogenization, variety continues to dominate. In fact, positing a hegemony of the critical editions against forms of regional, oral, performative resistance is not helpful. Orality insinuates itself, as Michel de Certeau puts it, into the network of a scriptural economy, and it is precisely through the opposition of writing and speaking, of viewing and doing, that modern practices legitimize themselves.[58]

It is ironic that Müller's *Wissenschaft*, which was critical of pretensions of racial superiority in the British nationalism of his time, was used in India to support a Hindu nationalism built on the racial superiority of the Hindu Aryans. The Indian philologists certainly used Müller's universalist arguments against the claim of racial and civilizational superiority of the British, but, more generally, they used philology in the way the Germans used it in their own country. Sanskrit philology provided them with the tools to dig up the origin and essence of the nation, that is, the Hindu nation. It also gave them a scientific language to exclude "latecomers," such as Muslims, as outsiders to the story of the nation.

The larger, discursive framework of Hindu nationalism, a formidable aspect of Indian modernity, has a realistic slant. It produces connections between scholarly pursuits such as philology, archaeology, and history; artistic pursuits such as literature, theater, and television; and political pursuits such as election campaigns and mass mobilizations. Together they produce a reality in which Indians have to live. This is not to say that all this is inevitable. Rather, the critical edition of India's historical landscape, which reached a high pitch in the recent destruction of Babar's Mosque in Ayodhya, is the site of struggle, the site of difference.

Aryan Origins

> At first, Balaram admitted to himself, he was baffled.
> The boy's head confused him utterly and for entirely
> unfamiliar reasons. Most heads were puzzling because
> they were so even. Often there was nothing, not the
> slightest undulation or bump to mark the major faculties
> and organs. Most heads, in a word, were dull, even
> boring. With Alu it was another matter altogether; it was
> like sitting down to a wedding feast after years of stewed
> rice. His head abounded with a profusion of knots and
> troughs, each more aggressively pronounced than the
> next and scattered about with an absolute disregard for
> the discoveries of phrenology. The array of bumps and
> protuberances grew cheerfully all over his head and
> showed no signs at all of dividing into distinct and
> recognizable organs—a wealth of new stimulating
> material. In time it prompted Balaram's paper on the
> Indistinctness of the Organs of the Brain (he sent it to
> the Bombay Natural History Society and to the Asiatic
> Society in Calcutta, but unaccountably it was never
> acknowledged).
> *(Amitav Ghosh, The Circle of Reason)*

IN HIS NOVEL, *The Circle of Reason*, Amitav Ghosh describes the passion
with which Balaram, schoolteacher in a small Bengali village, measures
the skull of his young nephew, Alu, in search of phrenological knowledge.[1] Balaram is an enthusiast for science and had discovered phrenology
during his college years in Calcutta. He reads the skull to see how the
human capacities of love, understanding, and sexual desire are developed
and how it can be classified. In other words, the skull is read to find
physical evidence for the moral character of the person. Besides being an
accomplished novelist Ghosh is also a trained anthropologist, and in the
novel he highlights one of the great obsessions of colonial ethnography:
phrenology, and anthropometry in general, as methods to determine ra-

cial types. It is an obsession, inherited by the current Anthropological Survey of India, although the methodology has changed. In its census of 1989 the Survey replaced cranial measurements with blood groups as indicators of racial difference.[2]

This chapter deals with the rise of race science in Victorian Britain and the use of it by liberal humanists, racist eugenicists, Hindu nationalists, criminologists, and Christian missionaries. It examines a variety of theories and ideologies that postulate a relation between habitat and physicality as well as between physicality and morality within a paradigm of scientific empiricism and evolutionary thought. It is often argued that the successes of nineteenth century science played a decisive role in the secularization of the British mind.[3] As discussed in chapter 3, this argument belongs, at least in part, to an Enlightenment mythology of the progress of rational thought. Scientific empiricism is, in fact, one of the foundations of spiritualist thought and, as such, of Theosophy. In this chapter we will see that science also played a decisive role in the legitimation of dark theories of racial difference, criminality, and colonial relations. In the previous chapters we have already seen that the science of race gradually replaced religion as the main marker of colonial difference after the Mutiny and after Darwin's discoveries. As will become evident, however, the story is not straightforward. Not only is there a great debate about the interpretation of race in the nineteenth century, with widely differing positions, but there is also the crucial link between race and morality which never leaves religion entirely out of the equation.[4]

A major step in the exposition is to differentiate between a science based on language and a science based on biology. The former connects language and race in the important theory of the Aryan race, perhaps the single most important theory in the area of race for both Britain and India. The great exponent of this belief in the nineteenth century is undoubtedly Friedrich Max Müller. Müller explicitly came to reject philology as the method to determine racial groups and their evolution. He does not reject the Aryan theory, however, but connects it with biological evidence of racial groupings in India. No exponent of this line of thought can compare to Max Müller, but there is great enthusiasm for it especially among British civil servants in India who are organizing the census. The single marker of the difference between linguistic and biological arguments about origins is obviously the towering figure of Darwin.

A second element in the exposition is to look at the political and practical implications of race science, both in the formulation of Aryanism and in the identification of racial identity and criminality. We begin at the very beginning, the romantic search for origins, which is the basis of the philological fascination with the Aryan myth.

THE ARYAN MYTH

As anthropologists know, societies have myths of origin. In Malinowski's view, they form charters for the way things are in the present. According to Edmund Leach, they create legitimations for certain current claims of political groups. In early modern Europe, these myths of origin become the subject of the emerging fields of legal, philological, and historical scholarship. This scholarship did not challenge the main frame of thought about origin in Europe, which was obviously biblical. As Thomas Trautmann observes, till the Brixham Cave excavation of 1859 and the almost simultaneous appearance of Darwin's *Origin of Species*, the evolution of nations was seen to have occurred within the biblical time frame of six thousand years.[5] In Britain a fascination with the history of invasions and the distinction between the Celts, the Saxons, and the Normans was added to the biblical myth. A myth of national origin was connected to the biblical myth of the origin of mankind. As elsewhere, these myths of origin had political import, especially ideas about the essential love of freedom of the Anglo-Saxon suffering under the Norman yoke and about the racial difference between Celts and Saxons, constantly invoked from the sixteenth century but increasingly popular in folklorist, antiquarian circles in the nineteenth century.

Debates about the nature of the polity, the distinctiveness of English civilization, and the "Irish question" were structured in the nineteenth century in reference to myths of racial origin. This was not peculiar to Britain, since a similar discussion is seen in France, one in which Ernest Renan played a dominant role. In fact, Renan had a considerable impact on Matthew Arnold, the great literary thinker about culture in the Victorian period.[6] Renan's work on Celtic literature celebrates its glories but at the same time decries its effeminacy, its dreamlike quality, and consequently its political ineffectiveness in ways that are very reminiscent of Hegel's description of Indian civilization. In line with Renan's view that inferior races should disappear, Arnold already proposed to found a chair at Oxford for the antiquarian study of the disappearing Celtic culture.[7] The position of the Irish as the Catholic Other in the British national imaginaire of the nineteenth century was racialized in philological ruminations about the origins of the Celts and the Saxons.

A crucial development in the thinking about race, language, and culture was the rise of comparative philology after Sir William Jones's articulation, in 1786, of the concept of the Indo-European language family. For Jones, a judge in the Calcutta High Court, Sanskrit scripture did not so much convey an alien civilization but the heritage of the descendants of Ham. He read the flood narrative in Sanskrit literature as confirming the biblical myth. For him and many other British Orientalists at the end of the eighteenth and beginning of the nineteenth century, India and its Hinduism belonged to a biblical world history of peoples. The main thrust of this monogenetic line of thought was that Indians were not essentially different from the British nor significantly inferior. This sympathetic view of India and its civilization is gradually marginalized in the nineteenth century through the attacks on Hinduism by Utilitarians and evangelicals alike. These attacks became increasingly racialized with the rise of comparative anatomy from the 1840s on and culminating in the popular polygenic racism of Robert Knox's *The Races of Man*, published in 1850. But only when language as the basis of scientific knowledge is replaced by biology does racial essentialism become hegemonic.

For the relationship between Indians and British, the scientific status of comparative linguistics proved very positive. English and Sanskrit were shown to belong to the same linguistic family, and it was assumed therefore that, ethnologically speaking, Englishmen and Indians were close kin. This was expressed even in a Sanskrit inscription commemorating the inauguration of the Indian Institute at Oxford in 1883:

> This building, devoted to Eastern sciences, was founded for the use of Aryas (Indians and Englishmen) by excellent and benevolent men desirous of encouraging knowledge. . . . By the favour of God may the learning and literature of India be ever held in honour; and may the mutual friendship of India and England constantly increase.[8]

This inscription was composed by the Boden Professor of Sanskrit at Oxford, Monier Monier-Williams, who otherwise was known for his critical, evangelical attitude toward India and Hinduism. It is clear from this that despite the Anglicist (Utilitarian and evangelical) victory in the beginning of the nineteenth century, comparative philology continued to instill a certain element of love and kinship with Hindu India in a section of British intellectual (and plebeian) opinion. It should also be observed that the concept of "Aryan," which was used for a number of racist purposes in the late nineteenth and twentieth centuries, still had a more positive connotation in 1883 as well.

The Sanskrit term *arya*, which means "honorable man," was used by Friedrich Max Müller to refer to what was otherwise known as the "Indo-European" language family. In a long exposition, in which he finds traces of the word *arya* in a great number of languages and discusses with interest the possible connection of the name *Ireland* with *arya*, Max Müller defends his choice of the term *Aryan* to designate the Indo-European languages as follows:

> As Comparative Philology has thus traced the ancient name of Arya from India to Europe, as the original title assumed by the Aryans before they left their common home, it is but natural that it should have been chosen as the technical term for the family of languages which was formerly designated as Indo-Germanic, Indo-European, Caucasian, or Japhetic.[9]

He may have come to use the term to avoid the nationalistic implications of the term *Indo-German*, which was in vogue in Germany.[10] It was always a considerable concern of Max Müller to avoid the impression that he was a German scholar and patriot working on German topics with a British salary in a British university. This is quite understandable considering the nationalist implications of the work on comparative linguistics. Müller's claims, however, were cosmopolitan: The Science of Language was the foundation of the Science of Man.[11]

The term *Aryan* made a number of oppositions, both inclusions and exclusions, possible. First, as we have seen, it expressed a kinship tie between the British and the Indians. Second, it represented perhaps the most pernicious opposition in the history of modern Europe, that between the Aryan language family and race, on the one hand, and the Semitic language family and race, on the other. Third, it expressed a pernicious opposition in Modern India between Aryan invaders into India, who had brought Brahmanical Sanskrit civilization, and the Others, primarily those in South India who spoke languages within the Dravidian language family but also all tribal groups, later to be classified as the adivasis or aboriginals. None of these oppositions were created or caused by the use of the term *Aryan*, but the scientific status given to the term by Max Müller gave existing opposition another salience and force.

Obviously the sharp distinction between Christians and Jews in medieval and early modern Europe has deep heterophobic roots that precede and go beyond comparative philology and the emergence of the Aryan myth. The point is, first, that the interest in Aryanism in Germany and elsewhere is not innocent of the conceptualization of the difference between Christians and Jews and, second, that the Sanskrit ideology, expressed in the term *arya*, could be appropriated for expressing the opposition between a master race and a slave people. The Sanskrit term *arya* in ancient India had already expressed an important difference between the three higher categories ("twice-born") of Hindu society and the fourth, excluded category of Shudra slaves.[12] Further, in terms of juridical entitlements and prohibitions, it was used to express a sharp domination of a people of masters over a people of slaves. The Sanskritist Sheldon Pollock argues convincingly that the extreme interest in comparative philology, which we find in nineteenth- and twentieth-century Germany, not only emerged out of a romantic quest for roots but also out of a desire to differentiate the Indo-Germans from the Semites. The Indologist Christian Lassen, student of the Schlegel brothers, wrote in 1845: "History teaches us that the Semites did not possess the harmonious balance of all forces of the spirit which characterized the Indo-Germans. Neither is philosophy a strong point with the Semites. All they have done is to borrow from the Indo-Germans, and it was only the Arabs who did this."[13] Whereas in the British case the emphasis was on the relationship between the British and Indians, in Germany (and elsewhere in Europe) it was the relationship between the Indo-European Aryans and the Semitic Jews that was stressed. In the German case, this led to the adoption of Aryanism in the official worldview of the Third Reich, where *Arier* were sharply distinguished from *Nichtarier* in the preparation of the Holocaust. Thus the scientific notion that language was the key to racial identification had a number of political implications still salient today.

In France it was the publication of the *Essay on the Inequality of Races* (1853–55) by Comte Gobineau that most clearly expressed the Aryan myth. In Gobineau's view, the Aryan race was the carrier of civilization as such. It is the Aryan blood that is capable of true civilization. The real danger, therefore, is in miscegenation through which blood comes to be diluted and civilization declines. Civilization may also not be transmitted by education and missionary work, but only by cross-breeding which, at the same time, is dangerous for the dominant Aryan race.[14] A decidedly pessimistic streak runs through Gobineau's writing in its expectation of civilizational degeneration. Gobineau's essay was not well received in France and seems to have gained a paradigmatic status in scientific racism only by hindsight. Much more influential, but essentially in agreement with Gobineau, were the writings of his friend, Ernest Renan, whose intellectual authority was international. Renan argued strongly that the Semitic race was a degenerate one and the Aryan race the newly chosen one. He seems a precursor of the Theosophists in his claim that Aryans were the Masters of the planet.[15] As we have already observed, in Britain Renan was accepted as a great authority by Matthew Arnold and others, while, of course, his notion of the link between language and race was initially shared by his friend, Max Müller.

In Britain the opposition between Jews and Christians was less important in the discourse of Aryanism than the much debated relation between the British and the Indians. Max Müller obviously wanted to express the kinship between the two with his famous remark that the same blood ran in the veins of English soldiers "as in the veins of the dark Bengalees." This view was supported by his general, idealistic theory of religion, which subsumed both Christianity and Hinduism but located it in the "Aryan tradition" of the Logos, the Word.[16] It was a view posing a certain religious universalism together with racial brotherhood and was popular among some Indian Christians, such as Krishna Mohan Banerjee (1813–1885), the author of the *Arian Witness; or, The Testimony of Arian Scriptures in Corroboration of Biblical History* (1875), and the Protestant missionary T. E. Slater (1840–1912).[17] In Britain, however, this kind of view became decidedly less popular after the Mutiny. Nevertheless, this shift in public opinion is not what made him reconsider the relationship between language and race. Rather, his reconsideration is based on an acknowledgment of a paradigmatic shift in scientific theory after Darwin's publications. The step he made from the determination of a family of languages to race followed from German philosophy and from Orientalist scholarship, but it was also fully acceptable to British ethnology which was dominated till the mid-nineteenth century by the theories of James Cowles Prichard. Coming from a Quaker background and touched by the evangelical revival, Prichard was a determined monogenist, defending the unity of mankind against the polygenist leanings of Scottish philosophers like Dugald Stewart.[18] Prichard worked on the explanation of physical differences between men, but he saw language as the most reliable indicator of racial affinity.[19] Language and physical features told the same story, but Prichard saw philology as the more reliable discipline.[20] However, Prichardian ethnology, already battered by the success of the polygenism of Robert Knox, would vanish from the academic scene after Darwin's discoveries and be replaced by a social evolutionism in which language would no longer occupy pride of place.[21]

In India the most far-reaching consequence of the Aryan myth was, in fact, not the positive impact it had on the relationship between the British and Indians but the negative impact it had internally. In an early paper on the relation between Sanskrit and the modern languages of India in

1847, Müller had developed a distinction between Sanskrit-derived languages and other languages. This distinction was linked to a theory of an invasion of light-skinned Aryans in an India populated by a race of dark-skinned aboriginals. Although these aboriginals were first turned into slaves, a great number of them had gradually been morally and physically civilized by the Aryan civilization, showing that race was not destiny.[22] In the same period a similar argument about the unity of aboriginal, non-Sanskritic languages was also advanced by British scholars in India, such as Brian Houghton Hodgson and the Rev. John Stevenson.[23] They all made a quick jump from linguistic evidence to physiological observations, such as the contrast between the light-skinned Aryans of North India and the dark-skinned people of South India, which was readily accepted not only by Müller but also by other Orientalists in this period such as Lassen.[24] The notion of a Brahmanic Aryan invasion in the South was foundational for the work done on South Indian languages by the missionary Robert Caldwell. In his *Comparative Grammar of the Dravidian or South-Indian Family of Languages*, published in 1856, Caldwell argued for the essential autonomy of the Dravidian culture, language, and race and for the essentially extraneous nature of Brahmanical Hinduism in the South. While this was clearly meant to pursue the traditional missionary attack on Brahmanism, it laid the foundation for a Dravidian movement that dominates South Indian politics still today.[25] The Aryan-Dravidian divide is one of the most salient ideological elements in Indian politics in the twentieth century. The other divide, obviously, is between the high "Aryan" castes and the low "non-Aryan" outcastes and tribals. Again the racial theory underpins political positions and is crucial in nationalist theories from the nineteenth century on.

A fascinating link between the Aryanist theories in India and in Europe is the theme of invasion. The mythology of invasion can be developed in at least two ways: First, the original inhabitants of the land are celebrated as the "owners of the land" who have a privileged access to the magical resources of the natural environment; second, the invaders are celebrated as valiant warriors, as deliverers of a higher, stronger civilization. In Britain and India the mythology took these forms simultaneously from a variety of perspectives. The Norman Conquest was the source of rich folklore traditions that were systematized and popularized in the nineteenth century. William the Conqueror, King Arthur, Ivanhoe, Richard Lionheart, Robin Hood, all familiar names of the days of conquest, became part of the national mythology of the island and its invasions. It is a story of conquest, resistance, and ultimate miscegenation of conquerors and vanquished. It is also the story of an attempt to find basic characteristics of the English people in the "ancient institutions" of the pre-Norman period. Another narrative development, mentioned earlier, is the story of the colonization of the Celts and the marginal position of the Irish, Scots, and Welsh. The Celts, as the original inhabitants of the land, were mythologized as both femininely weak and romantically connected to the land. The production of British identity was complemented with the simultaneous production of Irish, Welsh, and Scottish identities of which the first was particularly pronounced as the British colonial "Other." To the present day, the combination of religious antagonism and the history of British colonialism makes for a particularly violent mythology of invasion, possession, and identity in Ireland. The similarities between the colonization of Ireland and of India by the British have not escaped major figures of the Irish literary renaissance such as W. B. Yeats and, especially, James Cousins, later a Theosophist. Cousins even thought that Irish culture originated in pre-Christian Asian religions.[26] Such notions, however, have not drawn much attention from Indian nationalists.[27]

The theme of invasion is also crucial in the application of the Aryan theory in India. Max Müller's theory had it that an Aryan people, described in the Rg-Veda (composed between 1500 and 1000 B.C.) as tribes of horse-mounted fighters who worshipped sky-gods, had invaded the Indian plains. They subjugated the indigenous peoples and either pushed them to the margins (the hill tribes) or included them in their social system as a fourth category of slaves (*shudras*) after the three pure (and twice-born) categories of priests (*brahmans*), warriors (*kshatriyas*), and commoners (*vaishyas*). Müller proposed a two-race theory, light-skinned civilized Aryans and dark-skinned savages, who both mingled with and were excluded by the other, thereby forming the salient social distinctions found by the British in India. This story of invasion and racial history is fully accepted in India still today, but its civilizational interpretation is firmly challenged by both Dravidian speakers in the South and tribal groups (adivasis or aboriginals) who argue that their autochthony is the basis of their preeminence.

While the story of civilization being brought from outside fully applies to the dominant interpretation of the Aryan invasion, subsequent invasions were seen in a much bleaker light as the bringers of widespread destruction and barbarism. I am referring here to the common interpretation in India of the invasions by nomadic peoples from West and Central Asia. The invader Mahmud of Ghazni, the destroyer of Somnath, is perhaps the most common example of a villain in Indian history. These invaders, who were Muslim in terms of religion, became the ruling groups in North India from 1100 to 1800. The fact that Islam arrived in India from outside, as it were, brought by invading peoples, has given rise in colonial and modern India to the negative stigma that Muslims "do not belong." The difference in the interpretation of the Aryan invasion and the Muslim invasion neatly shows the two ways of using the "myth of invasion" in dealing with the past. Aryan means Hindu, equating language with race with religion, and thus excluding a large portion of the population not on the basis of language (such as in the case of Dravidian speakers) or ethnicity (such as tribal groups) but on the basis of their Islamic beliefs.

Originating in Britain's encounter with India, Aryanism became a commonplace in public discourse in Western Europe, including Britain, in the second half of the nineteenth century and the early part of the twentieth. Beyond that, it was developed not only in widespread anti-Semitism and fascist fantasies of the master race but also in the anti-imperialist thinking of the Theosophists. As I argue in chapter 3, the Theosophists were convinced that British imperialism was morally wrong, that Indian religions were spiritually superior, and that Indians had the right to self-rule. Annie Besant led many anti-imperialist activities in Britain and, after her arrival in India, became president of the Indian National Congress. Nevertheless, as Gauri Viswanathan points out, Besant and other Theosophists were firmly wedded to a theory of racial evolution.[28] The Theosophists hoped for the evolutionary emergence of universal brotherhood in which only spiritual hierarchy counted ("the wise are not equal to the ignorant"). Theosophy was a Universal Brotherhood of Humanity, according to its own logo, "without distinction of race, creed, sex, caste, or colour," but, as Viswanathan shows, Blavatsky developed an elaborate theory of racial evolution that was partly taken over by Besant. Blavatsky believed there was an evolutionary scheme of "five root races," the fifth being present now and dispersed over the seven continents and containing subraces, each representing a particular civilization. The highest subrace within the fifth root race was the Aryan and possessed the highest spirituality. This thinking was taken up by German reactionaries, such as the obscure group of "Ariosophists," who, in the years before the First World War, prophesied a coming era of German world rule.[29] They also adopted the swastika, an ancient Indian symbol of welcome and auspiciousness, which Blavatsky embraced as a Theosophical symbol and which was to play such an insidious role in the Nazi mythology. In fact, Blavatsky's writing amounts to an almost unreadable mythologizing that provided obscurantists of all types a treasury of myths and symbols leading to wild

143

speculations about racial difference and evolution. Annie Besant's interpretation of the racial theory, however, is in line with the more common racial theories of Matthew Arnold and Ernest Renan.[30] Like Arnold, Besant thought that cultural revival could be engendered by the invasion of a civilization coming from outside. In that sense, Besant supported the widespread imperialist theory that Hindu India had a golden Aryan past which had declined and had to be rescued through the agency of British colonialism. With Marx and so many others she shared the notion that imperialism was wrong in the short run but good in the long run. The differences in the evolution of the races and their spiritual miscegenation, brought about by the movement of peoples and imperialism, would lead in the end to a human brotherhood at a higher level of spirituality. Early Orientalist visions of Aryan brotherhood were developed in the writings of people as diverse as Max Müller and Annie Besant, with simultaneous anti-imperialist and Hindu revivalist implications.

From Language to Skulls

In 1874 Max Müller wrote a piece entitled "My Response to Mr Darwin," being a rejoinder to something Darwin's son, Leonard, had published criticizing lectures Max Müller had given on "Mr Darwin's Philosophy of Language." The issue is the vexed one of whether there is an essential difference between man and animal, and, if yes, whether that difference is located in the mind or, better, in the capacity for language.[31] This debate with Darwin junior highlights an essential theme of Victorian race science. The success of Darwin's evolutionary biology had reinforced a tendency already present in the intellectual opinion of Britain from the mid-nineteenth century, namely to assume a graduation from monkey to Negro to white Victorian man. This was a very old idea going back to Aristotle's scala naturae, yet it became linked in the eighteenth and nineteenth centuries to the notion that people with black skin were closer to monkeys than to white humans.[32]

Darwin and his colleague, Huxley, argued for the essential continuity between animals and humans. Their arguments derived some of their relevance from the important nineteenth-century science of comparative anatomy, which assumed a relation between brain structure and intelligence.[33] Huxley showed, in his *Evidence as to Man's Place in Nature* (1863), that there were no significant differences between the brain structure of man and that of monkey. This argument, of course, led to the famous exchange between Bishop Wilberforce and Thomas Huxley at Oxford in 1860 about the difference between man and monkey. Huxley's victory in the debate is generally interpreted as a victory of science over religion.[34] To me, that is an exaggerated view when we consider the ongoing discussion between Darwin and Wallace, the two founders of the theory of natural selection, about the much older issue of the interpretation of natural laws as either self-acting or expressions of God's will.[35] Wallace turned spiritualist in his search for "higher intelligence" in the evolution of man, much in the way of the Theosophists, but the problems he saw in Darwin's metaphor of "natural selection" were recognized as well by many other authoritative contributors to the debate. I find the relation to race science more important than the alleged "victory over religion." Evolutionary thought further legitimized the search for the missing link between monkey and Victorian man in other races. Imperial attitudes toward colonized people were thus linked to evolutionary biology. Max Müller's insistence on the faculty of language as an essential difference between humans and animals was thus an extremely significant anti-imperialist and antiracist intervention. He had already given up his idea that language was an indicator of race in the light of the Darwinian theory of biological evolution, but he continued to insist on the importance of language and linguistics.

Darwin had clarified his thought on human races in his *Descent of Man and Selection in Relation to Sex*, published in 1871 twelve years after *The Origin of Species*. Of course he again argued for the continuity between animals and humans, but he went one crucial step further to fill the gap between Victorian man and animals, and "savages" and "lower races."[36] There is little to suggest that he was a racist at heart, but he shared the racial thought of his time and did not use his new evolutionary ideas to transcend them. He also legitimized the evolutionary idea of progress from the barbaric state to the civilized state with his theory of natural selection, similar to what Herbert Spencer had suggested was "the survival of the fittest." Social Darwinism, with its vision of the "struggle between races," was not far from Darwin's own way of thinking.

Possibly the most important empirical element of race science, replacing linguistics in the second half of the nineteenth century, was comparative anatomy, especially craniometry, the measuring of skulls. The basic tenet of this science was that by measuring the shape of the skull one could ascertain the internal structure of the brain and thereby determine racial and individual differences in intelligence, temperament, and moral-

145

ity. Since the anatomist Pieter Camper, in the eighteenth century, had compared "facial angles" of different human races to those of an ape, head shapes had been measured in a number of ways with various results.[37] A major step toward systematization was taken by the Viennese physician Franz Joseph Gall (1757–1828) in his lectures on "craniology," a scientific method of investigating the skull in order to diagnose the internal state of one's mental faculties. This craniology or phrenology was further developed by Gall's assistant, Johann Gaspar Spurzheim (1776–1832), who played a major role in popularizing Gall's ideas in Britain. Phrenology was not the only form of research on skulls in the nineteenth century. Other forms of craniometry and more general anthropometry were incorporated into a field of racial anthropology, applied both at home and in the colonies. As Nancy Stepan observes, the European race is the race to which the "cephalic index," developed in 1844 by Anders Retzius, was most frequently applied.[38] Collignon divided the French into the brachycephalic Celtic people, the dolichocephalic Kymri from the North, and the dolichocephalic Mediterranean people.[39] In Britain the Anglo-Saxon type was distinguished from the Celtic type, as one might expect. Remarkable in this research is the notion that head shape is a stable indicator of race difference. Indeed, the simultaneous assumption of evolutionary progress and typological stability characterizes the very successful race science of the late nineteenth and early twentieth centuries. Another remarkable feature, shared by phrenology and forms of craniometry is the notion that one can read a person's or a race's character scientifically from the external appearance of the skull. That notion had democratic implications to the extent that anyone could read an individual's exterior without access to the disciplines of soul searching developed in the church or to the anatomical disciplines developed in the medical profession. At the same time it was a helpful notion for those who wanted to reform the penal system, since it afforded insight into the criminal intentions of people who tried to hide them.

In Britain, phrenology was made popular by George Combe's *Essays on Phrenology*, published in 1819. He founded the Phrenological Society in Edinburgh the following year. In 1822 Rammohan Roy, the great Indian thinker (see chapters 2 and 3), sent twelve Hindu crania to Edinburgh that were found, upon phrenological research, to show that "acquisitiveness and secretiveness" were well developed among Hindus. Rammohan Roy's skull was also studied by the Edinburgh phrenologists after his death in Bristol in 1833 and was found to show "dignity of character."[40]

Phrenology in Britain can be interpreted along similar lines as spiritualism (chapter 3).[41] It was a strongly materialist science that denied the existence of a mind separate from the brain's physical structure. This radical materialist empiricism gave phrenology anti-Christian implications that were taken up by both liberal reformers of education, prisons, and asylums and plebeian intellectuals. Phrenology was hugely popular and widely debated in all segments of society. George Combe's phrenological treatise *Of the Constitution of Man and Its Relation to External Objects* (1828) sold one hundred thousand copies by 1860 and was one of Britain's most widely circulated books of the nineteenth century.[42] As Roger Cooter points out, phrenology was as often rejected as a pseudo-science as it was accepted as a true science by medical and philosophical establishments.[43] Most important, however, it was a science popular outside the established scholarly world, appealing to enthusiasts among the general public fond of empiricism and experimentation that could not be controlled and monopolized by scientific elites. This enthusiasm found its expression in the spread of "phrenological societies" in Britain in the 1820s and the formation of the Phrenological Association in 1838.[44] By and large, these societies drew a firmly middle-class audience interested in the spread of respectability. Phrenology constituted "useful knowledge" in that it could assist societal reform. From the middle class it was spread to the "great unwashed" by introducing it into the education of, among others, mechanics.

One's character and morality could be read from the surface of the skull, as could one's health, both mental and physical. Phrenology had a notion of balance and harmony between the different parts of the brain, allowing for the possibility of self-improvement by eliminating bad habits such as drinking or sexual license. It also expressed a somewhat more Calvinistic notion of the limitations of one's own action, as given by the structure of one's brain. Cooter captures these aspects of phrenology aptly by calling it a "secular methodism" and by quoting the famous secularist G. J. Holyoake's claim that Combe's *Constitution of Man* was a "new Gospel of Practical Ethics."[45] As such, these two sides of phrenology also resonate with the major moral dilemma of the period, the contradiction between the idea of progressive improvement and the idea of innate, unchangeable mental and physical endowments inherent in race. It is a dilemma that is inherited in the twentieth century in the ongoing debate about nurture versus nature. Old debates were thus carried on in the modern language of education. Between the wars British schoolchildren's heads were routinely examined by means of anthropometric callipers, developed by Darwin's son, Leonard, the president of the Eugenics Society.[46] The gradual move from discourse on improvement to discourse on heredity in the second half of the nineteenth century, cited elsewhere in this book, was also notable in the understanding of skulls.

Not only was the population of Europe targeted by anthropometrists, however. India was considered by one of its most distinguished anthropologists cum civil servants, Sir Herbert Risley (1851–1911), an excellent place for this kind of research, since whereas in Europe a mixture of peoples had led to the formation of nations, in India "the process of fusion was long arrested . . . there is consequently no national type, and no nation in the ordinary sense of the word."[47] Risley's comment highlights out a major interest the British had in the lasting diversity of India's population, namely, its incapacity to form a nation. Risley had begun his scientific work in 1884, when the government of Bengal appointed him to survey the tribes and castes of that province. After that, he became responsible for the 1901 census, which he planned in accordance with the latest principles of ethnological research as developed in Britain. Administrators like Risley and his teacher and predecessor, William Hunter, director of statistics of the Indian government and compiler of the *Statistical Account of Bengal*, were also scholars who fully participated in the methodological and theoretical debates about race in the metropole.[48] In 1910 Risley was elected president of the Royal Anthropological Institute.

The main conceptual difficulty in the census operations, which the colonial government started in 1871–72, was how to classify the Indian population. Caste was the available indigenous category, but the problem was how to make it the basis of an All-India form of classification, as was clearly desired in an All-India modern governmentality envisaged by the colonial government. At least two procedures were required: the standardization of caste names and a standard All-India hierarchy of castes.[49] The early censuses used the *varna* categorization of Brahmanical text: Brahmans (priests), Kshatriyas (warriors), Vaishyas (commoners), and Shudras (the rest). The category comprising "the rest" was in fact the bulk of the population and had to be addressed for administrative purposes, and the Brahmanical classification was dropped for an occupational one in 1891.[50] The hierarchy of the occupational castes was explained in an evolutionary scheme, as developed in nineteenth-century thinking on the stages of human development. Again Risley moved away from occupational ranking because of the huge unclarities it conveyed. In his view, caste ranking should be understood in terms of religion and race.

The Brahman was considered the center of the caste universe and the relations that different castes maintained with the Brahman caste were taken to be the indicators of status in the caste hierarchy. It is striking how these principles of classification were reproduced in the later work on caste interactions by American anthropologists in the 1950s.[51]

Risley was searching for a scientific method to order the immense diversity of Indian society. He found it in anthropometry or, more specifically, in the nasal index as the scientific indicator of caste difference: "If we take a series of castes . . . and arrange them in order of the average nasal index, so that the caste with the finest nose shall be at the top, and that with the coarsest at the bottom of the list, it will be found that this order substantially corresponds with the accepted order of social procedure."[52] Anthropometry was not Risley's private hobby but, as we have seen above, one of the most serious objects of study at the time. Noses and crania were also obsessional objects of scientific inquiry for Edgar Thurston in his important *Castes and Tribes of Southern India* (1909) and for a great number of similarly inspired works. Thurston went so far as to wander through villages asking the villagers to strip and then measuring them with his "Lovibond Tintometer."[53] However bizarre this may sound today, the theoretical assumption in all this work was expressed in Risley's assertion that the "race sentiment" was the basis of the caste system. According to Risley, the race sentiment was not "a figment of the intolerant pride of the Brahman, but rests upon a foundation of fact which scientific methods confirm, that it has shaped the intricate grouping of the caste system, and has preserved the Aryan type in comparative purity throughout Northern India."[54] Crucial in Risley's argument was that he continued to build the theory of the Aryan-Dravidian divide, but now with anthropometrical evidence rather than philological confirmation. The political message behind this racial theory was that the British, like their "Aryan brethren" a few millennia before, had come to bring a higher civilization to India. Thus the theory not only gave the different castes a place in the hierarchy but also gave the British a legitimate place in India.

When Risley tried out his nasal index, the measurement of skulls had already been popular in India for half a century. The first British official to measure skulls was apparently William Sleeman, superintendent for the suppression of the criminal tribe the Thugs, a tribe prominent even today in the Western imaginaire. Already evident here is the connection between anthropometry and criminology, which is explored further in the next section. Tribes, then, as well as castes, were subjected to scientific inquiry about their racial composition. However, never did this inquiry become so sophisticated and thorough as in Risley's massive survey.

The huge significance of Risley's work was duly noted by the doyen of Indian anthropology, G. S. Ghurye, who severely criticized Risley's correlation between race and caste. In Ghurye's view, a long history of racial mingling made this kind of correlation impossible.[55] Ghurye had a fine eye for the politicization of caste that emerged as a consequence of the census operations: "The total result has been as we have seen, a livening up of the caste-spirit."[56] His focus and main concern was the rise of anti-Brahman movements both in his own state, Maharashtra, and in Tamil Nadu. These movements were fed by the ideological division between Aryans and non-Aryans, a division scientifically supported by Risley's theory and findings. To Ghurye, this was a great threat to Indian nationalism and an example of British divide-and-rule politics. Clearly scientific discourse on race in the metropole and the requirements of imperial politics fit nicely together, as will become more apparent when we examine, in the next section, the policing of criminal races.

RACE, CLASS, AND CRIMINALITY

In the Victorian period savages were compared either to children or to the lower classes. The famous journalist-investigator of city life, Henry Mayhew, described the urban poor as "wandering tribes in civilized society." They were seen as a "new city race." C.F.G. Masterman, in his *Heart of the Empire* (1901), described them as "stunted, narrow-chested, easily wearied; yet voluble, excitable, with little ballast, stamina, or endurance."[57] Schoolchildren were routinely measured by Francis Galton's anthropometric laboratory, and, in keeping with Galton's general views, the measurements correlated with social class. That the Irish were an inferior race on a par with other colonized races was a truism that further connected Britain's urban poor with the notion of race.

Here again we see the recurring Victorian ambivalence about heredity (nature) versus improvement (nurture). It was a nationalist imperative, however, that the urban poor were not only to be contained but had to be improved, had to change their lifestyles into those of the respectable middle class. Their criminality was regarded as a direct result of their morality, in which bad behavior (drinking) and bad heredity reinforced each other, and as a threat to respectable society. The state carried out the necessary civilizational project through legal means and the creation of labor colonies. The main impetus, however, came from evangelizing Christian movements. One of these was the Salvation Army, an organization that developed out of a Wesleyan revivalist movement in East London in 1878. General William Booth's *In Darkest England and the Way Out* (1890) explicitly connected the project of civilizing with that of Christianizing. Booth's adage: "Go for souls and go for the worst." The Salvation Army scoured urban slums, reaching out to alcoholics, destitute women, prostitutes, and other marginal characters in "notorious" city landmarks. Its methods were spectacular: the use of military uniforms, military hierarchy, and military discipline; open-air meetings in the streets, with people singing to coronets and drums; the indoor ritual of the "mercy seat," in which inner transformation was tied to the outward spectacle of penitent prostration. These methods were related to a particular moment in the public sphere in which new methods of publicity, melodrama, and oratory drew attention to the dangerous presence of the cities' "great unwashed" and the need to reform them.[58] The Salvation Army's "war cry" suited this particular moment in Britain and, in a peculiar way, was also relevant to the colonial project in India.

In the first half of the nineteenth century the British were very concerned with criminality in India's countryside, both banditry and vagrancy. Pindaris, Banjaras, Sannyasins, Fakirs, all kinds of migrant groups, often in religious garb, which especially mystified the British, roamed the hillsides begging, robbing, extorting, but primarily competing with the British in controlling the routes of travel and trade between urban centers. Added to this was the persistent anxiety that these groups were in fact supported by the nobility of independent kingdoms outside direct British control. The British were committed to suppress this flexible and mobile world and to restore their own authority. They accomplished this gradually by criminalizing and racializing peasant resistance against the new policies of taxation and policing. An interesting note is that many of the groups the British registered as "criminal" had been local or regional strongmen in the precolonial period. As such, they formed a concentration of power that had to be dismantled to give way to Pax Britannica, much as roving groups of ascetics had to be suppressed and controlled in the eighteenth century.[59] In fact, some groups that fit the "criminal" classification were identified as "martial" in cases where the British wanted a particular group to retain its power in a certain region.

Before the British succeeded in placing all criminality in India under the sign of "caste," "tribe," and "race" in the second half of the nineteenth century, they still attributed it to "religion." The best example of this is the complex phenomenon of the Thugs and the war on Thugs. The Thugs were a gang allegedly engaged in ritual murder. On October 16, 1830, an article appeared in *The Calcutta Literary Gazette* that revealed the horrible practices of the Thugs. They robbed and strangled travelers and offered them to the Goddess Kali, for which offering they received the Goddess's blessing. These were not individual cases but a well-organized network of thuggery. The author of this article, anonymously published, was Sir William Sleeman, a District Collector in Jabalpur, who subsequently was given the task of launching an anti-Thug campaign. With a guard of fifty cavalerists and fifty soldiers he set out to pursue the gangs of Thugs. By offering one thousand rupees to individuals for information leading to the arrest of suspected Thugs, Sleeman secured popular support for his efforts and was ultimately successful.

Who were the Thugs? A definition is elusive, since the only sources are the texts produced by William Sleeman himself, especially his *Ramaseeana; or, A Vocabulary of the Peculiar Language Used by the Thugs, with an Introduction and an Appendix Descriptive of the System Pursued by That Fraternity and of the Measures Which Have Been Adopted by the Supreme Government for Its Suppression*, published in 1836. As Martine van Woerkens points out in her book on the subject, fact and fiction, science and imagination, are so intertwined that in this case it is almost impossible to disentangle them.[60] Four elements converged in the way Thugs were imagined by the British. First, there was the fact of banditry in the countryside which made traveling a hazardous adventure. Second, the British felt a great disgust for the animal sacrifices made in worship of the terrifying Mother-Goddess Kali, in which scores of water buffalo and goats were slaughtered regularly at the temples of Kali. Third, a famous icon in the iconography of Kali shows her dancing, tongue protruding, with a string of skulls in one of her four hands on the corpse of Shiva. This horrific image stuck in the minds of the Protestant British whose tolerance for idolatry was quite low anyway. Fourth, the British were engaged in stamping out a number of "barbarous" Hindu practices, such as sati, or widow burning, and female infanticide. The combination of these four elements came together in the imagination of Thugs, bands of bandits who attacked travelers and engaged in the ritual of human sacrifice for Kali. It led not only to the successful career of William Sleeman in suppressing this phenomenon but also to a vivid fascination with these gangs in popular culture. It began with the success of Meadows Taylor's *Confessions of a Thug*, published in 1839, and continued in the cinematic sphere with George Stevens's movie *Gunga Din* (1939) and Steven Spielberg's *Indiana Jones and the Temple of Doom* (1984). Perhaps not a single theme signifies the relation between colonial imagination and Indian realities better than that of the Thugs.

Thugs were subjected to scientific scrutiny. Seven corpses of Thugs who had been hanged were decapitated by the medical doctor Henry Spry, Sleeman's cousin, and their heads sent to Edinburgh to be subjected to phrenological research by Robert Cox and Henry Combe. In an article in the *Edinburgh Journal of Phrenology*, published in 1837, their research shows that the criminal nature of the Thugs derived from the shape of their skulls. Nevertheless, Cox and Combe concur with Spry and Sleeman that the environment influences heredity; thus sons can be kept from following the criminal career of their fathers by changing the environment.[61] Indeed, Sleeman founded a school of arts and crafts in Jabalpur for the families of convicted Thugs.

The belief in Thugs as a criminal fraternity was gradually replaced by a view that criminality was directly related to the caste system, an assumption given importance in the second half of the nineteenth century. The British had "discovered" that criminality in India was not a personal vice; rather, it was inherent in one's caste or tribal identity. As the law member of the governor-general of India's Council, James Fitzjames Stephen, argued in 1871:

> Traders go by caste in India: a family of carpenters now will be a family of carpenters a century or five centuries hence, if they last so long ... If we keep this in mind when we speak of "professional criminals," we shall then realize what the term really does mean. It means a tribe whose ancestors were criminals from time immemorial, who are themselves destined by the usages of caste to commit crime, and whose descendants will be offenders against the law, until the whole tribe is exterminated or accounted for.[62]

Criminality, then, was both racial and occupational in India and, even more than in Britain, seemingly irredeemable. At the end of the nineteenth century the British tried to extend the Criminal Tribes Act to most of the regions under their control. At this peculiar juncture the Salvation Army, with all its experience in combating low life in the urban squalor of Britain's urban centers, enters the scene of Indian criminality.

Frederick Booth-Tucker had brought the Salvation Army to India in 1882. His activities, especially public processions and meetings in the streets, at first greatly embarrassed the British, who felt their imperial dignity was compromised by this sort of missionary activity. Booth-

Tucker and his companions were regularly stopped by the police, even given light prison sentences. This made them no less popular among the Indian public, which was as thrilled by the musical and evangelical performances of female Salvationists, "Hallelujah Lasses," as the British public had been.[63] Booth-Tucker dressed as an Indian *sadhu* with a saffron-colored *dhoti* and a turban, his wife dressed in a sari. He called himself Fakir Singh, and the Salvation Army received the Indian name Mukti Fauj. All this may have irritated respectable colonial officialdom, but it was relatively effective among the Indian population. Nevertheless, the great step forward in converting Indians came in early 1908 when the Salvation Army undertook "one of the greatest and most successful enterprises in the history of the Salvation Army in India—the transformation of criminal tribes to decent, law-abiding citizens."[64]

During a Salvation Army campaign in 1908, a Mr. Tweedy, commissioner of Rohilkhand, approached Booth-Tucker with the request to undertake the work of reforming the region's criminal tribes. The official story in the history of the Army's activities in India goes as follows:

A start was made by opening a settlement for 300 Doms who were under the charge of the police at Gorakhpur. A set of buildings, which had been police lines, was placed at the Army's disposal and Brigadier and Mrs. Hunter (Bahadur and Ratna Bai) were appointed to take charge of the settlement. The Doms were the most unpromising of human material, unruly, inveterate drunkards and gamblers. It was the practice when a Dom died to put a coin in the fist as token that there would be something with which to start gambling on the other side of the dark river. Domestic affairs were confusing to say the least; when a husband went to jail, as often happened, the wife would take to herself another husband "to protect her virtue," so she would say. When the first husband was released from jail he would claim his wife back, but if the second husband objected they would fight it out between them and the victor would win the wife. The children would seldom know who their real father was. To find work for the settlers was of paramount importance. When first they were told to work they laughed scornfully. "Work?" they said. "We never work, we dance and sing." It was indeed raw material the officers were dealing with.[65]

The account goes on to say that the Doms were taught how to use the Maxwell loom and how to do agricultural work. Not only in Rohilkhand did the Salvation Army acquire a role in the compulsory reeducation and supervision of criminal tribes and castes, but also in the Punjab and in

South India. In 1908 an abandoned fort in the Punjab was given to the Salvation Army and was used to contain Punjabi prisoners. As Jeffrey Cox points out, the Army worked as prison subcontractors in this and other cases.[66] The Salvation Army was so intrinsic to the criminal justice system that it even escorted prisoners to the Andaman Islands (a prison colony in the Bay of Bengal) and engaged in schemes to rehabilitate them there. Conversion, of course, includes not only indoctrination but also the question of preventing a relapse. To accomplish this, the Salvation Army simply secured for its endeavors a captive audience.

It is truly astonishing how this radical, antiestablishment Christian movement, antiracist in its open recruitment policies and regarded by the British as a racial embarrassment in India, had nevertheless become an instrument of imperial policing of the Indian population. It did not last long, however. In the 1920s, with the changing climate of Indian national-ist politics, the Salvation Army had to give up its imperial project to turn criminal tribes into cheap Christian labor.

CONCLUDING REMARKS

In the second half of the nineteenth century the British became a "ruling race," fit to control a vast empire. Their superiority was no longer based on their Protestantism and their prosperity but on the heredity of their racial characteristics. Heredity signified stability in imperial relations and thus formed an antidote to the challenge of uprisings like the Mutiny and the rise of anticolonial nationalism at the end of the Victorian period. The ideology of the master race was internally fraught with ambivalence and danger. Despite the enfranchisement of the Catholics and the Noncon-formists and the unification of the United Kingdom, a strong sense of internal division remained. This was best expressed in Disraeli's notion of the "two nations" and was reinforced by the linked processes of indus-trialization and urbanization. Primarily the urban poor were thought to form a different nation whose life was explored in ways resembling the exploits of Stanley and Livingstone in Africa. The main task of uplift and improvement, brought into the cities mainly by evangelical movements, was to make two nations into one, to spread middle-class morality to the rest of society.

Both the divisions and unity in Britain were theorized along the lines of language, culture, and race. To what extent did the Irish, Scots, and

Welsh differ from the English? According to Matthew Arnold, it was the Anglo-Saxon culture, not the Celtic culture, that formed the basis of powerful, political institutions. The English nation-state had to colonize the Celts by subsuming the Celtic contribution to national culture. Obviously this move to national unity was countered from the periphery by strong assertions of Irish and Welsh identity. These divisions and their unity were theorized in terms of comparative philology. They resemble the divisions and unity laid out in Indo-European scholarship between Indian and British cultures. In all these cases the relationship is never established or stable, but under constant negotiation.

A major element in the negotiation of imperial and national relations was the development of scientific arguments. The theory of the "Aryan race," as conceived by the early Müller, depended on linguistic arguments. It could be used for a variety of purposes: to oppose a Semitic race with an Aryan one; to show unity between the colonized Indians and the colonizing British; to oppose an Aryan master race in India with an aboriginal slave race, and so on. Darwin's theory of biological evolution showed the connection between language and race to be spurious but did little to eliminate the Aryan race theory. Rather, it reinforced the tendency to distinguish races on the basis of their evolutionary superiority or inferiority. This shows the extent to which science can be put to use for a variety of broader arguments. The development of science takes place in a changing historical context in which it is also applied and has moral and political impact.

Scientific empiricism in the guise of race science led to a number of arguments about racial difference and moral character, about nature and nurture. The most prominent representative of race science, phrenology, was applied to European as well as Indian races. Different races with diverse moral characters were discerned within nations. Phrenology's most significant application, however, was in the sphere of criminality. There, phrenology was used to determine the "moral stage" of the "criminal" underclass and to assist in the education and eugenicist improvement of that class. In India it was used to determine the racial characteristics that form the basis of caste differences and prevented the Indian population from becoming a nation. A nasal index, from the finest to the coarsest nose, proved the racial nature of caste difference in India. Again, like in Britain, this did not prevent ideas of improvement from taking shape.

Imperialism and nationalism had a common enemy: the racial and thus moral degeneration of a segment of the population of both colonizers and colonized. Science helped in contemplating this problem, but religion helped in solving it. The question of criminality and degeneracy among the poor of Britain's cities and of criminal castes and tribes was essentially the same.[67] Thus it should come as no surprise that the Salvation Army, with its vast experience in dealing with the urban underclass, was seen fit to battle criminality in India as well.

Conclusion

IN THE NINETEENTH CENTURY all kinds of attempts were made to show that modernity was rooted in a national past. Scientific inventions, political innovations, economic success, they all belonged to the biography of the nation, and the nation itself was traced to a hoary past. National character moved and motivated history. Religion, language, race, and gender were seen as aspects of national character and explained the relative prosperity, civilization, and freedom of a nation. The British, convincing themselves of their superiority, invented their oldest traditions in the second half of the nineteenth century. Liberty, for instance, was not understood as a modern political ideal but as an ancient British concept deeply rooted in history. Others would have to work hard to acquire it. This is not only a basic colonial assumption in John Stuart Mill's essay *On Liberty*, but it is also strikingly captured in the architect Lutyens's inscription in the gateway of the colonial government buildings in New Delhi: "Liberty will not descend to a People; A People must raise themselves to Liberty; It is a blessing which must be earned before it can be enjoyed." The invention of tradition in British nationalism is sometimes related to the English colonization of the Welsh, Scots, and Irish, but even then the analytical framework continues to be that of British national history with a serious neglect of empire.[1] When Linda Colley argues persuasively for the eighteenth and early nineteenth centuries when the British defined themselves as a nation "in reaction to the Other beyond their shores," that the Other is French and Catholic, one needs to add that increasingly in the nineteenth century the Other is also Indian and Hindu.[2]

In India, in the same period, one finds similar attempts to connect modernity to a hoary past. Swami Dayananda, for instance, argued that his reformist views of the Hindu caste system were based on the rationality and tolerance of an ancient Aryan golden age. While the great scientific and technological inventions of the nineteenth century were made in Britain and elsewhere in the West, Dayananda showed that they had already been present in the Vedas but were somehow tragically lost. Even Christ, according to a widespread and popular belief, was considered of Indian origin, in fact derived from Krishna. This reasoning has often been interpreted as a sign of an inferiority complex among the colonized, whereas metropolitan reasonings, similar in nature, are seldom seen to indicate a

158

superiority complex among colonizers. In fact, both British and Indian thoughts on origins belong to a history of colonial interactions and might be understood in the context of a shared colonial imaginaire.

It is much easier to recognize Britain's impact on India than vice versa. The nature of the British colonization of India is a subject of lively debate. It includes arguments stating an almost unilateral definition of the situation by the British as well as assertions positing a more "dialogic" development in which Indians are credited with more agency in constructing their history.[3] The extent to which British history has been shaped by the imperial conquest of India, however, is rarely discussed. Imperial history and national history are treated as different subjects. This makes possible the essentializations of rationality and racial and religious superiority, which are the foundation of nationalism and fundamentalism, as well as of sociological and historical theories of secularization, civilization, and cultural history. Sociological theory is not only the child of modern, industrial society, as is commonly assumed, it is also the child of empire.[4]

Britain's and India's close encounter has produced a number of remarkable parallel histories, fascinating chains of influences, and spectacular interpretations and misunderstandings. The two are sometimes connected by a single concept, such as "spirituality." One strand connects the translation of Indian religious and philosophical texts to German philosophy and philology.[5] Another connects British mysticism to an Orientalist interest in "Indian Wisdom." A third strand connects spiritualism, plebeian science, and political radicalism with anticolonial struggle. And still another connects an ethics of modern Christian social action with a new interpretation of Indian spirituality as "practical Vedanta," that is, social ethics as understood by Vivekananda and Gandhi. The issue here is to see that arguments about spirituality, both in Britain and India, were shaped by the imperial context and were not only academic but had a great impact both on British anticolonialism and pacifism and on India's nationalism and later leadership in the nonaligned movement after decolonization. The postcolonial predicament of plural societies and multiculturalism may well be understood in relation to a long colonial history of productive encounters.

The modernization and nationalization of Hinduism and Christianity makes it possible to use the universal category of "religion" for both, since they undergo similar transformations in different societal locations. This is not to say that discursive traditions of Protestantism and Catholicism, in all their varieties, or of Vaishnavism and Shaivism, in all their varieties as well, did not continue but that these traditions had to relate to the new societal form, that of the nation-state. Not everything is invented or reinvented; there are continuities, but the configurations in which these discursive traditions occur have changed dramatically in the nineteenth century. Hinduism and Christianity, as concepts, get a national salience in the imperial encounter. The universalism, claimed by the Enlightenment for its understanding of modernity, has to be rejected in its essential provincialism, but, at the same time, clearly the expansion of colonial power universalized the conditions under which concepts like liberty, secularity, and religion received their meaning.

Modernity has a global history. This does not imply a single origin of concepts and blueprints that are developed in the Enlightenment (both American and French) and exported and resisted, and adopted, elsewhere.[6] Nor does it imply the dialectic between an already finished idiom of modernity that confronts an already existing idiom of tradition, out of which a synthesis emerges.[7] Rather, it manifests a history of interactions out of which modernity, with its new historical problematic, arose, offering creative tensions, not solutions. Freedom and governance received a new, modern understanding not only from Herder's and Diderot's philosophical argument about the modern world in direct reference to migration, overseas colonies, and the mingling of populations, as convincingly shown by Anthony Pagden, but also, quite tangibly in the British case, from debates by Burke and his opponents about India.[8] A Eurocentric philosophical history of modernity, such as Charles Taylor's *Sources of the Self*, however brilliantly presented, ignores the importance of the global dimension of the issues it discusses.[9] This is especially evident in Taylor's treatment of civilizations as separate entities that may learn from one another. Although he emphasizes that modern notions of progress and social reform are a blend of Protestantism and Enlightenment, he is unaware of the extent to which the empire is the frame in which evangelicals and Utilitarians develop these notions.[10] Origins of modernity cannot be neatly located in Western civilization; they must be sought in the mess of encounters in which Indian begums, Hindu converts, and later Theosophical Universalists are all present.

Notes

INTRODUCTION

1. Edward Said, *Culture and Imperialism* (New York: Knopf, 1993).

2. Louis Dumont, *La Civilisation Indienne et Nous* (Paris: Armand Collin, 1975), 37.

3. Louis Dumont, *Homo Hierarchicus: The Caste System and Its Implications* (Chicago: University of Chicago Press, 1980). See my critique in "The Foreign Hand: Orientalist Discourse in Sociology and Communalism," in Carol A. Breckenridge and Peter van der Veer, eds., *Orientalism and the Postcolonial Predicament: Perspectives on South Asia* (Philadelphia: University of Pennsylvania Press, 1993), 23–44.

4. See Wilhelm Halbfass, *India and Europe: An Essay in Understanding* (Albany: State University of New York Press, 1988), 84–100; and Prasenjit Duara, *Rescuing History from the Nation: Questioning Narratives of Modern China* (Chicago: University of Chicago Press, 1995), 17–20.

5. See Daniel Thorner, "Marx on India and the Asiatic Mode of Production," *Contributions to Indian Sociology* 9 (1965): 33–66.

6. Nicholas B. Dirks, "History as a Sign of the Modern," *Public Culture* 2 (1990): 25–33.

7. Ingmar Westerman, "Authority and Utility: John Millar, James Mill, and the Politics of History, c. 1770–1836," dissertation defended in April 1999 at the University of Amsterdam.

8. John Pocock, "Modernity and Anti-Modernity in the Anglophone Political Tradition," in Shmuel Eisenstadt, ed., *Patterns of Modernity* (London, 1987).

9. See the brilliant discussion of Psalmanazar in Susan Stewart's *Crimes of Writing: Problems in the Containment of Representation* (Durham: Duke University Press, 1994).

10. James Mill, *History of British India*, ed. Horace Hayman Wilson (London: J. Madden; Piper, Stephenson, and Spence, 1858), 1:229.

11. T. B. Macaulay, *Speeches, with the Minute on Indian Education*, ed. G. M. Young (London: Oxford University Press, 1935).

12. Gauri Viswanathan, *Masks of Conquests: Literary Study and British Rule in India* (New York: Columbia University Press, 1989).

13. S. Lavin, *Unitarians and India: A Study in Encounter and Response* (Boston: Beacon Press, 1977).

14. Ajit Kumar Ray, *The Religious Ideas of Rammohun Roy: A Survey of his Writings Particularly in Persian, Sanskrit, and Bengali* (New Delhi: Kanak, 1976).

15. R. W. Connell, "Why is Classical Theory Classical?" *American Journal of Sociology* 102, no. 6 (1997): 1535.

16. Ibid., 1524.

17. Eric Wolf, *Europe and the People without History* (Berkeley: University of California Press, 1982).

18. Andre Gunder Frank, *ReOrient: Global Economy in the Asian Age* (Berkeley: University of California Press, 1998); idem, "Asian Age: ReOrient Historiography and Social Theory," *Wertheim Lecture 1998* (Amsterdam: CASA, 1998).

19. Gauri Viswanathan, "Raymond Williams and British Colonialism," *The Yale Journal of Criticism* 4, no. 2 (1991): 47–66.

20. Peter van Rooden, "Friedrich Schleiermachers *Reden über die Religion* en de historische bestudering van godsdienst," in *Theoretische Geschiedenis* 23 (1996): 419–38.

CHAPTER ONE
SECULARITY AND RELIGION

1. For useful introductions to the concept of secularization and the debate about it, see Bryan Wilson, *Religion in a Secular Society* (London: Weidenfeld and Nicholson, 1966); and Steve Bruce, ed., *Religion and Modernization: Sociologists and Historians Debate the Secularization Thesis* (Oxford: Clarendon, 1992).

2. See especially the multivolume *Fundamentalism Project*, edited by Martin Marty and Scott A. Appleby and published by the University of Chicago Press.

3. Jose Casanova, *Public Religions in the Modern World* (Chicago: University of Chicago Press, 1994).

4. John Wolffe, *God and Greater Britain: Religion and National Life in Britain and Ireland, 1843–1945.* (London: Routledge, 1994); Hugh McLeod, *Religion and the Working Class in Nineteenth-Century Britain* (London: Macmillan, 1984); David Hempton, *Religion and Political Culture* (Cambridge: Cambridge University Press, 1996).

5. See, for example, Ernest Gellner, *Nations and Nationalism* (Oxford: Blackwell, 1983).

6. T. N. Madan, "Secularism in Its Place," *Journal of Asian Studies* 46, no. 4 (1987): 747–59. See also his *Modern Myths, Locked Minds* (Delhi: Oxford University Press, 1997).

7. Madan, "Secularism in Its Place," 747.

8. Ibid., 753–54.

9. Owen Chadwick, *The Secularization of the European Mind in the 19th Century* (Cambridge: Cambridge University Press, 1975), 27.

10. Thomas Jefferson, in a letter to the Baptists of Danbury, Connecticut, January 1802, in *Jefferson's Writings*, ed. Merrill D. Peterson (New York: Library of America, 1984), 510.

11. See Keith Luria, "The Politics of Protestant Conversion to Catholicism in Seventeenth-Century France," in Peter van der Veer, ed., *Conversion to Modernities: The Globalization of Christianity* (New York: Routledge, 1996), 33–38.

12. John Stuart Mill, *Utilitarianism, On Liberty, Considerations on Representative Government*, ed. Geraint Williams (London: J. M. Dent, 1993), 69.

13. Charles Taylor, "Modes of Secularism," in Rajeev Bhargava, ed., *Secularism and Its Critics* (Delhi: Oxford University Press, 1998), 46.

14. Ibid., 44.

15. Peter Gay, *The Enlightenment: An Interpretation*, 2 vols. (New York: Knopf, 1966; 1969).

16. Robert E. Frykenberg, "The Emergence of 'Modern Hinduism,' " in Gunther Sontheimer and Hermann Kulke, eds., *Hinduism Reconsidered* (Delhi: Manohar, 1997), 90.

17. Ibid., 94.

18. Ibid.

19. C. J. Fuller, *Servants of the Goddess: The Priests of a South Indian Temple* (Cambridge: Cambridge University Press, 1984).

20. Arjun Appadurai, *Worship and Conflict under Colonial Rule: A South Indian Case* (Cambridge: Cambridge University Press, 1981); David Gilmartin, *Empire and Islam: Punjab and the Making of Pakistan* (Berkeley: University of California Press, 1988).

21. Nita Kumar, "Sanskrit Pandits and the Modernisation of Sanskrit Education in the Nineteenth to Twentieth Centuries," in William Radice, ed., *Swami Vivekananda and the Modernization of Hinduism* (Delhi: Oxford University Press, 1998), 54.

22. Sandria Freitag, *Collective Action and Community: Public Arenas and the Emergence of Communalism in North India* (Berkeley: University of California Press, 1989), 150.

23. Richard Fox Young, *Resistant Hinduism: Sanskrit Sources on Anti-Christian Apologetics in Early Nineteenth-Century India* (Vienna: De Nobili Research Library, 1981).

24. Talal Asad, *Genealogies of Religion* (Baltimore: The Johns Hopkins University Press, 1993).

25. Clifford Geertz, *The Interpretation of Cultures* (New York: Basic Books, 1973).

26. Asad, *Genealogies*, 19; Reinhart Koselleck, *Critique and Crisis: Enlightenment and the Pathogenesis of Modern Society* (Cambridge, Mass.: MIT Press, 1988).

27. Benedict Anderson, *Imagined Communities* (London: Verso, 1991), 24; Erich Auerbach, *Mimesis* (Garden City, N.Y.: Doubleday Anchor, 1957); Walter Benjamin, *Illuminations* (London: Fontana, 1973).

28. See Peter van der Veer, "Syncretism, Multiculturalism, and the Discourse of Tolerance," in Charles Stewart and Rosalind Shaw, eds., *Syncretism/Anti-Syncretism* (London: Routledge, 1994), 196–212.

29. Asad, *Genealogies*, 40–41.

30. See van der Veer, *Conversion to Modernities*.

31. For example, Heinrich von Stietencron, "Hinduism: On the Proper Use of a Deceptive Term," in Sontheimer and Kulke, *Hinduism Reconsidered*, 41.

32. Romila Thapar, "Syndicated Hinduism," in Sontheimer and Kulke, *Reconsidering Hinduism*, 65.

33. Jürgen Habermas, *Strukturwandlung der öffentlichkeit* (Neuwied, Berlin: Luchterhand 1962).

34. Margaret C. Jacobs, *Living the Enlightenment: Freemasonry and Politics in Eighteenth-Century Europe* (Oxford: Oxford University Press, 1992).

35. See also David Zaret, "Religion, Science, and Printing in the Public Sphere in Seventeenth-Century England," in Craig Calhoun, ed., *Habermas and the Public Sphere* (Cambridge, Mass.: MIT Press, 1992), 212–36.

CHAPTER TWO
THE MORAL STATE: RELIGION, NATION, AND EMPIRE

1. Quoted in Talal Asad, *Genealogies of Religion: Discipline and Reasons of Power in Christianity and Islam* (Baltimore: The Johns Hopkins University Press, 1993), 224.

2. See Hugh McLeod, "Protestantism and British National Identity, 1815–1945," in van der Veer and Lehmann, *Nation and Religion*, 44–71.

3. Quoted in Keith Robbins, "Religion and Identity in Modern British History," in Stuart Mews, ed., *Religion and National Identity: Studies in Church History*, vol. 18 (Oxford: Blackwell, 1982), 465.

4. John Eade, "Nationalism, Community, and the Islamization of Space in London," in Barbara Metcalf, ed., *Muslim Space* (Berkeley: University of California Press, 1997), 217–34.

5. Michael Hechter, *Internal Colonialism: The Celtic Fringe in British National Development, 1536–1966* (Berkeley: University of California Press, 1975).

6. Tom Nairn, *The Break-up of Britain: Crisis and Neo-Nationalism* (London: New Left Books, 1981).

7. Benedict Anderson, *Imagined Communities: Reflections on the Origin and Spread of Nationalism* (London: Verso, 1991).

8. Marcel Mauss, "La nation," in *Oeuvres* (Paris: Les Editions de Minuit, 1969) 3:592–93. Original from the 1920s.

9. Ibid., 596.

10. Ibid., 604.

11. Such a distinction is central in Clifford Geertz, "The Integrative Revolution: Primordial Sentiments and Civil Politics in the New States," in Clifford Geertz, *The Interpretation of Cultures* (New York: Basic Books, 1973), 255–311.

12. Michel Foucault, "The Subject and Power," *Critical Inquiry* 8, no. 4 (1982): 777–95.

13. Timothy Mitchell, "The Limits of the State: Beyond Statist Approaches and Their Critics," *American Political Science Review* 85 (1991): 93.

14. See, for the Netherlands, Peter van Rooden, "History, the Nation, and Religion: The Transformations of the Dutch Religious Past," in van der Veer and Lehmann, *Nation and Religion*, 96–112.

15. John Wolffe, *God and Greater Britain: Religion and National Life in Britain and Ireland, 1843–1945* (London: Routledge, 1994), 22.

16. Quoted in Boyd Hilton, *The Birth of Methodism in England: The Influence of Evangelicalism on Social and Economic Thought, 1795–1865* (Oxford: Clarendon, 1988), 209–10.

17. Quoted in Hilton, *The Age of Atonement*, 210.

18. Susan Thorne, *Protestant Ethics and the Spirit of Imperialism: British Congregationalists and the London Missionary Society, 1795–1925*, Ph.d. dissertation, University of Michigan (Ann Arbor: University Microfilms International, 1990), 67. The situation was similar in the Netherlands; see Peter van Rooden, "Nineteenth-Century Representations of Missionary Conversion and the Transformation of Western Christianity," in van der Veer, *Conversion to Modernities*, 65–89.

19. William Carey, *An Enquiry into the Obligations of Christians to Use Means for the Conversion of the Heathens* (Leicester: Ann Ireland, 1792).

20. Brian Stanley, "Christian Responses to the Indian Mutiny of 1857," in W. J. Sheils, ed., *Studies in Church History*, vol. 20: *The Church and War* (Oxford: Blackwell, 1983), 278.

21. Cf. David Hempton, *Religion and Political Culture in Britain and Ireland: From the Glorious Revolution to the Decline of Empire* (Cambridge: Cambridge University Press, 1996), 32–33, 71.

22. Hilton, *The Age of Atonement*, 26.

23. Ibid., 340.

24. Hugh Tinker, *The Ordeal of Love: C. F. Andrews and India* (Delhi: Oxford University Press, 1779).

25. Lynn Zastoupil, *John Stuart Mill and India* (Stanford: Stanford University Press, 1994).

26. Samuel Taylor Coleridge, *On the Constitution of the Church and State* (London: Hurst, Chance, 1830).

27. William E. Gladstone, *The State in Its Relations with the Church* (London: Hurst, Chance, 1838).

28. Gladstone, quoted in Helmstadter and Paul Phillips, eds., *Religion in Victorian Society: A Sourcebook of Documents* (Lanham, Md.: University Press of America, 1985), 82–89.

29. Hilton, *The Age of Atonement*, 341.

30. Thomas Arnold, *Principles of Church Reform* (London: Fellowes, 1833).

31. Zastoupil, *John Stuart Mill and India*.

32. Robbins, "Religion and Identity in Modern British History," 470–71.

33. This section is largely based on a discussion of Irish, Scottish, and Welsh nationalisms in Wolffe, *God and Greater Britain*.

34. Ibid., 69.

35. Ibid., 37.

36. John Henry Newman, *Apologia Pro Vita Sua* (London: Longman, 1864).

37. John Wolffe, *The Protestant Crusade in Great Britain, 1829–1860* (Oxford: Clarendon, 1991).

38. Ibid., 309.

39. Quoted in Robbins, "Religion and Identity in Modern British History," 471.

40. Robert J. C. Young, *Colonial Desire: Hybridity in Theory, Culture, and Race* (New York: Routledge, 1995), 47.

41. Quoted in Gauri Viswanathan, *Masks of Conquest: Literary Study and British Rule in India* (New York: Columbia University Press, 1989), 19.

42. Young, *Colonial Desire*, 71.

43. Chapter 6 further explores the question of race.

44. Viswanathan, *Masks of Conquest*, 102.

45. Geoffrey A. Oddie, *Hindu and Christian and South-East India* (London: Curzon, 1991), 57.

46. Brian Stanley, *The Bible and the Flag: Protestant Missions and British Imperialism in the Nineteenth and Twentieth Centuries* (Leicester: Apollos, 1990), 61.

47. Viswanathan, *Masks of Conquest*, 117.

48. Van der Veer, *Religious Nationalism*.

49. Thomas R. Metcalf, *Ideologies of the Raj* (Cambridge: Cambridge University Press, 1994), 95.

50. Gayatri Spivak, "Can the Subaltern Speak?" in Cary Nelson and Lawrence Grossberg, eds., *Marxism and the Interpretation of Culture* (Urbana: University of Illinois Press, 1988), 271–313.

51. Wilhelm Halbfass, *India and Europe: An Essay in Understanding* (Albany: SUNY Press, 1988): 205–6.

52. Lata Mani, "Contentious Traditions: The Debate on Sati in Colonial India," in KumKum Sangari and Sudesh Vaid, eds., *Recasting Women: Essays in Colonial History* (New Brunswick, N.J.: Rutgers University Press, 1989), 273–74.

53. Charles Taylor, *Sources of the Self: The Making of the Modern Identity* (Cambridge, Mass.: Harvard University Press, 1989), 273–74.

54. Ranajit Guha, *A Construction of Humanism in Colonial India: The Wertheim Lecture* (Amsterdam: CASA, 1993).

55. Cf. Sudipto Kaviraj, *The Unhappy Consciousness: Bankinchandra Chattopadhyay and the Formation of Nationalist Discourse in India* (Delhi: Oxford University Press, 1995), esp. chap. 4.

56. David Kopf, *The Brahmo Samaj and the Shaping of the Modern Indian Mind* (Princeton, N.J.: Princeton University Press, 1979).

57. Partha Chatterjee, *The Nation and Its Fragments: Colonial and Postcolonial Histories* (Princeton, N.J.: Princeton University Press, 1993).

58. In the next chapter I present a critical discussion of Chatterjee's views in relation to the construction of am anticolonial universal spiritualism.

59. Tapan Raychaudhuri, *Europe Reconsidered* (Delhi: Oxford University Press, 1988).

60. An elaborate analysis of Vivekananda's spirituality in relation to British spiritualism and theosophy follows in the next chapter.

61. Peter van der Veer, "Gender and Nation in Hindu Nationalism," in Hans Antlov and Stein Tonneson, eds., *Asian Forms of the Nation* (Richmond, Surrey, England: Curzon, 1996), 188–213.

62. Charles Dickens, "The Perils of Certain English Prisoners" (1857), quoted in Young, *Colonial Desire*, 120–21.

63. Quoted in Metcalf, *Ideologies of the Raj*, 48.

64. Nicholas B. Dirks, "The Conversion of Caste: Location, Translation, and Appropriation," in van der Veer, *Conversion to Modernities*, 115–37.

65. Kenneth Jones, *Arya Dharm: Hindu Consciousness in Nineteenth-Century Punjab* (Berkeley: University of California Press, 1976), 34.

66. Bernard Cohn, *An Anthropologist among the Historians* (Delhi: Oxford University Press, 1987).

67. Bernard Cohn and Nicholas Dirks, "Beyond the Fringe: The Nation-State, Colonialism, and the Technologies of Power," *Journal of Historical Sociology* 1 (1988): 244–30.

CHAPTER THREE
THE SPIRITS OF THE AGE: SPIRITUALISM AND POLITICAL RADICALISM

1. Kenneth W. Jones, *Arya Dharm* (Berkeley: University of California Press, 1989), 169–70.

2. Stefan Collini, *Public Moralists, Political Thought, and Intellectual Life in Britain, 1850–1930* (Oxford: Clarendon, 1991).

3. Catherine Hall, *White, Male, and Middle-Class* (Cambridge: Polity, 1992).

4. Sylvia Berti, "At the Roots of Unbelief," *Journal of the History of Ideas* (1995): 556.

5. E. P. Thompson, *Witness against the Beast: William Blake and the Moral Law* (Cambridge: Cambridge University Press, 1993), 109.

6. Quoted in Joscelyn Godwin, *The Theosophical Enlightenment* (Albany: SUNY Press, 1994), 61.

7. Logie Barrow, *Independent Spirits: Spiritualism and English Plebeians, 1850–1910* (London: Routledge & Kegan Paul, 1986), 4–6.

8. Ibid., 6.

9. Ibid., 157.

10. Alex Owen, *The Darkened Room: Women, Power, and Spiritualism in Late Nineteenth-Century England* (London: Virago, 1989).

11. Arthur Nethercott, *The First Five Lives of Annie Besant* (Chicago: University of Chicago Press, 1960), 349.

12. Ibid., 96.

13. Gauri Viswanathan, *Outside the Fold: Conversion, Modernity, and Belief* (Princeton, N.J.: Princeton University Press, 1998), 200.

14. Anthony Pagden, "The Effacement of Difference: Colonialism and the Origins of Nationalism in Diderot and Herder," in Gyan Prakash, ed., *After Colonialism: Imperial Histories and Postcolonial Displacements* (Princeton, N.J.: Princeton University Press, 1995), 129–53.

15. Quoted in Nethercott, *The Last Four Lives of Annie Besant*, 283.

16. Monier Monier-Williams, *Hinduism* (London: Society for Promoting Christian Knowledge, 1877), 186.

17. In Godwin, *The Theosophical Enlightenment*, 381.

18. Quoted in Partha Chatterjee, *The Nation and Its Fragments* (Princeton, N.J.: Princeton University Press, 1993), 38.

19. Barbara Metcalf, "Imagining Community: Polemical Debates in Colonial India," in Kenneth W. Jones, ed., *Religious Controversy in British India: Dialogues in South Asian Languages* (Albany: SUNY Press, 1992), 236.

20. J. N. Farquhar, *The Crown of Hinduism* (Oxford: Oxford University Press, 1913).

21. Reinhart Koselleck, *Futures Past* (Cambridge, Mass.: MIT Press, 1979).

22. Chatterjee, *The Nation and Its Fragments*, 8.

23. Lise McKean, *Divine Enterprise: Gurus and the Hindu Nationalist Movement* (Chicago: University of Chicago Press, 1996), xv.

24. Jeffrey Kripal, *Kali's Child: The Mystical and the Erotic in the Life and Teachings of Ramakrishna* (Chicago: University of Chicago Press, 1995).

25. Chatterjee, *The Nation and Its Fragments*, 57.

26. Kripal, *Kali's Child*, 30–32.

27. Jonathan Parry, *Death in Benaras* (Cambridge: Cambridge University Press, 1994); Alan Morinis, *Pilgrimage in the Bengali Tradition* (Delhi, Oxford University Press, 1984); Peter van der Veer, *Gods on Earth: The Management of Religious Experience in a North Indian Pilgrimage Centre* (London: Athlone, 1988).

28. Kripal, *Kali's Child*, 55.

29. Ibid., 2.

30. Chatterjee, *The Nation and Its Fragments*, 62–68.

31. Eric Ziolkowski, ed., *A Museum of Faiths: Histories and Legacies of the 1893 World's Parliament of Religions* (Atlanta: Scholars, 1993).

32. Sunrit Mullick, "Protap Chandra Majumdar and Swami Vivekananda at the Parliament of Religions: Two Interpretations of Hinduism and Universal Reli-

gion," in Eric Ziolkowski, ed., *A Museum of Faiths: Histories and Legacies of the 1893 World's Parliament of Religions* (Atlanta: Scholars, 1993), 221.

33. Van der Veer, *Religious Nationalism*, 1994.

34. Mircea Eliade has written an important study of yoga, placing it in the discipline of history of religions without even mentioning Vivekananda. His neglect of the historical context of his own work is all the more surprising considering that it was largely written in Calcutta under the supervision of the principal of Sanskrit College, Professor Surendranath Dasgupta. See Mircea Eliade, *Yoga: Immortality and Freedom* (Princeton, N.J.: Princeton University Press, 1958).

35. Lecture entitled "Common Bases of Hinduism," quoted in Shamita Basu, "Religious Revivalism as Nationalist Discourse: Swami Vivekananda and the Nineteenth-Century Neo-Hindu Movement in Bengal," Ph.D. dissertation, Roskilde University, Denmark, 1997, 76.

36. McKean, *Divine Enterprise*.

37. Gananath Obeyesekere, "Buddhism and Conscience: An Exploratory Essay," *Daedalus* 120 (1991): 221.

38. Geoffrey Oddie, *Hindu and Christian in South-East India* (London: Curzon, 1991), 196–98.

39. McKean, *Divine Enterprise*.

40. Friedrich Nietzsche, *Jenseits von Gut und Bose*, in *Werke in Drei Banden, Zweiter Band* (hrsg. von Karl Schlechta) (München: Carl Hansen Verlag, 1960), 616.

41. Gauri Viswanathan, "Reading Theosophy, Writing Secularism," paper presented at a conference entitled "Religion and Modernity: Rethinking Secularization," Bellagio, 1999.

42. Peter Pels, "Spiritual Facts and Super-Visions: The 'Conversion' of Alfred Russell Wallace," *Etnofoor* 8, no. 2 (1995): 69–91.

43. Van der Veer, *Gods on Earth*.

CHAPTER FOUR
MORAL MUSCLE: MASCULINITY AND ITS RELIGIOUS USES

1. Catherine Hall, *White, Male, and Middle Class* (Cambridge: Polity, 1992), 76–94.

2. Ashis Nandy, *The Intimate Enemy: Loss and Recovery of Self under Colonialsim* (Delhi: Oxford University Press, 1983).

3. Mrnalini Sinha, *Colonial Masculinity: The "Manly Englishman" and the "Effeminate Bengali" in the Late Nineteenth Century* (Manchester: Manchester University Press, 1995).

4. Ibid., 8.

5. Brian Stanley, "Christian Responses to the Indian Mutiny," in W. J. Shiels, ed., *The Church and War*, 277–91 (Oxford: Basil Blackwell, 1983).

6. Ibid., 280.

7. Ibid., 288.

8. Benita Parry, *Delusions and Discoveries* (London: Penguin, 1972), 127.

9. Thomas Metcalf, *Ideologies of the Raj* (Cambridge: Cambridge University Press, 1994), 163.

10. Ibid., 199.

11. Hall, *White, Male, and Middle Class*, 270.

12. Norman Vance, *The Sinews of the Spirit: The Ideal of Christian Manliness in Victorian Literature and Religion* (Cambridge: Cambridge University Press, 1985), 59–69.

13. Ibid., 65.

14. Ibid., 81.

15. Donald Hall, *Muscular Christianity: Embodying the Victorian Age* (Cambridge: Cambridge University Press, 1994), 52.

16. Vance, *The Sinews of the Spirit*, 169–71.

17. Judith Walkowitz, *City of Dreadful Delight: Narratives of Sexual Danger in Late-Victorian London* (Chicago: University of Chicago Press, 1992), 74.

18. Vance, *The Sinews of the Spirit*, 172.

19. Ibid., 187.

20. Allen Warren, "Citizens of the Empire: Baden-Powell, Scouts and Guides, and an Imperial Ideal," in John MacKenzie, ed., *Imperialism and Popular Culture*, 242 (Manchester: Manchester University Press, 1986).

21. Michael Rosenthal, *The Character Factory: Baden-Powell and the Origins of the Boy Scout Movement* (New York: Pantheon, 1986), 133.

22. Ibid., 281.

23. Ibid., 179.

24. Ibid., 262.

25. Thomas Laqueur, *Religion and Respectability* (New Haven: Yale University Press, 1976), 15.

26. Ibid., 232–33.

27. Ibid., 235–36.

28. Dennis Allen, "Young England: Muscular Christianity and the Politics of the Body in *Tom Brown's Schooldays*," in Hall, *Muscular Christianity*, 119.

29. David Newsome, *Godliness and Good Learning: Four Studies on a Victorian Ideal* (London: John Murray, 1961), 35.

30. Lytton Strachey, *Eminent Victorians* (New York: Harcourt-Brace, 1918), 214.

31. Allen, "Young England," 130.

32. J. A. Mangan, *The Games Ethic and Imperialism* (London: Viking, 1985), 21.

33. Ibid., 123.

34. Ibid., 25.

35. Ibid., 39.

36. *Spectator*, October 8, 1898, quoted in Hugh McLeod, "Protestantism and British National Identity, 1815–1945," in Peter van der Veer and Hartmut Lehmann, eds., *Nation and Religion: Perspectives on Europe and Asia*, 52 (Princeton, N.J.: Princeton University Press, 1999).

37. J. A. Mangan, *The Cultural Bond: Sport, Empire, Society* (London: Frank Cass, 1992), 2.

38. Metcalf, *Ideologies of the Raj*, 146–48.

39. Said, "Introduction," *Rudyard Kipling: Kim*, 14.

40. Baden Powell, September 4, 1937, quoted in Rosenthal, *Character Factory*, 266.

41. Quoted in Sinha, *Colonial Masculinity*, 15–16.

42. Ronald Inden, *Imagining India* (Oxford: Basil Blackwell, 1990), 94–95.

43. Patrick Brantlinger, *Rule of Darkness: British Literature and Imperialism, 1830–1914* (Ithaca: Cornell University Press, 1988), 161–62.

44. Sinha, *Colonial Masculinity*, 158.

45. Ibid., 164.

46. Walkowitz, *City of Dreadful Delight*.

47. Ibid., 132–34.

48. Quoted in John Rosselli, "The Self-Image of Effeteness: Physical Education and Nationalism in Nineteenth-Century Bengal," *Past and Present* 86 (1980): 123.

49. David Lelyveld, *Aligarh's First Generation* (Princeton, N.J.: Princeton University Press, 1978), 117.

50. Tony Mason, "Football on the Maidan: Cultural Imperialism in Calcutta," in Mangan, *The Cultural Bond*, 142–54.

51. Arjun Appadurai, "Playing with Modernity: The Decolonization of Indian Cricket," in Breckenridge, *Consuming Modernity*, 25–26.

52. Peter van der Veer, *Gods on Earth: The Management of Religious Experience in a North Indian Pilgrimage Center* (London: Athlone, 1988).

53. Joseph Alter, *The Wrestler's Body: Identity and Ideology in North India* (Berkeley: University of California Press, 1992).

54. Peter van der Veer, "The Power of Detachment: Disciplines of Body and Mind in the Ramanandi Order," *American Ethnologist* 16 (1989): 458–70.

55. Alter, *The Wrestler's Body*, 237–59.

56. Ibid., 246.

57. Indira Chowdhury-Sengupta, "The Effeminate and the Masculine: Nationalism and the Concept of Race in Colonial Bengal," in Peter Robb, ed., *The Concept of Race in South Asia*, 282–304 (Delhi, Oxford University Press, 1995).

58. Pradip Kumar Datta, " 'Dying Hindus': Production of Hindu Communal Common Sense in Early 20th Century Bengal," *Economic and Political Weekly*, June 19, 1993, 1305–19.

59. George Mosse, *Nationalism and Sexuality* (New York: Howard Fertig, 1975).

60. Sumit Sarkar, "Indian Nationalism and the Politics of Hindutva," in David Ludden, ed., *Contesting the Nation: Religion, Community, and the Politics of Democracy in India*, 275 (Philadelphia: University of Pennsylvania Press, 1996).

61. Thomas Blom Hansen, "Recuperating Masculinity: Hindu Nationalism, Violence, and the Exorcism of the Muslim 'Other,' " *Critique of Anthropology* 16, no. 2 (1996): 145.

62. Rosselli, "The Self-Image of Effeteness," 130.

63. Thomas Blom Hansen, *The Saffron Wave: Democracy and Hindu Nationalism in Modern India* (Princeton, N.J.: Princeton University Press, 1999).

CHAPTER FIVE
MONUMENTAL TEXTS: ORIENTALISM AND THE CRITICAL EDITION OF
INDIA'S NATIONAL HERITAGE

1. Nirad C. Chaudhuri, *Scholar Extraordinary: The Life of Professor the Rt. Hon. Friedrich Max Müller, P.C.* (New York: Oxford University Press, 1974), 5.

2. (Friedrich) Max Müller, *Chips from a German Workshop*, vol. 4 (New York: Scribner, 1876), 7.

3. Thomas Nipperdey, *Nachdenken über die deutsche Geschichte* (München: C. H. Beck, 1986), 140–55.

4. For a description of these controversies, see Chaudhuri, *Scholar Extraordinary*, 220–29.

5. Stefan Collini, Donald Winch, and John Burrow, *That Noble Science of Politics* (Cambridge: Cambridge University Press, 1983).

6. Monier Monier-Williams, *The Study of Sanskrit in Relation to Missionary Work in India* (London: Oxford University Press, 1861), 54.

7. Müller, *Chips*, 241.

8. (Friedrich) Max Müller, *Last Essays* (London: Longmans, 1901), 337.

9. (Friedrich) Max Müller, *Theosophy or Psychological Religion* (London: Longmans, 1903), 4.

10. Ibid., 6.

11. Ibid., 10–11.

12. (Friedrich) Max Müller, *Auld Lang Syne: My Indian Friends* (New York: Scribner, 1899), xxiii.

13. Ibid., xxiv–xxv.

14. Ibid., x.

15. Berhard S. Cohn, *An Anthropologist among the Historians* (Oxford: Oxford University Press, 1987), 652.

16. Ibid.

17. David Ludden, "Orientalist Empiricism: Transformations of Colonial Knowledge," in Carol A. Breckenridge and Peter van der Veer, eds., *Orientalism and the Postcolonial Predicament: Perspectives on South Asia*, 250–79 (Philadelphia: University of Pennsylvania Press, 1993).

18. Rosanne Rocher, "British Orientalism in the Eighteenth Century: The Dialectics of Knowledge and Government," in Breckenridge and van der Veer, *Orientalism*, 220.

19. Berhard S. Cohn, *Colonialism and Its Forms of Knowledge* (Princeton, N.J.: Princeton University Press, 1996), 57–76.

20. Nicholas B. Dirks, "Colonial Histories and Native Informants: Biography of an Archive," in Breckenridge and van der Veer, *Orientalism*, 279–314.

21. Thomas Trautmann, *Aryans and British India* (Berkeley: University of California Press, 1997).

22. Sheldon Pollock, "Deep Orientalism? Notes on Sanskrit and Power Beyond the Raj," in Breckenridge and van der Veer, *Orientalism*, 76–134.

23. Trautmann, *Aryans and British India*, 1997.

24. (Friedrich) Max Müller, *Last Essays*, 218–50.

25. Müller, *Auld Lang Syne*.

26. Ibid., 105.

27. David Hult, "Reading it Right: The Ideology of Text Editing," in Steven Nichols, ed., *The New Criticism* (Baltimore: The Johns Hopkins University Press, 1990), 118.

28. Of these manuscripts, those in Bengali numbered 32; Grantha, 31; Telugu, 28; Malayalam, 26; Nepali, 5; Sarada, 3; Maithili, 1; Kannada, 1; and Nandinagari, 1.

29. V. S. Sukthankar, *Critical Studies in the Mahabharata* (Poona: Bhandarkar Oriental Research Institute, 1944), 43.

30. Ibid., 43.

31. Ibid., 108.

32. Ibid., 438.

33. Jack Goody, *The Domestication of the Savage Mind* (Cambridge: Cambridge University Press, 1977).

34. Benedict Anderson, *Imagined Communities* (London, Verso, 1991).

35. Sandria Freitag, *Collective Action and Community* (Berkeley: University of California Press, 1993).

36. Thomas Coburn, " 'Scripture in India': Towards a Typology of the Word in Hindu Life," in Miriam Levering, ed., *Rethinking Scripture* (Albany: State University of New York Press, 1989).

37. Alf Hiltebeitel, *The Cult of Draupadi* (Chicago: University of Chicago Press, 1988), 135.

38. Sukthankar, *Critical Studies*, 83–89.

39. Peter van der Veer, *Religious Nationalism* (Berkeley: University of California Press, 1994), 165–93.

40. B. G. Tilak, *Srimad Bhagavadgita Rahasy*, trans. B. S. Sukthankar, 2 vols. (Poona: Bhandarkar Oriental Research Institute, 1935–36), 831.

41. Sukthankar, *Critical Studies*, 9.

42. Ibid., 493.

43. Sheldon Pollock, "The Ramayana Text and the Critical Edition," in Robert Goldman, ed., *The Ramayana of Valmiki* (Princeton, N.J.: Princeton University Press, 1984), 91.

44. Paula Richman, *Many Ramayanas* (Berkeley: University of California Press, 1990); Philip Lutgendorf, *The Life of a Text* (Berkeley: University of California Press, 1991).

45. Shahid Amin, "Gandhi as Mahatma," in Ranajit Guha and Gayatri Spivak, eds., *Selected Subaltern Studies* (New York: Oxford University Press, 1988).

46. Partha Chatterjee, *The Nation and Its Fragments* (Princeton, N.J.: Princeton University Press, 1993), 113.

47. B. P. Sinha, "Indian Tradition and Archeology," *Puratattva* 14 (1984): 109.

48. B. B. Lal, "Was Ayodhya a Mythical City?" *Puratattva* 10 (1978): 45.

49. Romila Thapar, "Puranic Lineages and Archeological Cultures," *Puratattva* 8 (1978): 86.

50. Madeleine Biardeau, "The Story of Arjuna Kartavirya without reconstruction," *Purana* 12, no. 2 (1970): 286–303.

51. Jacques Derrida, *Writing and Difference* (London: Routledge and Kegan Paul, 1978), 278–95.

52. Jacques Derrida, *Of Grammatology* (Baltimore: The Johns Hopkins University Press, 1976).

53. Jonathan Boyarin, ed., *The Ethnography of Reading* (Berkeley: University of California Press, 1993).

54. Lutgendorf, *Life of a Text*, 39, 40.

55. Purnima Mankekar, "Television Tales and a Woman's Rage: A Nationalist Recasting of Draupadi's Disrobing," *Public Culture* 5 (1993): 569–492.

56. Aijaz Ahmad, *In Theory* (London: Verso, 1992), 243–87.

57. Vinay Dharwadker, "Orientalism and the Study of Indian Literatures," in Breckenridge and van der Veer, *Orientalism*, 163.

58. Michel de Certeau, *The Practice of Everyday Life* (Berkeley: University of California Press, 1984), 132.

CHAPTER SIX
ARYAN ORIGINS

1. Amitav Ghosh, *The Circle of Reason* (London: Granta, 1986), 8–9.

2. Crispin Bates, "Race, Caste, and Tribe in Central India: The Early Origins of Indian Anthropometry," in Peter Robb, ed., *The Concept of Race in South Asia*, 219 (Delhi: Oxford University Press, 1995).

3. Owen Chadwick, *The Secularization of the European Mind in the 19th Century* (Cambridge: Cambridge University Press, 1975).

4. Susan Bayly, "Race in Britain and India," in van der Veer and Lehmann, *Nation and Religion*, 71–96.

5. Thomas Trautmann, *Aryans and British India* (Berkeley: University of California Press, 1997), 193.

6. Robert Young, *Colonial Desire* (London: Routledge, 1995), 70, 71.

7. Ibid., 71.

8. Trautmann, *Aryans and British India*, 4.

9. (Friedrich) Max Müller, *Lectures on the Science of Language*, vol. 1 (London: Longmans, Green, 1861 [last vol. in series, 1885]), 289.

10. One of the first Englishmen to use the term *Aryan* to refer to Indo-European tribes is the ethnologist James Cowles Pritchard (1786–1848) in his *Natural History of Man* (1843), a work dedicated to the Prussian ambassador C.C.J. Bunsen (1791–1860), who was a friend and benefactor of Max Müller; see Joan Leopold, "British Applications of the Aryan Theory of Race to India, 1850–1870," *The English Historical Review* 89 (1974): 278–603.

11. Ibid., 2:7.

12. Sheldon Pollock, "Deep Orientalism," in Breckenridge and van der Veer, *Orientalism*, 108.

13. Quoted in Leon Poliakov, *The Aryan Myth* (London: Chatto, 1974), 197.

14. See the discussion in Young, *Colonial Desire*, 99–118.

15. Poliakov, *The Aryan Myth*, 208. Gauri Viswanathan also argues that Annie Besant was strongly influenced by Renan, in his *Outside the Fold* (Princeton, N.J.: Princeton University Press, 1998), 199.

16. Martin Maw, *Visions of India: Fulfillment Theology, the Aryan Race Theory, and the Work of British Protestant Missionaries in India* (Frankfurt: Peter Lang, 1990), 32.

17. Ibid., 46.

18. G. W. Stocking, *Victorian Anthropology* (New York: The Free Press, 1987), 49.

19. Stocking, *Victorian Anthropology*, 51.

20. Ibid., 133.

21. Ibid., 166–67.

22. Ibid., 176.

23. Ibid., 160. See also Peter Pels, "The Rise and Fall of the Indian Aborigines: Orientalism, Anglicism, and the Emergence of an Ethnology of India, 1833–1869," in Peter Pels and Oscar Salemink, eds, *Colonial Subjects: Essays on the Practical History of Anthropology* (Ann Arbor: University of Michigan Press, 1999), 82–116.

24. Poliakov, *The Aryan Myth*, 197.

25. Nicholas Dirks, "The Conversion of Caste: Location, Translation, and Appropriation," in van der Veer, *Conversion to Modernities*, 115–37.

26. Viswanathan, *Outside the Fold*, 206.

27. A claim that the Welsh and Hindus were cognate was expressed at the visit of Dwarkanath Tagore to the Welsh Association of Abergavenny in 1842 but did not elicit much interest from Tagore. See Joan Leopold, *British Applications*, 581.

28. Viswanathan, *Outside the Fold*, 205.

29. Nicholas Goodrich-Clarke, *The Occult Roots of Nazism: Secret Aryan Cults and Their Influence on Nazi Ideology; The Ariosophists of Austria and Germany, 1890–1935* (New York: New York University Press, 1985).

30. Viswanathan, *Outside the Fold*, 199–200.

31. For Müller's admiring but inconsistent position in relation to Darwin and his theories, see Gregory Schrempp, "The Re-Education of Friedrich Max Müller: Intellectual Appropriation and Epistemological Antinomy in Mid-Victorian Evolutionary Thought," *Man(NS)* 18 (1983): 90–110.

32. Nancy Stepan, *The Idea of Race in Science* (London: Macmillan, 1982), 6–10.

33. Ibid., 14.

34. Chadwick, *The Secularization of the European Mind*, 174 ff.

35. Robert M. Young, *Darwin's Metaphor* (Cambridge: Cambridge University Press, 1985), 100–104.

36. Stepan, *The Idea of Race*, 53.

37. Poliakov, *The Aryan Myth*, 162.

38. Stepan, *The Idea of Race*, 97.

39. Ibid., 98.

40. Bates, "Race, Caste, and Tribe," 232.

41. Peter Pels, "Occult Truths: Race, Conjecture, and Theosophy in Victorian Anthropology," in R. Handler and G. W. Stocking, eds., *Excluded Ancestors*, Vol 9: *History of Anthropology* (Madison: University of Wisconsin Press, forthcoming).

42. Roger Cooter, *The Cultural Meaning of Popular Science: Phrenology and the Organization of Consent in Nineteenth-Century Britain* (Cambridge: Cambridge University Press, 1984), 28.

43. Ibid., 120.

44. Ibid., 92.

45. George Jacob Holyoake, *Sixty Years of an Agitator's Life* (1892), quoted in Cooter, *The Cultural Meaning of Popular Science*, 196.

46. Ibid., 259.

47. Quoted in Christopher Pinney, "Classification and Fantasy in the Photographic Construction of Caste and Tribe," *Visual Anthropology* 3 (1990): 261.

48. Susan Bayly, "Caste and Race in Colonial Ethnography," in Peter Robb, ed., *The Concept of Race in South Asia* (Delhi: Oxford University Press, 1997), 172.

49. Rashmi Pant, "The Cognitive Status of Caste in Colonial Ethnography: A Review of Some Literature on the North West Provinces and Oudh," *The Indian Economic and Social History Review* 24, no. 2 (1987): 151.

50. Ibid., 155.

51. McKim Marriott, "Interactional and Attributional Theories of Caste Ranking," *Man in India* 39, no. 2 (1959): 92–107.

52. H. H. Risley, *The Tribes and Castes of Bengal,* 4 vols. (Calcutta: Bengal Secretariat Press, 1891), xxxiv; quoted in Cristopher Pinney, "Classification and Fantasy in the Photographic Construction of Caste and Tribe," *Visual Anthropology* 3 (1990): 267.

53. Crispin Bates, "Race, Caste, and Tribe in Central India," in Robb, *The Concept of Race,* 247.

54. Quoted in B. S. Cohn, *An Anthropologist among Historians and Other Essays* (Delhi: Oxford University Press, 1987), 247.

55. Nicholas Dirks, "Recasting Tamil Society," in C. Fuller, *Caste Today* (Delhi: Oxford University Press, 1997), 265.

56. G. S. Ghurye, *Caste and Race in India* (London: Kegan Paul, 1932); quoted in Cohn, *An Anthropologist among Historians,* 241.

57. Quoted in Henrika Kuklick, *The Savage Within* (Cambridge: Cambridge University Press, 1991), 101.

58. Judith Walkowitz, *City of Dreadful Delight* (Chicago: University of Chicago Press, 1992).

59. Van der Veer, *Gods on Earth.*

60. Martine van Woerkens, *Le Voyageur etrangle. L'Inde des Thugs, le colonialisme et l'imaginaire* (Paris: Bibliotheque Albin Michel, 1995).

61. Ibid., 272.

62. Quoted in Rachel Tolen, "Colonizing and Transforming the Criminal Tribesman: The Salvation Army in British India," *American Ethnologist* 18, no. 1 (1991): 109.

63. Walkowitz, *City of Dreadful Delight,* 75.

64. Solveig Smith, *By Love Compelled: The Salvation Army's One Hundred Years in India and Adjacent Lands* (London: Salvation Publishing and Supplies, 1981), 103.

65. Ibid., 104.

66. Jeffrey Cox, "The Salvation Army and Imperial Power in Early-Twentieth Century Punjab," paper presented at a conference on religion and nationalism in Amsterdam, November 1995.

67. See also Robert Colls, "Englishness and the Political Culture," in Robert Colls and Philip Dodd, eds., *Englishness: Politics and Culture, 1880–1920* (London: Croom Helm, 1986), 46–47.

CONCLUSION

1. See, for instance, Colls and Dodd, *Englishness.*

2. Linda Colley, *Britons: Forging the Nation, 1707–1837* (New Haven: Yale University Press, 1992), 6.

3. Nicholas B. Dirks, *The Hollow Crown: Ethnohistory of an Indian Kingdom* (Cambridge: Cambridge University Press, 1987); Eugene F. Irschick, *Dialogue and*

History: Constructing South India, 1795–1895 (Berkeley: University of California Press), 1994.

4. R. W. Connell, "Why Is Classical Theory Classical?" *American Journal of Sociology* 102, no. 6 (1997): 1511–57.

5. Wilhelm Halbfass, *India and Europe: An Essay in Understanding* (Albany: City University of New York Press, 1988).

6. E.g., Benedict Anderson's diffusionism in *Imagined Communities*.

7. For instance, Ranajit Guha, "Dominance without Hegemony and Its Historiography," *Subaltern Studies*, Vol 4: *Writings on South Asian History and Society* (Delhi: Oxford University Press, 1989), 210–309.

8. Anthony Pagden, "The Effacement of Difference: Colonialism and the Origins of Nationalism in Diderot and Herder," in Gyan Prakash, ed., *After Colonialism: Imperial Histories and Postcolonial Displacements* (Princeton, N.J.: Princeton University Press, 1995), 129–53; Sara Suleri, *The Rhetoric of English India* (Chicago: University of Chicago Press, 1992).

9. Charles Taylor, *Sources of the Self: The Making of the Modern Identity* (Cambridge, Mass.: Harvard University Press, 1989).

10. Ibid., 397–99.

Bibliography

Ahmad, Aijaz. *In Theory*. London: Verso, 1992.

Allen, Dennis. 1994 "Young England: Muscular Christianity and the Politics of the Body in *Tom Brown's Schooldays*." In Donald E. Hall, ed., *Muscular Christianity: Embodying the Victorian Age*, 114–33. Cambridge: Cambridge University Press, 1994.

Alter, Joseph. *The Wrestler's Body: Identity and Ideology in North India*. Berkeley: University of California Press, 1992.

Amin, Shahid. "Gandhi as Mahatma." In Ranajit Guha and Gayatri Spivak, eds., *Selected Subaltern Studies*, 288–351. New York: Oxford University Press, 1988.

Anderson, Benedict. *Imagined Communities*. London: Verso, 1991.

Appadurai, Arjun. *Worship and Conflict under Colonial Rule: A South Indian Case*. Cambridge: Cambridge University Press, 1981.

———. "Playing with Modernity: The Decolonization of Indian Cricket." In Carol A. Breckenridge, ed., *Consuming Modernity*, 23–49. Minneapolis: University of Minnesota Press, 1995.

Arnold, Thomas. *Principles of Church Reform*. London: Fellowes, 1833.

Asad, Talal. *Genealogies of Religion*. Baltimore: The Johns Hopkins University Press, 1993.

Auerbach, Erich. *Mimesis*. Garden City, N.Y.: Doubleday Anchor, 1957.

Barrow, Logie. *Independent Spirits: Spiritualism and English Plebeians, 1850–1910*. London: Routledge and Kegan Paul, 1986.

Basu, Shamita. "Religious Revivalism as Nationalist Discourse: Swami Vivekananda and the Nineteenth-Century Neo-Hindu Movement in Bengal," Ph.D. dissertation defended at Roskilde University, Denmark, in 1997.

Bates, Crispin. "Race, Caste and Tribe in Central India: The Early Origins of Indian Anthropometry." In Peter Robb, ed., *The Concept of Race in South Asia*. Delhi: Oxford University Press, 1995.

Bayly, Susan. "Caste and Race in Colonial Ethnography." In Peter Robb, ed., *The Concept of Race in South Asia*. Delhi: Oxford University Press, 1997.

———. "Race in Britain and India." In Peter van der Veer and Hartmut Lehmann, eds., *Nation and Religion*. Princeton: Princeton University Press, 1999.

Bebbington, D. W. *Evangelism in Modern Britain*. London: Unwin Hyman, 1989.

Benjamin, Walter. *Illuminations*. London: Fontana, 1973.

Berti, Silvia. "At the Roots of Unbelief." *Journal of the History of Ideas* (1995): 555–65.

Biardeau, M. "The Story of Arjuna Kartavirya without Reconstruction." *Purana* 12, no. 2 (1970): 286–303.

Boyarin, Jonathan, ed. *The Ethnography of Reading*. Berkeley: University of California Press, 1993.

Brantlinger, Patrick. *Rule of Darkness: British Literature and Imperialism, 1830–1914*. Ithaca: Cornell University Press, 1988.

Breckenridge, Carol A., and Peter van der Veer, eds. *Orientalism and the Postcolonial Predicament: Perspectives on South Asia*. Philadelphia: University of Pennsylvania Press, 1993.

Bruce, Steve, ed., *Religion and Modernization: Sociologists and Historians Debate the Secularization Thesis*. Oxford: Clarendon, 1992.

Carey, William. *An Enquiry into the Obligations of Christians to Use Means for the Conversion of the Heathens*. Leicester: Ann Ireland, 1792.

Casanova, Jose. *Public Religions in the Modern World*. Chicago: University of Chicago Press, 1994.

Chadwick, Owen. *The Secularization of the European Mind in the 19th Century*. Cambridge: Cambridge University Press, 1975.

Chatterjee, Partha. *The Nation and Its Fragments*. Princeton, N.J.: Princeton University Press, 1993.

Chauduri, Nirad C. *Scholar Extraordinary:The Life of Professor the Rt. Hon. Friedrich Max Müller, P.C.*. New York: Oxford University Press, 1974.

Chowdhury-Sengupta, Indira. "The Effeminate and the Masculine: Nationalism and the Concept of Race in Colonial Bengal." In Peter Robb, ed., *The Concept of Race in South Asia*, 282–304. Delhi: Oxford University Press, 1995.

Coburn, Thomas. " 'Scripture in India': Toward a Typology of the Word in Hindu Life." In Miriam Levering, ed., *Rethinking Scripture*. Albany: State University of New York Press, 1989.

Cohn, Bernard S. *An Anthropologist among the Historians and Other Essays*. Delhi: Oxford University Press, 1987.

———. "Law and the Colonial State." In June Starr and Jane Collier, eds., *History and Power in the Study of Law*, 131–52. Ithaca: Cornell University Press, 1989.

———. *Colonialism and Its Forms of Knowledge*. Princeton, N.J.: Princeton University Press, 1996.

Cohn, Bernard, and Nicholas Dirks. "Beyond the Fringe: The Nation State, Colonialism, and the Technologies of Power." *Journal of Historical Sociology* 1, no. 2 (1988): 224–30.

Coleridge, Samuel Taylor. *On the Constitution of the Church and State*. London: Hurst, Chance, 1830.

Colley, Linda. *Britons: Forging the Nation, 1707–1837*. New Haven: Yale University Press, 1992.

Collini, Stefan. *Public Moralists: Political Thought and Intellectual Life in Britain, 1850–1930*. Oxford: Clarendon, 1991.

Collini, Stefan, Donald Winch, and John Burrow. *That Noble Science of Politics*. Cambridge: Cambridge University Press, 1983.

Colls, Robert, and Philip Dodd, eds., *Englishness: Politics and Culture, 1880–1920*. London: Croom Helm, 1986.

Cooter, Roger. *The Cultural Meaning of Popular Science: Phrenology and the Organization of Consent in Nineteenth-Century Britain*. Cambridge: Cambridge University Press, 1984.

Connell, R. W. "Why is Classical Theory Classical?" *American Journal of Sociology* 102, no. 6 (1997).

Cox, Jeffrey. "The Salvation Army and Imperial Power in Early Twentieth-Century Punjab." Paper presented at a conference on religion and nationalism, Amsterdam, November 1995.

Datta, Pradip Kumar. " 'Dying Hindus'; Production of Hindu Communal Common Sense in Early 20th Century Bengal." *Economic and Political Weekly*, June 19, 1993, 1305–19.

De Certeau, Michel. *The Practice of Everyday Life*. Berkeley: University of California Press, 1984.

Derrida, Jacques. *Of Grammatology*. Baltimore: The Johns Hopkins University Press, 1976.

———. *Writing and Difference*. London: Routledge and Kegan Paul, 1978.

Dharwadker, Vinay. 1993 "Orientalism and the Study of Indian Literatures." In Carol A. Breckenridge and Peter van der Veer, eds., *Orientalism and the Postcolonial Predicament: Perspectives in South Asia*. Philadelphia: University of Pennsylvania Press, 1993.

Dirks, Nicholas B. *The Hollow Crown: Ethnohistory of an Indian Kingdom*. Cambridge: Cambridge University Press, 1987.

———. "History as a Sign of the Modern," *Public Culture* 2 (1990).

———. "Colonial Histories and Native Informants: Biography of an Archive." In Carol A. Breckenridge and Peter van der Veer, eds., *Orientalism and the Postcolonial Predicament*. Philadelphia: University of Pennsylvania Press, 1993.

———. "The Conversion of Caste: Location, Translation, and Appropriation." In Peter van der Veer, ed., *Conversion to Modernities: The Globalization of Christianity*, 115–37. New York: Routledge, 1996.

———. "Recasting Tamil Society." In C. Fuller, ed., *Caste Today*. Delhi: Oxford University Press, 1997.

Duara, Prasenjit. *Rescuing History from the Nation: Questioning Narratives of Modern China*. Chicago: University of Chicago Press, 1995.

Dumont, Louis. *La Civilisation Indienne et Nous*. Paris: Armand Collin, 1975.

———. *Homo Hierarchicus: The Caste System and Its Implications*. Chicago: University of Chicago Press, 1980.

Eade, John. "Nationalism, Community, and the Islamization of Space in London." In Barbara Metcalf, ed., *Muslim Space*. Berkeley: University of California Press, 1997.

181

Eliade, Mircea. *Yoga: Immortality and Freedom*. Princeton, N.J.: Princeton University Press, 1958.

Farquhar, J. N. *The Crown of Hinduism*. London: Oxford University Press, 1915.

Foucault, Michel. "The Subject and Power," *Critical Inquiry* 8, 4, 1982.

Frank, Andre Gundur. *ReOrient: Global Economy in the Asian Age*. Berkeley: University of California Press, 1998.

Freitag, Sandria. *Collective Action and Community*. Berkeley: University of California Press, 1993.

Frykenberg, Robert E. "The Emergence of 'Modern Hinduism.'" In Gunther Sontheimer and Hermann Kulke, eds., *Hinduism Reconsidered*. Delhi: Manohar, 1997.

Fuller, C. J. *Servants of the Goddess: The Priests of a South Indian Temple*. Cambridge: Cambridge University Press, 1984.

Garnett, Jane, and Colin Matthew. *Revival and Religion since 1700*. London: Hambledon, 1993.

Gay, Peter. *The Enlightenment: An Interpretation*, 2 vols. New York: Knopf, 1966.

Geertz, Clifford. *The Interpretation of Cultures*. New York: Basic Books, 1973.

Gellner, Ernest. *Nations and Nationalism*. Oxford: Blackwell, 1983.

Ghosh, Amitav. *The Circle of Reason*. London: Granta, 1986.

Gilmartin, David. *Empire and Islam: Punjab and the Making of Pakistan*. Berkeley: University of California Press, 1988.

Gladstone, William E. *The State in Its Relations with the Church*. London: Hurst, Chance, 1838.

Godwin, Joscelyn. *The Theosophical Enlightenment*. Albany: State University of New York Suny Press, 1994.

Goodrich-Clarke, Nicholas. *The Occult Roots of Nazism: Secret Aryan Cults and Their Influence on Nazi Ideology: The Ariosophists of Austria and Germany, 1890–1935*. New York: New York University Press, 1985.

Goody, Jack. *The Domestication of the Savage Mind*. Cambridge: Cambridge University Press, 1977.

Guha, Ranajit. "Dominance without Hegemony and Its Historiography." In *Subaltern Studies*, vol. 4. Delhi: Oxford University Press, 1989.

———. "A Construction of Humanism in Colonial India." *Wertheim Lecture*, Amsterdam: Centre for Asian Studies, Amsterdam (CASA), 1993.

Habermas, Jürgen. *The Structural Transformation of the Public Sphere: An Inquiry into a Category of Bourgeois Society*. Cambridge, Mass.: MIT Press, 1962; translated, 1989.

Halbfass, Wilhelm. *India and Europe*. Albany: State University of New York Press, 1988.

Hall, Catherine. *White, Male, and Middle-Class*. Cambridge: Polity, 1992.

Hall, Donald. *Muscular Christianity*. Cambridge: Cambridge University Press, 1994.

Handler, R., and G.W. Stocking, eds. *Excluded Ancestors*. Madison: University of Wisconsin Press, 2000.

Hansen, Thomas Blom. "Recuperating Masculinity: Hindu Nationalism, Violence, and the Exorcism of the Muslim 'Other'." *Critique of Anthropology*, 16, no. 2 (1996): 137–72.

———. *The Saffron Wave: Democracy and Hindu Nationalism in Modern India*. Princeton, N.J.: Princeton University Press, 1999.

Hechter, Michael. *Internal Colonialism: The Celtic Fringe in British National Development, 1536–1966*. Berkeley: University of California Press, 1975.

Helmstadter, Richard, and Paul Phillips, eds. *Religion in Victorian Society: A Sourcebook of Documents*. Lanham, Md.: University Press of America, 1985.

Hempton, David. *Religion and Political Culture in Britain and Ireland: From the Glorious Revolution to the Decline of Empire*. Cambridge: Cambridge University Press, 1996.

Hiltebeitel, Alf. *The Cult of Draupadi*. Chicago: University of Chicago Press, 1988.

Hilton, Boyd. *The Age of Atonement: The Influence of Evangelicalism on Social and Economic Thought, 1795–1865*. Oxford: Clarendon, 1988.

Hult, David. "Reading It Right: The Ideology of Text Editing." In Steven Nichols, ed., *The New Criticism*. Baltimore: The Johns Hopkins University Press, 1990.

Inden, Ronald. *Imagining India*. Oxford: Basil Blackwell, 1990.

Irschick, Eugene F. *Dialogue and History: Constructing South India, 1795–1895*. Berkeley: University of California Press, 1994.

Jacobs, Margaret. "Private Beliefs in Public Temples: The New Religiosity of the Eighteenth Century." *Social Research* 59, no. 1 (1992): 59–84.

Jacobs, Margaret C. *Living the Enlightenment: Freemasonry and Politics in Eighteenth-Century Europe*. Oxford: Oxford University Press, 1992.

Jones, Kenneth. *Arya Dharm*. Berkeley: University of California Press, 1976.

———. *Religious Controversy in India*. Albany: State University of New York Press, 1992.

Jones, Kenneth W. *Arya Dharm*. Berkeley: University of California Press, 1989.

Kanitkar, Helen. "Real True Boys: Moulding the Cadets of Imperialism." In Andrea Cornwall and Nancy Lindisfarne, eds., *Dislocating Masculinity*. London: Routledge, 1994.

Kaviraj, Sudipto. *The Unhappy Consciousness: Bankimchandra Chattopadhyay and the Formation of Nationalist Discourse in India*. Delhi: Oxford University Press, 1995.

Knights, Ben. *The Idea of the Clerisy in the 19th Century*. Cambridge: Cambridge University Press, 1978.

Kopf, David. *The Brahmo Samaj and the Shaping of the Modern Indian Mind*. Princeton, N.J.: Princeton University Press, 1979.

Koselleck, Reinhart. *Futures Past*. Cambridge, Mass: MIT Press, 1979.

Koselleck, Reinhart. *Critique and Crisis: Enlightenment and the Pathogenesis of Modern Society.* Cambridge, Mass.: MIT Press, 1988.

Kripal, Jeffrey. *Kali's Child. The Mystical and the Erotic in the Life and Teachings of Ramakrishna.* Chicago: Chicago University Press, 1995.

Kuklick, Henrika. *The Savage Within.* Cambridge: Cambridge University Press, 1991.

Kumar, Nita. "Sanskrit Pandits and the Modernisation of Sanskrit Education in the Nineteenth to Twentieth Centuries." In William Radice, ed., *Swami Vivekananda and the Modernization of Hinduism.* Delhi: Oxford University Press, 1998.

Lal, B.B. "Was Ayodhya a Mythical City?" *Puratattva* 10 (1979–80): 45–49.

Laqueur, Thomas. *Religion and Respectability.* New Haven: Yale University Press, 1976.

Lavin, S. *Unitarians and India: A Study in Encounter and Response.* Boston: Beacon Press, 1977.

Lelyveld, David. *Aligarh's First Generation.* Princeton, N.J.: Princeton University Press, 1978.

Leopold, Joan. "British Applications of the Aryan Theory of Race to India, 1850–1870," *The English Historical Review* 89, 1974.

Ludden, David. "Orientalist Empiricism: Transformations of Colonial Knowledge." In Carol A. Breckenridge and Peter van der Veer, eds., *Orientalism and the Postcolonial Predicament: Perspectives on South Asia,* 250–79. Philadelphia: University of Pennsylvania Press, 1993.

Luria, Keith. "The Politics of Protestant Conversion to Catholicism in Seventeenth-Century France." In Peter van der Veer, ed., *Conversion to Modernities: The Globalization of Christianity.* New York: Routledge, 1996.

Lutgendorf, Philip. *The Life of a Text.* Berkeley: University of California Press, 1991.

Macaulay, T.B. *Speeches, with the Minute on Indian Education,* ed. G. M. Young. London: Oxford University Press, 1935.

MacKenzie, John. *Imperialism and Popular Culture.* Manchester: Manchester University Press, 1986.

Madan, T. N. "Secularism in Its Place." *Journal of Asian Studies* 46, no. 4 (1987): 747–59.

Mangan, J.A. *The Games Ethic and Imperialism.* London: Viking, 1985.

———. *The Cultural Bond: Sport, Empire, Society.* London: Frank Cass, 1992.

Mani, Lata. "Contentious Traditions: The Debate on *Sati* in Colonial India." In Kumkum Sangari and Sudesh Vaid, eds., *Recasting Women,* 88–127. New Brunswick, N.J.: Rutgers University Press, 1990.

Mankekar, Purnima. "Television Tales and a Woman's Rage: A Nationalist Recasting of Draupadi's 'Disrobing.' " *Public Culture* 5 (1993): 469–92.

Marriott, McKim. "Interactional and Attributional Theories of Caste Ranking," *Man in India* 39, no. 2, 1959.

Mason, Tony. "Football on the Maidan: Cultural Imperialism in Calcutta." In J. A. Mangan, ed., *The Cultural Bond: Sport, Empire, Society*, 142–54. London: Frank Cass, 1992.

Mauss, Marcel. "La Nation" (1920). In *Oeuvres*, 3:573–639. Paris: Les Editions de Minuit, 1969.

Maw, Martin. *Visions of India: Fulfillment Theology, the Aryan Race Theory, and the Work of British Protestant Missionaries in India*. Frankfurt: Peter Lang, 1990.

McKean, Lise. *Divine Enterprise: Gurus and the Hindu Nationalist Movement*. Chicago: University of Chicago Press, 1996.

McLeod, Hugh. *Religion and the Working Class in Nineteenth-Century Britain*. London: Macmillan, 1984.

———. "Protestantism and British National Identity, 1815–1945." In Peter van der Veer and Hartmut Lehmann, eds., *Nation and Religion*. Princeton, N.J.: Princeton University Press, 1999.

Metcalf, Barbara. "Imagining Community: Polemical Debates in Colonial India." In Kenneth W. Jones, ed., *Religious Controversy in British India: Dialogues in South Asian Languages*, 229–41. Albany: State University of New York Press, 1992.

Metcalf, Thomas. *Ideologies of the Raj*. Cambridge: Cambridge University Press, 1994.

Mill, James. *History of British India*. ed. Horace Hayman Wilson. London: J. Madden; Piper, Stephenson, and Spence, 1858.

Mill, John Stuart. *Utilitarianism, On Liberty, Considerations on Representative Government*, ed. Geraint Williams. London: J.M. Dent, 1993.

Mitchell, Timothy. "The Limits of the State: Beyond Statist Approaches and Their Critics." *American Political Science Review* 85, no. 1 (1991): 77–97.

Monier-Williams, Monier. *Hinduism*. London: Society for Promoting Christian Knowledge, 1877.

Morinis, Alan. *Pilgrimage in the Bengali Tradition*. Delhi: Oxford University Press, 1984.

Mosse, George. *Nationalism and Sexuality*. New York: Howard Fertig, 1975.

———. *The Image of Man*. London: Oxford University Press, 1996.

Müller, Friedrich Max. *Chips from a German Workshop*. Vol. 4. New York: Scribner, 1876.

———. *Auld Lang Syne: My Indian Friends*. New York: Scribner, 1899.

———. *Last Essays*. London: Longmans, 1901.

———. *Theosophy or Psychological Religion*. London: Longmans, 1903.

Mullick, Sunrit. "Protap Chandra Majumdar and Swami Vivekananda at the Parliament of Religions: Two Interpretations of Hinduism and Universal Religion." In Eric Ziolkowski, ed., *A Museum of Faiths: Histories and Legacies of the 1893 World's Parliament of Religions*. Atlanta: Scholars Press, 1993.

Nairn, Tom. *The Break-Up of Britain: Crisis and Neo-Nationalism.* London: New Left Books, 1981.

Nandy, Ashis. *The Intimate Enemy: Loss and Recovery of Self under Colonialism.* Delhi: Oxford University Press, 1983.

Nethercott, Arthur. *The First Five Lives of Annie Besant.* Chicago: University of Chicago Press, 1960.

———. *The Last Four Lives of Annie Besant.* Chicago: University of Chicago Press, 1963.

Newman, John Henry. *Apologia Pro Vita Sua.* London: Longman, 1864.

Newsome, David. *Godliness and Good Learning: Four Studies on a Victorian Ideal.* London: John Murray, 1961.

Nietzsche, Friedrich. *Jenseits von Gut und Bose.* In von Karl Schlechta, ed., *Werke in Drei Banden; Zweiter Band,* 563–761. Munchen: Carl Hanser Verlag, 1960.

Nipperdey, Thomas. *Nachdenken über die deutsche Geschichte.* Munchen: C. H. Beck, 1986.

Obeyesekere, Gananath. "Buddhism and Conscience: An Exploratory Essay." *Daedalus* 120, no. 3 (1991): 219–38.

Oddie, Geoffrey. *Hindu and Christian and South-East India.* London: Curzon, 1991.

Owen, Alex. *The Darkened Room: Women, Power, and Spiritualism in Late Victorian England.* London: Virago, 1989.

Pagden, Anthony. "The Effacement of Difference: Colonialism and the Origins of Nationalism in Diderot and Herder." In Gyan Prakash, ed., *After Colonialism: Imperial Histories and Postcolonial Displacements.* Princeton, N.J.: Princeton University Press, 1995.

Pant, Rashmi. "The Cognitive Status of Caste in Colonial Ethnography: A Review of Some Literature on the North West Provinces," *The Indian Economic and Social History Review* 24, no. 2, 1987.

Parry, Benita. *Delusions and Discoveries.* London: Penguin, 1972.

Parry, Jonathan. *Death in Benares.* Cambridge: Cambridge University Press, 1994.

———. "The Brahmanical Tradition and the Technology of the Intellect." In Joanna Overing, ed., *Reason and Morality,* 200–225. London: Tavistock, 1985.

Pels, Peter. "The Rise and Fall of the Indian Aborigines: Orientalism, Anglicism, and the Emergence of an Ethnology of India, 1833–1869." In Peter Pels and Oscar Salemink, eds., *Colonial Subjects: Essays on the Practical History of Anthropology.* Ann Arbor: University of Michigan Press, 1999.

———. "Occult Truths: Race, Conjecture, and Theosophy in Victorian Anthropology." In R. Handler and G. W. Stocking, eds., *Excluded Ancestors, Invertible Traditions.* Vol. 9: *History of Anthropology.* Madison: University of Wisconsin Press, 2000.

Pinney, Christopher. "Classification and Fantasy in the Photographic Construction of Caste and Tribe," *Visual Anthropology* 3, 1990.

Pocock, John. "Modernity and Anti-Modernity in the Anglophone Political Tradition." In Shmuel Eisenstadt, ed., *Patterns of Modernity*. London: F. Pinter, 1987.

Poliakov, Leon. *The Aryan Myth*. London: Chatto, 1974.

Pollock, Sheldon. "The Ramayana Text and the Critical Edition." In Robert Goldman, trans., *The Ramayana of Valmiki*, 82–93. Princeton, N.J.: Princeton University Press, 1984.

———. "Deep Orientalism? Notes on Sanskrit and Power Beyond the Raj." In Carol A. Breckenridge and Peter van der Veer, eds., *Orientalism and the Postcolonial Predicament: Perspectives on South Asia*. Philadelphia: University of Pennsylvania Press, 1993.

Ray, Ajit Kumar. *The Religious Ideas of Rammohun Roy: A Survey of His Writings Particularly in Persian, Sanskrit, and Bengali*. New Delhi: Kanak, 1976.

Raychaudhuri, Tapan. *Europe Reconsidered*. Delhi: Oxford University Press, 1988.

Richman, Paula, ed. *Many Ramayanas*. Berkeley: University of California Press, 1990.

Robbins, Keith. "Religion and Identity in Modern British History." In Stuart Mews, ed., *Studies in Church History*. Vol. 18: *Religion and National Identity*, 465–89. Oxford: Basil Blackwell, 1982.

Rocher, Rosanne. "British Orientalism in the Eighteenth Century: The Dialectics of Knowledge and Government." In Carol A. Breckenridge and Peter van der Veer, eds., *Orientalism and the Postcolonial Predicament: Perspectives on South Asia*, 215–50. Philadelphia: University of Pennsylvania Press, 1993.

Rosenthal, Michael. *The Character Factory: Baden-Powell and the Origins of the Boy Scout Movement*. New York: Pantheon, 1986.

Rosselli, John. "The Self-Image of Effeteness: Physical Education and Nationalism in Nineteenth-Century Bengal," *Past and Present* 86, 1980.

Said, Edward. *Orientalism*. New York: Vintage, 1978.

———. "Introduction." In Rudyard Kipling, *Kim*. Harmondsworth: Penguin, 1987.

———. *Culture and Imperialism*. New York: Knopf, 1993.

Sarkar, Sumit. "Indian Nationalism and the Politics of Hindutva." In David Ludden, ed., *Contesting the Nation: Religion, Community, and the Politics of Democracy in India*. Philadelphia: University of Pennsylvania Press, 1996.

Schrempp, Gregory. "The Re-Education of Friedrich Max Muller: Intellectual Appropriation and Epistemological Antinomy in Mid-Victorian Evolutionary Thought," *Man (NS)* 18, 1983.

Sinha, B. P. "Indian Tradition and Archaeology." *Puratattva* 14 (1984): 109.

Sinha, Mrnalini. *Colonial Masculinity: The 'Manly Englishman' and the 'Effeminate Bengali' in the Late Nineteenth Century*. Manchester: Manchester University Press, 1995.

Smith, Solveig. *By Love Compelled: The Salvation Army's One Hundred Years in India and Adjacent Lands*. London: Salvation Publishing and Supplies, 1981.

187

Spivak, Gayatri. "Can the Subaltern Speak." In Cary Nelson and Lawrence Grossberg, eds., *Marxism and the Interpretation of Culture*, 271–313. Urbana: University of Illinois Press, 1988.

Stanley, Brian. "Christian Responses to the Indian Mutiny of 1857." In W. J. Shiels, ed., *The Church and War*, 277–291. Oxford: Basil Blackwell, 1983.

———. *The Bible and the Flag: Protestant Missions and British Imperialism in the Nineteenth and Twentieth Centuries*. Leicester: Apollos, 1990.

Stepan, Nancy. *The Idea of Race in Science*. London: Macmillan, 1982.

Stewart, Susan. *Crimes of Writing: Problems in the Containment of Representation*. Durham, N.C.: Duke University Press, 1994.

Stocking, G. W. *Victorian Anthropology*. New York: The Free Press, 1987.

Strachey, Lytton. *Eminent Victorians*. New York: Harcourt-Brace, 1918.

Sukthankar, V. S. *Critical Studies in the Mahabharata*. Poona: Bhandarkar Oriental Research Institute, 1944.

Suleri, Sara. *The Rethoric of English India*. Chicago: University of Chicago Press, 1992.

Taylor, Charles. *Sources of the Self*. Cambridge, Mass.: Harvard University Press, 1989.

———. "Modes of Secularism." In Rajeev Bhargava, ed., *Secularism and Its Critics*. Delhi: Oxford University Press, 1998.

Thapar, Romila. "Puranic Lineages and Archaeological Cultures." *Puratattva* 8 (1978).

———. "The Ramayana Syndrome." *Seminar* 353 (1989): 71–75.

———. "A Historical Perspective on the Story of Rama." In Sarvepalli Gopal, ed., *Anatomy of a Confrontation*, 141–163. New Delhi: Viking, 1991.

———. "Syndicated Hinduism." In Günther Sontheimer and Hermann Kulke, eds., *Reconsidering Hinduism*. Delhi: Manohar, 1997.

Thompson, E. P. *Alien Homage*. Delhi: Oxford University Press, 1993.

———. *Witness against the Beast: William Blake and the Moral Law*. Cambridge: Cambridge University Press, 1993.

Thorne, Susan. *Protestant Ethics and the Spirit of Imperialism: British Congregationalists and the London Missionary Society, 1795–1925*. Ann Arbor: University Microfilms, 1990.

Thorner, Daniel. "Marx on India and the Asiatic Mode of Production," *Contributions to Indian Sociology* 9, 1965.

Tilak, B. G. *Srimad Bhagavadgita Rahasya*. Translated by B. S. Sukthankar. Poona, 1935–36.

Tinker, Hugh. *The Ordeal of Love: C. F. Andrews and India*. Delhi: Oxford University Press, 1979.

Tolen, Rachel. "Colonizing and Transforming the Criminal Tribesman: The Salvation Army in British India," *American Ethnologist* 18, 1, 1991.

Trautmann, Thomas. *Aryans and British India*. Berkeley: University of California Press, 1997.

van der Veer, Peter: *Gods on Earth*. London: Athlone, 1988.

———. "The Power of Detachment: Disciplines of Body and Mind in the Ramanandi Order." *American Ethnologist* 16 (1989): 458–70.

———. "The Foreign Hand: Orientalist Discourse in Sociology and Communalism." In Carol A. Breckenridge and Peter van der Veer, eds., *Orientalism and the Postcolonial Predicament: Perspectives on South Asia*. Philadelphia: University of Pennsylvania Press, 1993.

———. *Religious Nationalism: Hindus and Muslims in India*. Berkeley: University of California Press, 1994a.

———. "Syncretism, Multiculturalism, and the Discourse of Tolerance: the Case of India." In Charles Stuart and Rosalind Shaw, eds., *Syncretism/Anti-Syncretism*, 196–212. London: Routledge, 1994b.

———. "Gender and Nation in Hindu Nationalism." In Hans Antlov and Stein Tonneson, eds., *Asian Forms of the Nation*, 188–213. London: Curzon, 1996.

———. ed. *Conversion to Modernities: The Globalization of Christianity*. New York: Routledge, 1996.

Van Rooden, Peter. "Friedrich Schleiermacher's *Reden über die Religion* en de historische bestudering van godsdienst," *Theoretische Geschiedenis* 23, 1996.

———. "Nineteenth-Century Representations of Missionary Conversion and the Transformation of Western Christianity." In Peter van der Veer, ed., *Conversion to Modernities*, New York: Routledge, 1996.

———. "History, the Nation, and Religion: The Transformation of the Dutch Religious Past." In Peter van der Veer and Hartmut Lehmann, eds., *Nation and Religion*. Princeton, N.J.: Princeton University Press, 1999.

van Woerkens, Martine. *Le Voyageur étranglé. L'Inde des Thugs, le colonialisme et l'imaginaire*. Paris: Bibliotheque Albin Michel, 1995.

Vance, Norman. *The Sinews of the Spirit*. Cambridge: Cambridge University Press, 1985.

Viswanathan, Gauri. *Masks of Conquest: Literary Study and British Rule in India*. New York: Columbia University Press, 1989.

———. "Raymond Williams and British Colonialism," *The Yale Journal of Criticism* 4, no. 2, 1991.

———. *Outside the Fold: Conversion, Modernity, and Belief*. Princeton, N.J.: Princeton University Press, 1998.

Von Stietencron, Heinrich. "Hinduism: On the Proper Use of a Deceptive Term. In Günther Sontheimer and Hermann Kulke, eds., *Hinduism Reconsidered*. Delhi: Manohar, 1997.

Walkowitz, Judith. *City of Dreadful Delight: Narratives of Sexual Danger in Late-Victorian London*. Chicago: University of Chicago Press, 1992.

Warren, Allen. "Citizens of the Empire: Baden-Powell, Scouts and Guides, and an Imperial Ideal." In John MacKenzie, ed., *Imperialism and Popular Culture*, 232–52. Manchester: Manchester University Press, 1986.

189

Westerman, Ingmar. "Authority and Utility: John Millar, James Mill, and the Politics of History, c. 1770–1836," dissertation defended at the University of Amsterdam, 1999.

Wilson, Bryan. *Religion in a Secular Society.* London: Weidenfeld and Nicholson, 1966.

Wolf, Eric. *Europe and the People without History.* Berkeley: University of California Press, 1982.

Wolffe, John. *The Protestant Crusade in Great Britain, 1829–1860.* Oxford: Clarendon, 1991.

———. *God and Greater Britain: Religion and National Life in Britain and Ireland, 1843–1945.* London: Routledge, 1994.

Young, Richard Fox. *Resistant Hinduism: Sanskrit Sources on Anti-Christian Apologetics in Early Nineteenth Century India.* Vienna: De Nobili Research Library, 1981.

Young, Robert M. *Darwin's Metaphor.* Cambridge: Cambridge University Press, 1985.

Young, Robert. *Colonial Desire: Hybridity in Theory, Culture, and Race.* New York: Routledge, 1995.

Zaret, David. "Religion, Science, and Printing in the Public Spheres in Seventeenth-Century England." In Craig Calhoun, ed., *Habermas and the Public Sphere*, 212–36. Cambridge, Mass: MIT Press, 1992.

Zastoupil, Lynn. *John Stuart Mill and India.* Stanford: Stanford University Press, 1994.

Ziolkowski, Eric, ed. *A Museum of Faiths: Histories and Legacies of the 1893 World's Parliament of Religions.* Atlanta: Scholars Press, 1993.

Žižek, Slavoj. *The Sublime Object of Ideology.* London: Verso, 1989.

Index

191

First orientalists:

-Sir William Jones 1794
    comes from a law project, deriving legal/colonial
    practices from sanskrit/hindu text

-modern anti-muslim sentiment & islamaphobia
hot the same phenomena but overlapping